Flood Tide

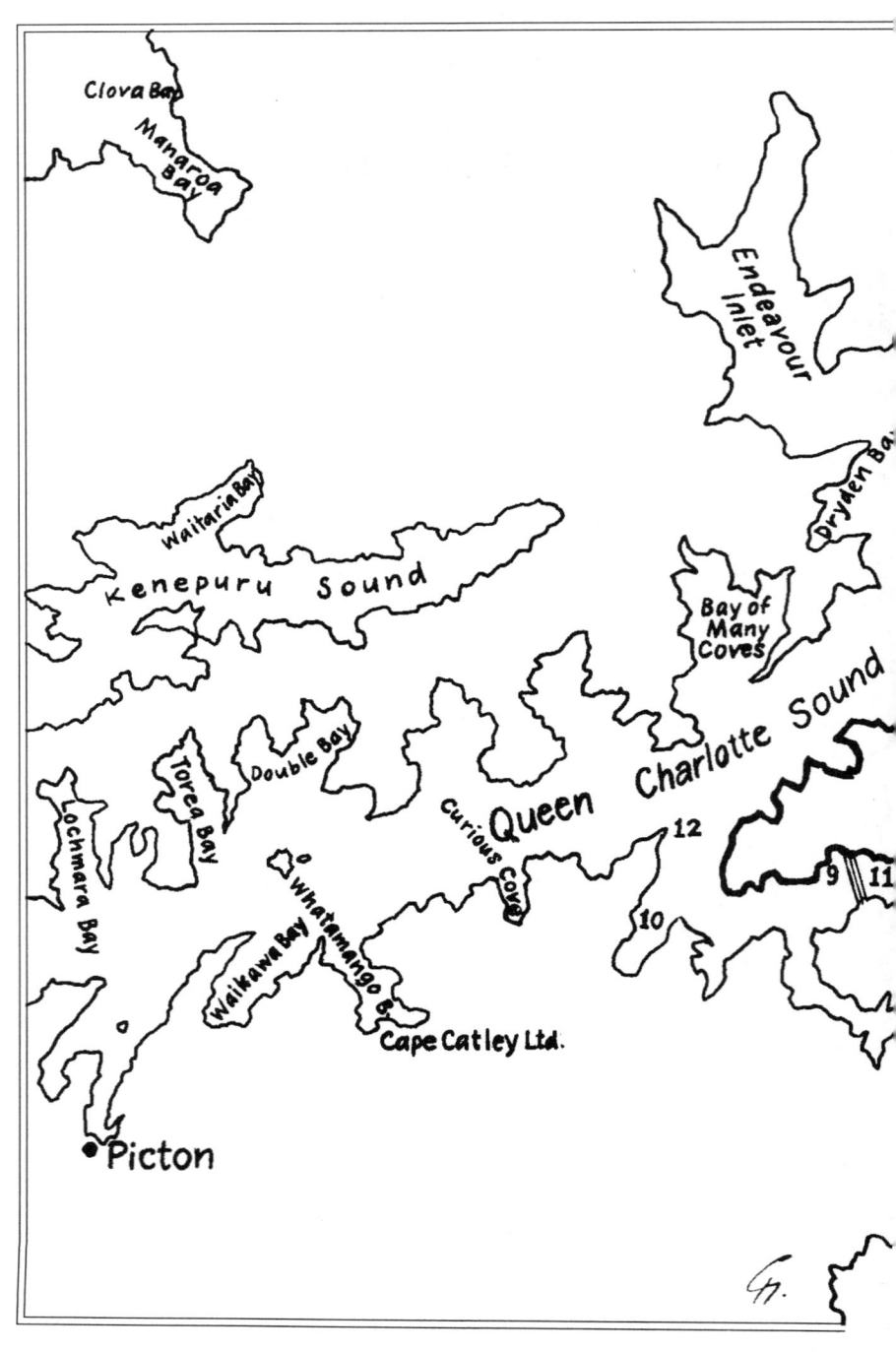

Clova Bay
Manaroa Bay
Endeavour Inlet
Dryden Bay
Waitaria Bay
Kenepuru Sound
Bay of Many Coves
Double Bay
Torea Bay
Queen Charlotte Sound
Lochmara Bay
Curious Cove
12
9
11
Whatamango B.
10
Waikawa Bay
Cape Catley Ltd.
Picton

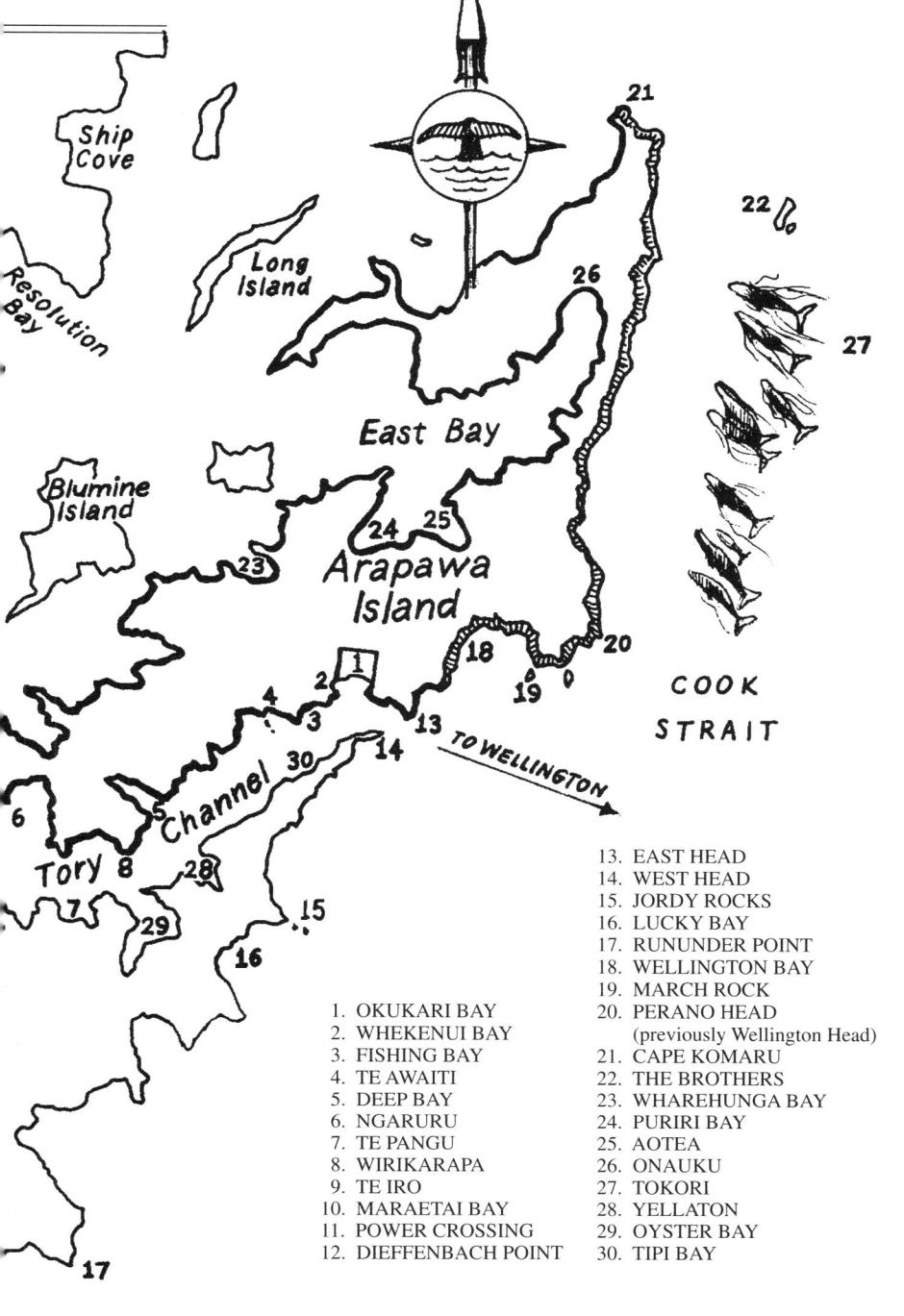

Ship Cove

Resolution Bay

Long Island

East Bay

Blumine Island

Arapawa Island

Tory Channel

COOK STRAIT

TO WELLINGTON

21
22
26
27
24 25
23
18
20
19
1
2
4
3
13
30
14
6
8
28
7
29
15
16
17

1. OKUKARI BAY
2. WHEKENUI BAY
3. FISHING BAY
4. TE AWAITI
5. DEEP BAY
6. NGARURU
7. TE PANGU
8. WIRIKARAPA
9. TE IRO
10. MARAETAI BAY
11. POWER CROSSING
12. DIEFFENBACH POINT

13. EAST HEAD
14. WEST HEAD
15. JORDY ROCKS
16. LUCKY BAY
17. RUNUNDER POINT
18. WELLINGTON BAY
19. MARCH ROCK
20. PERANO HEAD
    (previously Wellington Head)
21. CAPE KOMARU
22. THE BROTHERS
23. WHAREHUNGA BAY
24. PURIRI BAY
25. AOTEA
26. ONAUKU
27. TOKORI
28. YELLATON
29. OYSTER BAY
30. TIPI BAY

FLOOD
TIDE

by

Heather Heberley

CAPE CATLEY LTD

First published August 1997
Second edition September 1997
CAPE CATLEY LTD
Whatamango Bay, Queen Charlotte Sound
New Zealand

Design by Bill Wieben
Cover photograph by Ian Garrod
Typeset by Coral Orsman
Printed in Hong Kong

ISBN: 0-908561-61-X

Contents

In memory of William John (Bill) Gibb

14-5-1947 - 25-10-1996

"A kind, strong, brave man of the sea, who didn't suffer fools, who cared deeply for people."

Acknowledgements

THE PERSON who made this book happen is Christine Cole Catley, my editor, publisher and mentor, but best of all my friend. It was her encouragement that made me start to write again and I thank her sincerely for her faith in me.

While writing this book I have been amazed at people's willingness to help me with my research. I would like to thank all those many people I contacted, either by phone or letter. Their generosity in passing on their knowledge has made it easier for me to write the history of Okukari and the Heberley family.

When I walked into Blenheim's Land Titles Office to search for deed titles I was grateful for Jane Brennan's help in guiding me to the right places. She began the search for me, and made my task much less daunting both in the Land Titles office and LINZ (Land Information of New Zealand). Altogether this book has been an incredible learning experience for me, such as when I spent time at the Waikawa Marae archives, and at the Picton Museum. A handful of people are working so hard to hold our history for future generations, and I'd like to congratulate them on their achievements. My special thanks go to Mike Taylor for the information he has given to me.

Once again my thanks to Gary Hebley, descendant of Frederick Heberley, Worser Heberley's brother, for the map of our area. I liked the first one so much I have used it again, with additions. Gary also drew the decorative heading in the recipe section.

Ian Garrod is another I must thank once again for taking the photo for the cover. His photo appeared on the cover of *Weather Permitting*, and to create something similar, but different, he came out to our bay in his small open speedboat on a very cold southerly day. The photo was taken from the place where I have so often watched for the return of my Joe and sons Joe and James, when they've been caught out in the Straits in a southerly or they have been out in a search or rescue in atrocious conditions.

I've discovered that people love to share history and in the process I've met some wonderful people. When the Marlborough Historical Society came up to Okukari Bay on one of their outings recently I was particularly grateful to one of their members, Jack Andrews. He helped me immensely with information.

Tom Gullery, an ex-whaler, made one of my town days pleasurable as I sat with him in his room at Picton's Seaview Rest Home and listened to some of his memories.

I'd like to thank Marcia Rowe, my neighbour from Aotea, who has walked 10 kilometres each way to help me when things have been getting on top of me while I've been writing this book. Her hard work and sense of humour have always put me back on track.

And my good friend Maureen Stewart, who came with me on my North Island author-tour, made the 1760 kilometres fun. I couldn't have done it without her and I'm grateful.

I had no idea that I would receive so many letters from people who read my first book, *Weather Permitting*. My grandchildren loved gathering up stamps from Switzerland, Tanzania, Kenya, the Shetland Islands, Canada, the USA, Australia and England, as well as more than 400 from all over New Zealand. It has been these letters which have made me want to write a sequel. From the bottom of my heart I thank everyone who wrote to me so supportively about my dear father's suicide after my mother's death in a car accident. Writing about that event in my life, together with your letters, at last healed the wound.

Once again I must thank my family for providing the stories. All I have done is write them down. I couldn't have written another book without their friendship and love.

Lastly I must thank one very special person. Joe Heberley QSM. I cannot describe my feelings when he was named in the Queen's Birthday Honours list in 1996. He is a brave, honest and fair man of the sea but best of all he is my husband. He has given me the inspiration to write my story.

Heather Heberley

Living in the Sounds

Correspondence School essay by Angela Heberley, aged 10, 1996

WE LIVE on Arapawa Island in the Marlborough Sounds, in a bay called Okukari which is right at the entrance to Tory Channel.

Arapawa Island is 7487 hectares, and it used to have lots of farms on it but now there are only a few left and my grandparents own one of them. Three families live here in the bay, on the farm. They are my grandparents, Heather and Joe Heberley (he is called Grumps), Dad's brother James and his wife, Lisa, and their two children, Haydn, 5, and Danielle, 3, and then there's us, Joe and Joy Heberley, and my sister Rachael who is going to boarding school next year, and me.

My dad is a fisherman and a farmer. So are Grumps and Uncle James. Sometimes when Dad's crewman has a weekend off, we go fishing with him. I really enjoy helping on the boat.

They catch crayfish in pots, which are steel frames covered with nylon netting. Groper and school shark are caught on long-lines, with lots of hooks on them, and they troll for tuna by towing coloured lures behind the boat on long nylon lines.

Our crayfish are kept alive in wooden crates that float in the bay until they are full. Then they are taken to Picton and packed in wood wool (thin shavings of wood) in plastic cases to keep them alive, and sent to a crayfish plant in Oamaru. Then they are flown to Japan for the live crayfish market.

Groper and shark are kept in big ice holds on the boats. They are unloaded in Picton and taken to Nelson by truck in bulk bins covered in ice to keep them fresh.

On the farm we have crossbred and merino sheep and hereford cattle. At lambing time Rachael and I go round the sheep every morning, checking them to make sure there are no sheep down, having trouble lambing. Quite often we find a lamb that hasn't got a mother, so it becomes a pet. When they get bigger, everyone thinks they are pests. One, who is called Bud, loves biscuits and always finds a way into someone's yard and eats the garden.

I like rowing in the dinghy around the bay and out to Dad when he puts the *Fugitive* on the moorings for the night. I have been rowing since I was seven. My granddad taught me how. I am not allowed to row when it is a strong northerly wind because I might get blown out into Cook Strait.

I have joined Lone Girl Guides. I am a Lone Guide because I live too far away from town so I can't go to an active pack. Instead we go to special Lone days and camps, about once a term, and get a newsletter every month.

I really enjoy living here on the island because it is close to the sea and I think it is beautiful.

Angela Heberley

CHAPTER ONE

With the Tide

There is a tide in the affairs of men
Which, taken at the flood, leads on to fortune;
Omitted, all the voyage of their life
Is bound in shallows and in miseries.
Shakespeare, *Julius Caesar*, Act 4, Scene 3

MY LIFE is the tide. It can't be stopped. I have grabbed the tide with both hands.

I've thought so often that if I hadn't married Joe, if I hadn't begun my married life with the youngest whale-gunner in the Southern Hemisphere, if I hadn't moved from Auckland to an island in the Marlborough Sounds, if I hadn't gone fishing, if I hadn't worked in the woolshed, if I hadn't been involved in the many sea rescues with Joe and our two sons in one of the most dangerous and unpredictable places in the world - then my life in contrast would have been 'bound in shallows', though I don't know about the 'miseries'.

One day in July 1995 I finished writing my first book. When I pressed that last full stop, wrote 'the end' and drew a smiling face, I had no idea about all the things that were to come. As the mailboat was steaming into our bay on Arapawa Island I was still trying to squeeze the manuscript into the envelope. I'd promised my publisher that it would be in the mail that day and I was determined it would be. I resisted drawing another smiling face on the envelope. I didn't have the time, and the staff in the Picton mailroom wouldn't have understood my joy. I had finished.

Our red mailboat was waiting as I ran down the track from our house and along the wharf. The wash slapped lightly against the sand and I heard squawks of displeasure from the seagulls as the ripples lifted over the rocks in the middle of our beach, disrupting their search for food. A quick exchange of mailbags, a wave to the passengers on board and the boat was reversing from the wharf before turning and heading across the bay to Whekenui.

As I walked back up to the house with the mailbag under my arm, a feeling of overwhelming loss came over me. So often strangers had asked me, "What do you do all day out there?" - and now I found I was asking myself the same question. What was I going to do all day now I wasn't working on my book? It was my life I'd been working on, and now it was gone.

Not even the mail or daily newspapers lifted my spirits. I felt lost.

My gardens were overgrown and over the last 10 months the inside household chores had become secondary to my book but I couldn't bring myself to do a thing. Our son Joe knew what my problem was. "You've got post-book depression, Mum."

A phone call a few days later from publisher Chris Cole Catley had me back on track again when she told me she thought the book was great. "The facts are down, but now more of your thoughts and more of your feelings, please. Don't write so tightly," I was told.

So I hadn't finished after all. I'd been faxing chapters as I wrote them, for subediting, but it turned out this was only the first subbing, especially as I'd written the chapters out of order as subjects occurred to me.

The joy - I had my book back once more. The confidence I had gained using my word processor enabled me to recall chapters to the screen, and I relived them once again. Surrounded by my diaries, newspaper cuttings, photos, correspondence lessons, school reports and letters I'd kept, I'd feel myself climbing back into that particular time frame.

The first days when I'd struggled to work my word processor had me wondering seriously if I'd ever master it. The memories of those days still make me laugh.

I'd bought it secondhand and had arrived in Okukari Bay with the machine packed in two cartons, plus an instruction book. I had written two chapters in longhand and I was dying to type them, with two fingers, just so I could see what my words looked like when typed. I didn't have time to read the instruction book though I did glance at it. I wanted to start typing that very moment, but first the machine had to be set up. Margins, tabs, auto return, justify, save settings, auto indent - all these words were foreign to me and so I called on Joe's wife, Joy, to teach me their meaning. At last I could begin.

"The beauty of this machine," I was told by the instruction book, "is that all your work can be stored on disks." It seemed all that was left for me to do was press the right key and I'd have my writing on a disk. No one had told me that I had to know how to find it once I had it stored.

The tangles I got myself into reduced me to tears of frustration. This machine was as bad as that coal range I'd struggled with in my early years at Okukari. It controlled me completely.

In desperation I called on Young Joe. He's a whizz on his computer, which is much more elaborate than mine, so I hoped he could help me. All I wanted to be able to do was put the words I'd written on to a disk, and then, when I needed to, be able to recall them. Somewhere, lurking inside my machine, there were the two chapters I'd typed.

I was ordered out of the room when Young Joe came to figure out how to work my word processor. "Give me half an hour," is all he said. When he came out I was told it was more difficult than he'd thought but if I kept fiddling around on it I'd soon pick it up. "I'll take the instruction book home with me and have a read and come back tomorrow night. We'll sort it out."

First light found me at the machine, trying to master it. I'd stored phrases and tried unsuccessfully to recall them when, suddenly, up on the screen came the words, 'Heather, please learn how to use your machine.' I was stunned. It even knows my name, I thought. Then commonsense took over and I knew exactly what my son had been doing the night before. He'd put the message in, hoping I'd recall it.

Gradually I learnt how to store, and then recall, what I'd written. I found my two missing chapters and the book grew. As I finished each block of writing I always printed it out, mindful of the two chapters that had remained lost for the first few days, but then I had another problem. Experts told me I should have a back-up disk. Now I was terrified that if I attempted to copy the disk I might lose the lot, and so the 104,000 words that made up my book travelled New Zealand. I took my disk with me wherever I went, right up to the time the proofed copy of the book was in the printers' hands in Hong Kong.

Three months after I'd thought I'd finished my book, lambing was over, shearing finished, the lambs tailed, the main editing and putting-together of the chapters was done, and my book was completed. This time I knew it was right. Without being aware of it at the time I had written a complete circle. Post-book depression was gone and as I read through the chapters I felt a surge of elation. It was what I'd wanted to say.

Paul Palmer, a friend and professional photographer, came and stayed at our home and while he was with us his camera worked overtime. Later, with Paul's photos, plus a large suitcase full of my photo albums and loose photos, I came into Picton and stayed with Chris at her Whatamango Bay home in Queen Charlotte Sound. From a lifetime of photos we selected what we believed told the best story. Then the captions were thought up. Photos that told me many stories had to be able to tell strangers the same stories. My mind buzzed, and sleep eluded me that night as memories evoked from the hundreds of long ago photos flashed through my mind.

In the beginning the cover seemed unimportant. I'd had the name, *Weather Permitting*, in my mind for years, but I'd forgotten about the cover. Chris hadn't. There had been various ideas. Then, "One with you on the front, I feel." And so I found myself, one cold southerly day, down on the beach in Picton Harbour. Ian Garrod from Picton's Happy Snappa gave me the only experience in my life of having a 'photo shoot'. It wasn't Ian's fault that to get that one photo that I felt was perfect for my book he had to take 36 shots.

I'd never thought about what goes into publishing a book. Someone wrote a book - and there it was in the bookshop. But there's more to it than that.

Mine was different to begin with, because I'd written chapters out of order, as subjects came to me. After all, I've always been a 'list lady' and it was natural for instance to make lists of things like searches and rescues, or mustering and shearing anecdotes, and then write about them. What happened then was like the putting together of a big patchwork quilt. Where should this chapter go, or that? How should they be linked?

When I visited my Sounds publisher I found her dining table and part of the carpet covered with my chapters, in the process of being moved around. I learned bits and pieces about type faces and paper, unit costs and bookshop discounts and even things like 'widow lines' which really intrigued me. This means a short line standing all by itself forlornly - poor little widow! - at, say, the last paragraph of a page. It doesn't look right, so the words and spaces have to be juggled around so readers are no longer troubled even subliminally by widows standing alone.

A red letter day was 19 March 1996. That's when the advance copies of my book arrived in Picton. Chris rang me, sounding very pleased. When I told her that Joe with Young Joe and James were in Picton unloading fish, she wrapped up two books and took them down to our boat, getting Joe's promise he wasn't to look at them or show them to anyone. The unwrapping was to be my privilege.

At home my day dragged. Not even the view from my windows gave me any pleasure. Tory Channel lay between me and my book. It might as well have been a steel barrier 100 feet high. Apart from the proofs of the colour photos and a fax 12 feet long from Hong Kong, with all the photos and captions, I hadn't seen the book since it left Okukari. I yearned to hold the end result in my hands.

I sat at the kitchen table, watching the hills and water in the channel grow black as red clouds lost their golden rims, and the sky, hills and sea melted into each other. This view, my wonderful painting that has been with me all my years at Okukari, sprang to life when I saw the silhouette of our fishing boat, *Te Wai*, turn Wirikarapa light and head up Tory Channel. The next 20 minutes were some of the longest I have spent. I was waiting there when she arrived at the wharf.

All sorts of feelings rushed through me when I held my book for the first time. Eighteen months earlier it was still a dream. Thirty-three years of my life, the years of my marriage, were sandwiched inside these pages. I'd written of things I'd hardly spoken about to anyone before. What would people think? How would my friends react?

The following day, in the midst of these jumbled thoughts, I read my book from cover to cover. Now I was terrified. I saw it as disjointed, childish, a book no one would want to read. A phone call to Chris made me feel better. "Honey," she told me, "if I'd thought it was like that I wouldn't have published it."

I had to believe her words to believe in myself. I had to push misgivings aside as my diary began to fill with dates for interviews, which were part of the book's promotion. Books don't sell themselves these days, I was told. People have to be told about them. Magazines, papers, radio and television. Some interviews were even to take place before the 'family and friends' launching in Picton, but most were to be after that.

My very first magazine interview was by telephone. I wondered if it was an April Fool's Day joke when the phone rang at lunchtime on 1 April and Cheryl Lilly introduced herself. I knew her name from Four Corners in *North & South* magazine, and I immediately felt anxious. When she told me she'd ring back later it was worse. I couldn't enjoy my lunch at all and every time the phone rang I became more and more anxious. When I finally spoke with Cheryl I was struck by her friendly personality and I actually enjoyed that interview.

I wasn't so sure about my next two. They were lined up for me in Wellington and I was to catch the *Lynx*, the fast ferry, to Wellington on April 11. Lisa, our younger son James's wife, came with me and brought their older child, Haydn, then four years old. The fast ferry was a first for me. I loved the speed of the trip across the Strait but as we steamed up Tory Channel I felt sympathy for those residents who are affected by the huge wash the ferry creates. I like to think we could do two things - keep this service, and prevent the damage to the shoreline and the bottom of the channel.

Wellington became a different city as Haydn's wide eyes took in the sights. When a little voice asked "Who lives in those castles?" the tall grey buildings became magical places to me as well. In the fast-moving crowds a little hand wrapped tightly around mine. I laughed when Haydn asked the old question, "What do all these people do all day? Where are they going?"

My first appointment was with Jane Bowron at the *Sunday Star Times*. The closer I got to Press House, the more nervous I became. It was as bad as going for a job interview. When I'd written my book, no one had told me these sorts of things were part of it. I had a picture of Jane in my mind as being tall, dark, slim and probably very austere. I met a charming woman who was the complete opposite. When I told her this she admitted to being surprised at how different I was, and I wondered if she'd expected to see me in jeans, Swanndri and gumboots.

This interview was fun. I was amazed at how intrigued people were with my life story. One of the questions I was asked made me think hard. "Are women more capable than men?"

I believe strongly in my answer. "Yes. They can turn their hands to anything, only missing out on equalling male physical strength."

When Jane asked if I had a religious belief, or had I meditated to help me over the bad times I'd written about, especially in those early years, I knew the answer without having to think. I hadn't had time to call on a god.

My next appointment was also at Press House. This was to be for an article in *Contact*, the all-Wellington community newspaper. They wanted a photograph, and I found myself standing on the footpath of

Boulcott Street, at the back of Press House, holding my book up to my face and trying to act normally, even though I was dressed in unfamiliar clothes and black leather shoes. Even my handbag felt foreign, slung over my shoulder. Car drivers shouted at me and tooted their horns as they passed. I grinned at the thought that they probably thought I was a model.

I was beginning to feel weighed down by the people and the traffic. The minute the interview was over, I raced to the front of the building where Lisa and Haydn were waiting for me.

Childhood memories had me suggesting that we took an electric unit to Johnsonville where I'd visited my grandparents. I remembered the tunnels that had made us late after an earthquake as they all had to be checked to make sure there wasn't any structural damage. In James Smiths' department store I'd watched as staff had swept up the plaster that had fallen off the ceilings and I had been thankful that Auckland didn't have these earthquakes.

Haydn's excited voice, telling Lisa and me about the red and green lights he could see, cars at crossings, more tunnels, another train and finally Wellington Station jolted me back to the present.

The return trip on the *Lynx* and the final leg of our trip up the Sounds seemed to take forever. When we at last arrived back to the peace of Okukari I whispered a prayer that I might always be healed by this place I love.

I'd no sooner caught my breath after my day in Wellington than I had a call from Jackie Maher, a reporter on TV's Paul Holmes show. She had read my book and wanted to make a programme. In the space of one phone call it was all arranged. Jackie, with Ivars Berzins her camera person, would meet us in Picton when we unloaded fish on 15 April, and then they were coming back to Okukari with us.

As my diary filled I found myself trying to hold on to my way of life. I guess I was an island innocent but I felt I was being swallowed up in the publicity, and I wasn't ready for it. I didn't want to change. The phone always rang at meal times when I was dishing up, and Joe's digestive system suffered from the burnt dinners. Three more television interviews were confirmed before I'd got through the first one, and this didn't help either. I realised the only way I was going to get through this whole promotion thing was to take one day at a time, and so, when my publisher sent me the pages of the author-tour itinerary which Catriona McEwan of McMedia Marketing had initiated and she'd added on to, I followed my own advice. Throughout the tour I always focused on one page, never looking ahead to the next page until I had to.

I still had to get through my television debut. At least the day was fine and as the shark or lemonfish and groper were unloaded the camera seemed to be filming all the time. My husband and sons became adept at making themselves scarce in front of a rolling camera, showing their faces only when necessary. Then it was my turn and I found myself wired for sound. To my surprise they had picked up that part of my book about what had to be packed into a short visit to Picton, so I was filmed shopping, always with my lists, and trying as usual to fit a whole day into half a day.

When we returned to our bay and unloaded the stores from the boat to the wharf at Okukari I remembered how it used to be when we arrived home with a month's supply of stores and everything had to be rowed ashore no matter what the weather. Ivars had told me his camera was worth more than $70,000. I was glad it didn't have to balance on the seat of an eight-foot dinghy that always had water sloshing around in its bottom as we were rowed ashore. These days we have a wharf. Everything can be piled on to the four-wheel motorbike and trailer, then driven to the shed that was built for the generator, and carried inside. The concrete engine bed where the generator sat is still in the shed. I'm still grateful that I don't have to swing the handle to start the generator before going inside, praying that it would start and I'd have electricity. The paper work involved in getting Arapawa Island reticulated, the money we paid for our capital contribution and the $1,900 we still pay annually, plus our units, are worth it. Being able to turn on a light with a flick of a switch still means as much to me as it did on 7 April 1982, Reticulation Day.

Having visitors in the bay doesn't guarantee a quiet relaxed evening, as Ivars and Jackie were to find out. The stores were all packed away and the next day was being planned. Filming would begin early in the morning as that's often the best light, I was told. Then we noticed a small fire across the bay over at Whekenui. The farm manager was burning scrub on the bank above the wharf. As we watched, the strong nor-westerly fanned the flames. "It'll sweep around the cliffs and into the trees around Gunyah if he doesn't watch out," Joe said as he peered through binoculars.

Joe Perano, the founder of Perano Whaling, had built the house,

Gunyah, for his wife Pattie, in 1945. It was part of history. It couldn't burn, I thought.

"She'll be tinder-dry. Go up like matchwood."

Joe's words made me cold. I realised that history burns the same as anything else.

The fire officer in Joe wouldn't let him watch the flames as they licked closer to the old house, and five minutes later Jackie and I found ourselves on our own, with the men on their way over the hill on the motorbike. Joe thought they'd probably be able to beat out the fire but if he needed the fire pump I was told he'd ring from Whekenui and I was to have it ready for him.

Thick clouds of grey smoke took the place of bright orange flames as the men went to work, and, while we watched, slowly the smoke died away. The men arrived home for dinner - just another day for us, but a different kind of day for our visitors.

Early next morning was clear and bright, perfect for fishing in Cook Strait and perfect for filming at Okukari. The channel was at its very best and the early light created a painting as beautiful as in any art gallery. Ivars was already at work, capturing the beauty of a yellow rose, its petals laden with dew.

Some of the next five hours I'd rather not remember. Especially when, out of the blue, I was asked to play my piano. Since writing my book I'd been so busy catching up with other things that the only times I'd touched it was to practise the music I was to play each month at Picton's Holy Trinity Church. And it needed tuning. But nothing put Jackie off so I played some Mozart, knowing how the piano would sound to a trained ear. Later, when I watched the Holmes Show on television, I was aware that the music was right for the programme. I tried to shut my ears to the dull notes, and promised myself to have the piano tuned.

I had read how, in film-making, it's said that the best bits are left on the cutting-room floor, and by the end of the day I believed it. The camera rolled all day, enough for a documentary, and I was told it was all to get just six minutes of air time. Old photos were pored over, family portraits of Joe's great-great-grandfather, James (Worser) Heberley and his wife, Te Wai, were filmed. My lounge was filled with photos balanced on chairs, the camera standing on its tripod, and boxes of photos which we'd searched through for the most suitable. The interview with Joe and me was nerve-wracking. Even though Jackie assured us she would use only the best footage I found it so hard to be natural when I answered some of the questions. I'd become tongue-tied, and we'd have to start again. I'd be told that it was nearly over and that I should just bear with it a little longer - words the dentist uses when I'd be beginning to wish I'd had a local anaesthetic after all.

When at last I was told that that was it, I could wonder why ever I had been so worried. Now I could enjoy the experience in retrospect and as Jackie and Ivars pulled away from our wharf in the boat and I waved goodbye I felt I was a Cinderella, shedding the glamour of television and becoming plain Heather Heberley of Okukari who lives in the first house on the right as you come in Tory Channel - and I revelled in it.

Three days to go before the Picton book launching on Saturday. Precious days to gather myself together. I needed this time to myself, and when Joe left to go into Picton I was happy to be on my own. I tried to write my speech and ended up just making a list of people I had to thank, hoping the other words would come on the night. Just thinking about the launching made my heart pound and hands shake. No, I definitely was not a public person. Too much of Okukari had seeped into my blood over the last 33 years. I was happiest in my own company, with my family, definitely not standing up in front of a crowd to speak.

That day I couldn't concentrate. I drifted from one thing to another. After giving up on my speech I dragged out the books I had to sign, but even then I found myself flipping back and forth through pages, reliving so many memories, so much of my life. I wept as once again I went through my parents' deaths, then laughed at myself as I read about my first attempt at a steamed pudding that our pet pig wouldn't eat. The Correspondence School years, the loneliness and fear as I've waited for my men when they've been out in a storm searching for a missing boat, so many events crowded my mind and I had to pull myself together before Joe arrived home. I didn't think he'd under-stand if he came home to a blubbing wife who was supposed to be excited on the eve of her book launch.

At night I prayed that I'd sleep through to morning, but I woke at 4.15am. My mind was so busy I was amazed when I drifted back to sleep and woke once more at 5.30am. I rehearsed my speech to four walls until I could see the first light through the curtains. Joe's rhythmic breathing told me he was still asleep and I slid carefully out of bed, tiptoed down the hall and sat in the dawn light of the kitchen, waiting for the peace that always comes as I drink in the beauty of the morning.

The water in the bay was flat glassy calm. Patches of ruffles from feeding fish were all that changed the surface, while out in the channel only the turbulent water at Wheke Rock, below Gunyah, disturbed the surface. The mass of water could be seen moving down Tory Channel as the last of the flood tide pushed slowly into all the bays, stealing the sand at the top of the tide. The early passenger ferry from Picton rumbled up the channel. A rain shower passed over and the sound of it on the roof was an invasion. I needed quiet time alone today.

Marcia and Roy Rowe had also had an early start to their day as they were worried that the track out of Aotea on the Queen Charlotte side of Arapawa Island might have become too slippery with the rain, so they left home with two hours to spare in case they had to walk. I was thrilled to see the bike driving down the farm road on our side of the island, with Marcia riding pillion, her pack bulging with their town clothes. The thought of wearing clothes other than jeans, shirts and sneakers had everyone on the boats laughing in happy anticipation of the day ahead. As we were picking up quite a few friends on the way in to the book launch, Joe had decided to take both boats to Picton. When we steamed out of our bay the noise from two engines reverberated and I watched as the ripples we had made dressed the bay in a white frothy collar as they hit the white sand.

Just because it was the day my book was being launched made little difference to a day in Picton. I had my usual lists of things I needed and things I had to do. My first stop was the bookshop to stock up with stationery for the office. I lifted my hand to push the door open - and stopped. The window was full of my books. Nothing would make me go into that shop. I was too embarrassed. Imagine if someone recognised me, I thought. That particular list was put back in my purse until my next trip to Picton.

My sister Betty from Auckland, Aunt Willa from Hamilton and cousins from Taumarunui, Palmerston North and Wellington were due on the Interislander that berthed at 12.30pm, and once they were all in Picton the festive mood began to build. But so did the tight knot in the pit of my stomach. Even the usual relaxing time at the hairdresser didn't help. It only brought me an hour closer to 5pm. I felt I was on a roller coaster that wouldn't stop until it came to the time when I had to make a speech in front of so many people, even if they were mostly family and friends. What worried me even more was realising that people were going to be able to buy my book and read all about me.

By 3pm I was a mess. My head ached and the knot in my stomach was making me feel sick. I wanted to be sociable and join in the conversations that were bubbling around me but I'd reached the stage when I knew I had to get away from people. Through the buzzing in my head I heard Joe tell Pauline he was taking me back to the boat where I could lie down in the cool before getting dressed. It was a zombie who drove with Joe down to the boat which was still tied up in Picton. Climbing out of the car on the wharf, I took deep breaths of the fresh salt air and could feel my head starting to belong to my body. I sat in the shade on the deck, my hands wrapped around a cup of tea, feeling the nervous tension drain away just by being on the sea, watching boats pull in and out of the wharves and the antics of the seabirds as they paddled around, their bright beady eyes trying to catch those of a young fisherman, hoping he'd throw them a piece of his bait.

Joe's voice telling me it was time to get changed brought me out of my reverie. I wanted to be dressed when everyone arrived back at the boats before we steamed them round into Waikawa Bay and tied up at the boating club where the book would be launched. My mind still wanted to shut out the present, and, as I enjoyed the luxury of a shower on the *Te Wai*, memories of all the other boats we've had crowded in. The *Heather*, our first, and *Tineke*, both now sold, and *Fugitive* which we still own, none of these had showers. Today we wouldn't dream of having a boat built without one, but as I mused I realised fishing has changed. Our men have to go much further afield to fish now, and the boats have to be more comfortable. Their standards have changed, too.

As we steamed into the Waikawa Marina, I had to face up to the present. The Waikawa Bay Boating Club was straight ahead. Our boats were tied up immediately in front of the building, and my mind stored the picture it made in the late afternoon sun. The usual Sounds fare of crayfish, paua patties, smoked salmon and groper throats and cheeks, along with other food which friends had prepared for me, was off-loaded and carried into the kitchen for the staff to position on plates. I walked into the building.

The first thing that caught my eye as I glanced around was the lectern. My imagination working overtime saw it as a malevolent presence, standing on its own up on the dais with the microphone hooked alongside it. The past caught up with me again as I remembered having those same feelings when I saw my coal range in my first years at Okukari.

Then I saw the flowers. A living card of flowers had come from friends in Australia and written on the card was the name of my book, *Weather Permitting*. And there were more flowers other people had sent me. It was the jolt I needed to make me realise that tonight I was among friends and they all wished me well. Among all the people arriving and lots of hugs, squashing my beautiful red corsage which Chris had pinned on me, I watched my grandchildren beginning to pass around plates of food, their faces beaming with pleasure at being included in Grandma's special night. All my family was here and my heart felt as if it would burst when I saw them altogether, still close and loving. My own family.

I had been told that speeches would start about 6pm and that first hour went too quickly. Listening to Chris's speech followed by one from Doug Kidd, our local MP, I couldn't begin to imagine how mine would sound. They were so professional. Then it was Pauline's turn. My youngest was to launch my book.

Her words had me sitting back and enjoying the moment. The mother in me took over from the author and a warmth encompassed my whole being. It wasn't only pride. It was every feeling a mother ever feels in a lifetime. Pauline's speech was built up after she had talked to all her siblings. It was part of them all, and I knew I'd finally been given the answer I'd asked myself over the years when teaching correspondence lessons. I had taught them well. They were all one hundred percent.

Then it was my turn. After the first panic, words flowed, and being a practised list lady I found it easier to remember all those I had to thank. The hard part of the evening was over. Now it was time to remember my publisher's motto, "Have fun."

The 90-minute boat trip up the Sounds had us leaving Waikawa at 9.30pm and when we left the wharf those who didn't have to travel by boat lined the rails of the decking outside the boating club, farewelling us with the Mexican Wave. The warmth and emotion brought a lump to my throat and as we steamed slowly through the marina I thought what a wonderful ending to the night.

That night still held unexpected magic. As the light faded behind us, new lights lit up the sea. Dolphins, with their distinguishing longer beaks than the smaller porpoises, became our companions. They swam around the two boats, their black shapes lit up by the phosphorescence in the water. As they rolled and dived, liquid silver shadows melted from sight, then burst up through the darkness as they broached the surface to begin their show again. No one noticed the cold as we stood out on the deck spellbound, and the usual trip home seemed to be over in no time at all.

Once we were in the house all I could think was that I'd crossed the first bridge. Relief washed over me. I'd written a book, it was launched, nothing surely could ever be as nerve-wracking as tonight. Not even the author-lunches lined up in my diary - at which I'd only just realised I had to speak. For now I could forget them. As sleep took over, I felt that my day at Okukari tomorrow would set me up for the busy month that lay ahead.

CHAPTER TWO

A Distinctly New World

THE NIGHT before my first literary luncheon, to be held in Blenheim, I lay in bed and listened to a southerly storm. The stillness before it hit had been enough to wake me. Then came the roar of the wind as it raced up the channel. I could picture the spray lifting off the tops of the waves and I felt the force of the salt-laden wind as it slammed against the windows. The noise of the seas crashing on the beach made me worry that I might be weatherbound tomorrow. Quite appropriate, I thought, if the weather kept the author of *Weather Permitting* at home.

Unable to sleep I wandered out to the lounge and sat in the darkness, watching the sheets of lightning light up my painting. My eyes weren't adjusted to the darkness before the thunder rumbled around the hills. There was no break before another sheet of lightning lit up the hills in sharp relief and another clap of thunder shook the house.

In my garden I caught glimpses of tall conifers being battered by the wind. Another flash showed the last of my beautiful summer dahlias flattened. The wind stretched the leaves of the flax bushes horizontally and they took on the appearance of giant squids, their clutching tentacles wrapping around the smaller shrubs and stripping them of their leaves. The darkness hid some of the destruction, but I knew.

With every storm I promise myself that I'm giving up gardening. I tell myself it's not worth the heartache or expense. But once the sun comes out I find myself outside cleaning up the debris, losing count of the number of times I fill up the wheelbarrow with torn branches and smashed flowers, and at the same time making a mental list of plants and shrubs to buy when I next go to Picton. I have learnt by trial and error what grows and survives, and I've learnt to close my eyes to the more beautiful hybrids and stick to the hardier shrubs. I am finding more and more pleasure from conifers and their shades of green are gradually taking over from the bright flowers I have tried to grow year after year. My dahlias grow well among the shrubs. That night the cold, not tiredness, drove me back to the warmth of my bed and I lay wishing the night would end.

Hannah, a friend staying with us and who lives about as far away from the sea as anyone in New Zealand can, looked very bleary-eyed at breakfast. "I've been lying awake all night, wondering how we get off the wharf on to the boat," she told me. Breakfast time didn't cheer Hannah up. With an "I might be seasick," she decided it was better not to eat.

Once again all our town clothes were packed into a bag and with Joe calling out and telling us to be ready on the wharf when he brought in the boat, he left the house.

In my entire life I can count on one hand the times I've worn a corsage. The night of my book launching was one of those times and I'd looked after my flowers, hoping to wear them again at the luncheon. I sat the flowers on a saucer and covered them with plastic wrap to protect them from the weather. I'd carry these down to the boat myself.

A big swell was running and the seas were crashing over the wharf, just as Hannah had feared. Joe nudged the boat in, yelling at Hannah to jump. I watched as she balanced on one foot while urging the other to leave the safety of the wharf and jump on to the heaving deck. I knew Joe meant what he said when he told Hannah that you either leap aboard and go with the boat or stay behind. She did it.

The bags were thrown after her and then it was my turn. I'd hardly landed before Joe pushed the throttle hard down and we reversed out from the wharf. Waves broke over the stern and water sloshed over the deck. By the time I had all the bags in the wheelhouse my newly shampooed and blow-waved hair was full of salt water, I was soaking wet and worst of all the wind had flicked the wrap off my corsage and it was ruined. I was so angry as I dried myself and tried to repair the damage to my corsage that I took it out on Joe. "Just once," I cried, "let me arrive somewhere without the windswept look!"

But after 33 years I doubt if I ever will. Joe had the last word and stopped me by quoting what he'd read on the back of my book cover. "It's a love story. You're not meant to growl at me."

This luncheon went well and I did find speaking to about 80 people a little easier although I still had to overcome the dry mouth syndrome, and the sea of faces in front of me made my mind a blank at the start. But there were many people I knew and when I was presented with flowers the warm love of friends buoyed me up and the afternoon actually passed too quickly. It was great to meet up with people with whom I'd shared dreams at the two writing courses I'd attended with Christine Cole Catley, and, as I talked with them later, there was wonder that I, the shyest one in the class, had her name on a book first. But best of all was the comment I heard many times that afternoon - "Now I've heard you speak I'm going home to write the book I've wanted to for years."

The next day at Okukari I spent packing. Both Joe and I were going to the 38th national conference of the New Zealand Federation of Commercial Fishermen. This was to be held in Nelson and my book was going to be presented on the evening of the fundraising auction for the Shipwreck Society. Following the three days of conference, Joe would be coming back home on his own.

My author-tour would begin by picking up my friend Maureen Stewart in Picton, then going by ferry to Wellington. Maureen has been my friend and Picton lifeline since the days when I had four children, very close together, and dreaded leaving my island and taking them all to Picton when I had to do essential shopping. When my editor and publisher couldn't leave her one-woman publishing enterprise to travel with me on my author-tour, Maureen naturally was the person I turned to.

Now I needed a suitcase with enough clothes for 15 days. Deciding on the most suitable was a problem. My wardrobe was stretched to the limit. I needed clothes to wear at the conference and then for author luncheons, signings in bookshop, newspaper and radio interviews and television. Clothes for warm Auckland days and clothes for colder days. As my wardrobe emptied and my suitcase bulged I kept an eye on my itinerary, trying to work out what I could wear each day. The enormity of all the travelling ahead washed over me. After the 15 days away I'd have one weekend at home, and then another 14 days around the South Island. At least Joe had promised to come south with me.

I sat on the floor surrounded with clothes I didn't need and thought about the last few days. Locally, my book was a winner. Bookshops loved it in Marlborough. This was so exciting I couldn't really believe it. But now I had to help sell the book over all New Zealand and I wondered if I was capable of doing this. People, traffic and noise. The three things I'd hungered for in those early days at Okukari now had me wishing I didn't have to face them. It would be a distinctly new world. I knew that, but as yet I had no idea what it would really be like.

All the wishing in the world didn't stop another day dawning and another boat trip down the Sounds to Picton. By the time we left home the early morning fog had cleared in Tory Channel, and as we neared Picton the fog was lifting off the water and lying in pockets on the shore. The sun rose behind us as we steamed down Queen Charlotte Sound and made a golden pathway on the bronze sea. Droplets lifting off the water that churned up behind the stern caught the sun's rays and formed mini-rainbows. Other boats with sea birds swooping and diving in their wake were blackened in the bright light.

I sat on the stern, taking in the beauty and storing it in my mind for the days ahead. The sun shining through the tree tops and the flat calm water with the reflections of moored boats in the harbour made me catch my breath. It brought back memories of that beautiful, unforgettable day on which my mother was killed in 1977, and I wished as I expect I will always wish that she could be sharing this time with me.

At the conference we again found more new faces, replacements for many of the older fishermen who have pulled out of the industry, some who have been lost at sea and others who have died. The fishermen and wives who attend conferences work hard, and the evening is time for them to have fun.

Dick Hall, an executive member of the Picton Fishermen's Association, has run the fundraising auction at conferences as long as I can remember, and we'd asked him to present my book during this year's auction. I knew he'd do it well but I dreaded to think what story he might dredge up. He'd been toastmaster at two of our family weddings, and at these I'd been reminded of quite a few incidents I'd rather forget. Half way through the auction, *Weather Permitting* was launched.

Dick told everyone that he was disappointed not to read of the following incident in my book - it was about a trip I'd made on a Cook Strait ferry. I knew it! I knew he'd go and tell this. It was the most embarrassing thing I've ever done in my entire life. I didn't write about it as I imagined the person involved might read my book. If I'd been a snail I'd have crawled into my shell and hidden. Dick had told this story at our daughter Pauline's wedding to Dene, and as I listened to it again I thought I'd better tell my side in this book before Dick tells it another time with more embellishments and actings-out.

It actually happened like this. Joe and I had been to Auckland in our car. On the way back we'd stopped off in Wellington as I wanted to catch up with a cousin. Joe wasn't coming with me. He said he didn't want to hear us natter for an hour and was happy to go and have a beer.

Our hour passed very quickly and I suddenly found I was going to be late to meet up with Joe. I couldn't believe it when my usually undemonstrative husband rushed up, hugged me tightly and kissed me.

"Thank goodness you're back. That creep over there has been following me. Let's get to hell out of here."

We scuttled down the street and in between my bursts of laughter I heard the rest of the story.

"I went downstairs to this pub." We found out later it was where the gay community gathered. "This guy kept watching me. I downed my beer and took off. He followed me." I had to laugh as I imagined my Joe being picked up by a stranger - and a male.

It was no laughing matter, an indignant Joe told me as he looked around again to see if he was still being followed. In the car and driving to the ferry terminal, Joe was still on edge and I don't think he relaxed until we were steaming out of Wellington harbour, the memory of his encounter fading with the buildings.

The weather is the most important news item for men of the sea and the closer we got to home the more urgent was his need to study it. When he told me he would go to the lounge for the news and wait for the weather map to come on television, I curled up on a seat with a book.

He seemed to have been gone for ages and I thought I'd go and look for him. There he was, leaning against a bulkhead at the back of the lounge, watching the weather map. In the semi-darkness he was easy to pick out in his brown corduroy trousers and cream Arran jersey. He looked totally relaxed, his afternoon ordeal forgotten. I crept up to his back, wrapped my arms around his waist, then ran my hands right down his front, snuggling my chin on his shoulder, and in my deepest, sexiest voice I whispered, "How much?"

He swung round. It was not Joe.

All I could stutter was that I thought he was my husband. His reply, "I only wish I was," is etched in my memory.

I raced back to my seat to wait for Joe. I couldn't bear to look up when he arrived but sat with my eyes glued to my book. Passengers with vehicles were told to go and get in their cars but I was too embarrassed to leave the seat in case my stranger recognised me. I pretended nothing was wrong. Then Joe noticed I was reading my book upside down. So I told him, and whenever a possible man passed by he'd prod me and ask if this was the man I'd propositioned.

It is a story quite a few of my family and friends dine out on to this day - especially Dick Hall.

As I waited for the laughter at Dick's version at conference to die down before I made my speech, my eyes took in the room. Nerves left me. I was among friends brought together because of one thing - their love of the sea. At sea many are bitter rivals in the competitive age fishing has come to, but while at conference they are a united group working for the good of the industry and preserving fish stock in New Zealand.

Two of my books were donated to be used for fundraising for our special charity, the Shipwreck Society. One book was auctioned after my speech, and Michele Leith of Northern Fish Quota Trading Limited paid $120 for it.

The second book was saved until the function on the last night, the night when all the hard work of the conference is forgotten and everyone has fun. The Shipwreck Society benefited by $240 from the second book which was bought by Sir Tipene O'Regan. Dick Hall had found out it was our thirty-third wedding anniversary and ordered me to pay $25 into the bucket that was filling rapidly with forfeits as he related stories about many fishermen or their partners, and we had to pay up.

Over the years some rather unusual things have been offered for auction. We've had a shovel and a tie, but the most extraordinary thing to date has been a Lifesaver peppermint. It was presented to Dick to be auctioned and it seemed that many people wanted to purchase a peppermint with a hole in the middle. At the conclusion of the bidding a Whitianga fisherman, with support from several backers, proudly held his prize aloft with the promise it would be framed and brought back for next year's auction. It cost him $252. A lot of money for a peppermint, but so little to give in the face of the loss of family or friends at sea, and these families are the ones who benefit from the fishermen who have fun at the auctions.

The following morning I received the first of what were to become hundreds of phone calls from people who had read my book. Not only women. It appeared that men too were enjoying reading about life on an island in the Marlborough Sounds. I couldn't believe that strangers would take the trouble to ring: not only direct dialling but calls on my cellphone and toll calls from all over New Zealand. One Saturday morning at home the phone rang and it was a fisherman from the Chatham Islands. He'd read my book and taken the time to ring and tell me how it was so like his own life. But, he added, he'd never had a piano stuck in a doorway.

Sunday 28 April - and the first day of my author-tour. I tried to quell my apprehension. Joe and I arrived back in Picton in time to pick up Maureen and her luggage, and drop Joe off. He was to wait for our sons to arrive as they were unloading fish later in the day. I watched him walk down the wharf to yarn with some of the local fishermen and wished that I too was going back to Okukari. Instead I had more than 1700 kilometres in front of me before I'd be home again. Maureen and I drove to the ferry terminal. Once aboard we met up with Chris Cole Catley who was also travelling to Wellington to help us get into the rhythm of the tour, as she put it, and we were able to finalise dates on my itinerary. She had added more engagements to it during the past week and I took in a deep breath as my eyes scanned all the events over the next fortnight. As Maureen and I went down to the car deck on our arrival in Wellington, every step I took tapped out Chris's words, "You can do it. Have fun. Have fun."

The night at my cousin's home in Wellington was far too short - the hours go so quickly when you don't want them to - and it seemed to be no time until I found myself, with Maureen, walking up the street to my first live radio interview. This was with Mike Yardley on Newstalk ZB. Later Maureen told me how my footsteps became slower and slower as we neared the station. I was so nervous I couldn't swallow and my throat was closing up. Going up in the lift I closed my eyes and tried to stop the pounding of my heart. It felt as if it was at the base of my throat, trying to leap out of my body, and one of my eyes was affected. It was twitching.

I wonder if these confident media people have any idea how nervous their interview subjects can get. Somehow I don't think I can be the only one. But Mike Yardley put me at my ease and although I was still very nervous I was surprised when the interview was over and he told me how long we'd been talking. The 20 minutes had flown. I came out of the studio on a high, and in the reception area I noticed my name among others on the board welcoming Newstalk ZB's guests for that day.

"Who's Bill Bailey?" I asked. A scruffy man turned around from the desk.

"Me. Haven't you heard of me?"

When I told him the only Bill Bailey I'd heard of was in the song, 'Won't you come home Bill Bailey', he started singing it and Maureen and I joined in.

"I'm a comedian. I sing and play my guitar. Come and hear me tonight," he called out to us as we stepped into the waiting lift.

The day was filled with another newspaper interview and two more radio interviews, one live and another to be played at a later date. At the end of the day I turned over the first page of my itinerary and felt relieved. The nerves were still there before each interview but it became apparent on that first day that all I had to do was answer the questions I was asked, and they were all about my own life. I don't know what I had been expecting and dreading. Imagination does strange things. As I gained more confidence I discovered that I could direct the interviews to questions that I'd like to be asked, and I began to enjoy them.

Palmerston North, Hastings and then on to Napier. Newspaper interview rooms merged into one another and there were the radio interviews and stopping at bookshops for book signings. I met relatives, friends of the Heberley family and people whose relatives had whaled with Joe or his father. I wrote down names so I'd be able to remember to tell the family when I arrived home.

Maureen and I drove from Hastings to Napier the morning of another author-luncheon. The proceeds from the luncheon were for the Save the Children Fund. It was freezing cold when we arrived in Napier and the first thing on our agenda was to find the public toilets. A sign on Marine Parade showed us where they were.

We paid for what we got. Twenty cents each gave us clean toilets, toilet paper, and a clean hand basin with a spotless mirror over it. It also gave us a man sitting in a box-like room with three sides which came down only to the top of his stool. His job was to take your money and point left for the women or right for the men. I was doing my hair when I noticed his buttocks beneath the too-short wall, and when his phone rang I couldn't contain my laughter any more as I remarked to Maureen that maybe someone was booking a toilet.

Half an hour before the luncheon I thought I'd lost my glasses. A race back to our parked vehicle didn't find them and so it was a quick visit to a chemist's shop to buy a pair of off-the-rack glasses. The relief when I could see my notes again calmed down the panic which had taken over my body. I found my lost glasses later, but a spare pair was great to have.

At the luncheon I had a wonderful surprise. I was introduced to Gary Hebley, the designer of the map in the front of my book, and the recipe section heading. To put a face to a name and be able to thank him personally gave me great satisfaction. Gary is related to the Heberleys through Frederick Heberley. James (Worser) and Frederick were brothers. Word of mouth created many variations of the surname, Heberley, including Ebberly, Haverly and Ebley. The name, Frederick Heblery, is given on a copy of his daughter Maria's birth certificate dated 1849. Frederick's surname became Hebley. As for the others at the luncheon, the many questions asked after my talk made me realise just how interested people were in our island way of life.

Gisborne, where we were to stay with fishing friends, was a three-hour drive away. I was glad I didn't have to drive. In fact Maureen did all the driving, leaving me free to go over what was next on my itinerary, and relax. I was exhausted when we arrived. It dawned on me that I had been away from Okukari for more than a week, and I hadn't seen Joe for four days. I longed to be around my family once more so I disregarded the cost of toll calls and after a session on the telephone felt much better. In Gisborne our friends wanted to take us out for dinner - it would be a special treat for me. But all I wanted to do was flop in front of the fire, with no make-up, shoes or stockings, and wearing jeans and a sloppy jersey. In the bedroom Maureen and I were sharing I felt like having a really good howl, and said to Maureen how I'd love to stay in tonight.

"Leave it to me," said Maureen and five minutes later she was back telling me Colin and Jill were happy to stay in. They thought we would have liked to go out. Takeaways, washed down with red wine and the companionship of friends, were the ingredients for just the kind of evening I wanted.

All this time I had no idea what was happening to my book. Were people actually buying it? I looked at the countryside and the people in the streets and it all seemed unreal. Was my book real? Perhaps I was imagining it all. I had to shake myself because it was time for my first appointment in Gisborne, with the *Gisborne Herald*. Here I was interviewed by Barbara Scott. By remarkable chance Barbara had been brought up at Wharehunga, ('house where a child is born'), just over the hill from Okukari. We had immediate affinity. The Sounds of her childhood were now my Sounds. This was one interview I specially loved as we covered the years she had missed and the years I had gained.

Next door to the *Gisborne Herald* was Muir's Bookshop. Anne Muir had arranged a literary luncheon, the proceeds of which were to go to the Shipwreck Society. At the shop I learnt that I had been advertised as New Zealand's answer to Australia's Sara Henderson and it made me feel very vulnerable. Could I possibly compete in her league, I asked myself?

But in the bookshop I had the answer to my fearful imaginings. Chris had sent a fax to me. Sales were booming over New Zealand. People were loving my book, she said. I left the shop walking on air, knowing that now I could face the more than 100 people who had booked for the luncheon.

All the travelling hadn't stopped my hair from growing and I longed to spend time with a hairdresser. This couldn't be organised before the luncheon but with the rest of the afternoon free in Gisborne I found a hairdresser. Snippets of conversation from the two operators washed over me as I lay back in the chair. My tired body didn't bother to listen until I heard one girl saying how she'd had "a real messed-up luncheon" - she'd gone to the new Gisborne-Tatapouri Sports Fishing Club rooms on the wharf. "Was told it was full. Some author or something they told me."

That evening I watched the Paul Holmes show on television. We knew the programme that Jackie and Ivars had filmed was going to be brought to air that night and the suspense as we waited was sickening. Questions without answers flashed through my mind. What would be on it? How would it sound? How would we look? Would Okukari be portrayed as I see it? But from the start to the finish I was enthralled. Two strangers had put together a show for television which captured the soul of Okukari - even an out-of-tune piano.

Our next stop was Auckland. It was the furthest place from home but I knew I was on countdown now so I could face the fast lane much more assertively. That was until I had my only dreadful interview with a newspaper.

The interview room was small and I felt claustrophobic shut in with this arrogant, and very chauvinistic, male. He spoke down to me the whole time. He asked me why people would want to read what he was going to write about me. "What would make them stop at the page and read it?"

He told me he hadn't read the book and I felt like telling him that if he read it he might find an answer to that question. His questions battered me and I felt like a log being tumbled in the rip outside the channel entrance, being pushed in all directions, not knowing how to answer. He seemed to delight in making me feel small. Then he asked me what was the climax of the book. "Every book has a build-up to its peak, then drops to the end, doesn't it?"

I was white-hot with anger and my legs felt like jelly. "Whose life ever builds up to a crescendo and then fades?" I shot back at him. "Has yours?" There was a silence. He changed, and the article in the paper a few days later turned out to be one of the best. I wondered if it had happened because I weakened and admitted to the warm feeling I got when I arrived in Auckland on a Saturday afternoon and saw the harbour bridge and the yachts on the harbour, while all the time claiming to have lost all love for the city I'd been brought up in.

That interview was soon forgotten as I went from one radio station to another, all the while writing little notes about each interview. I found myself becoming adept at moulding myself to the type of listener I was speaking to. From Auckland it was Hamilton and my first regional television interview. One thing in my favour was that it was pre-recorded which was just as well as I dropped the microphone off my lap. I didn't know whether to keep on talking or bend down and pick it up but I was told it was fine. That part would be covered with the use of photos taken from the book. More book signings, a talk in Cambridge, back to Hamilton and from there to Taupo where we were to stay overnight.

We left the roar of the Huka Falls behind, and the early morning fog rising off the Waikato river at the outlet of Lake Taupo wreathed the trees in grey. Plumes of steam rose along the shore of the lake, blotting out the far shore. I thought of home and that I'd be there in 12 hours.

As we drove down the country I made a grocery list. I intended to buy groceries at a North Island supermarket because as soon as we arrived in Picton I'd be boarding another boat to come home. Twice the cellphone rang. Lisa and Joy knew I'd be bringing home stores and needed one or two items. Although I'd not made out a list for two weeks I realised I'd become a different kind of list lady when I'd ticked off the last of the North Island engagements and turned the page for the start of the South Island tour.

Cook Strait was flat calm and as we neared Tory Channel entrance Maureen and I went out on to the ferry's deck. The *Te Wai*, our aluminium fishing boat, was steaming towards the channel entrance and we waved out to my son James, and his crew - not that they recognised us. Birds followed in *Te Wai*'s wake, skimming the surface of the water as they waited for the scraps of fish washed through the scuppers in the bulwarks as the decks were hosed down.

A group of men came over and asked us if we knew the men aboard the boat and the fish they'd be catching. They target groper this time of the year and catch a few shark, as well, I told them, and added that we lived inside the entrance and that we'd soon be passing our home. And when they saw our bay I was asked the same question I'd been asked hundreds of times over the years. "How do you keep yourself busy?"

I grinned to myself but Maureen had the best answer that has ever been given. "She's written a book. It's called *Weather Permitting*."

If only I'd had lots of copies in my bag - but - I sold the only copy I had with me and made a mental note to carry two or three spare copies with me in future.

Pauline met me in Picton with a bunch of red roses. "Dad asked me to pick them up. He's missed you, Mum." I was glad I had flowers to bury my face in. Now I didn't have to be busy and I had two days being myself before Joe and I were to leave on the South Island leg. I felt myself letting go inside. I was exhausted. Along with my luggage, groceries and roses, Pauline carried another carton aboard the boat. "From Dene and me. It's your Mother's Day." Inside were biscuits and cakes she'd baked for me, knowing how much her father liked home cooking and how little time I'd have to do any over the weekend.

People often ask me if I get annoyed about having to pass our bay on the ferry, spend another hour aboard, and then turn around and travel back to Okukari by small boat. In the early years it did frustrate me. Especially when the children were younger, I would have loved to have been able to climb aboard the ferry outside our bay.

My father-in-law, Charlie, had told me how the *Tamahine* used to slow down in Tory Channel and pick up passengers or let them off. Charlie's parents, Ada and Arthur Heberley, ran a guesthouse in Oyster Bay, Tory Channel. When guests were arriving, rather than make the trip into Picton, Arthur or one of his sons would take their boat, *Oria*, out into the channel when the *Tamahine* was due. She would slow down and her bow wave helped hold the smaller *Oria* into the ship. Both boats kept moving ahead slowly. A gangway was lowered on to the *Oria*'s deck, and up to 20 guests were often brought off with their luggage in this way. At the end of their holiday the process was reversed.

Hugo and Leila Terrill were Ruby Heberley's maternal grandparents. They ran a guesthouse in Eerie Bay, Tory Channel. They used to transport their guests in the same manner and often one boat from either Oyster Bay or Eerie Bay would pick up the guests and take them out to the *Tamahine*. Once my father-in-law was carrying luggage aboard for the guests when he discovered the gangway was up and he was on his way to Wellington. On his return across Cook Strait he left the ship in Picton.

Charlie had regaled me with stories about what happened if there were only one person travelling. Then the crew of the *Tamahine* wouldn't lower the gangplank. Instead the traveller had to jump off a frequently rolling boat to grab the rope ladder dangling down the *Tamahine*'s topsides, and then clamber up its wooden rungs on to the deck. Stories like that made me quite happy to endure the boat ride to Picton.

In one of the letters I received after *Weather Permitting* was published, I learned that people were horrified to watch Ada Heberley skimming up the rope ladder when they were staying at Oyster Bay many years ago. I tried to imagine the courage it must have taken. This wouldn't have been a woman in jeans, a sloppy sweat shirt and sneakers. From photos, I knew this would have been a lady in leather shoes, stockings, skirt and blouse, or dress, probably with a long overcoat, her purse hanging off her arm. If only her generation had been able to find the time to write, what a story they could have told.

On this occasion, when I returned from Auckland, it was dark when the boat pulled in at the wharf at Okukari and I had to shake off my reminiscing and throw my luggage off the boat up on to the wharf. My red roses I handed to Rachael, our oldest granddaughter, and my cakes and biscuits to Angela, her younger sister, who had come down to meet me with Joe, and of course Quita, my long-haired black and white chihuahua. Three farm dogs were off the chain and they frantically tried to jump up and greet me with their wet tongues. They jumped over my bags and groceries and Joe roared at them to clear off. As he backed up the wharf they barked at the bike tyres in an excited frenzy but after the last fortnight it all seemed a gentle chaos.

Joe had kept me up to date about all the letters that I'd been receiving and I was dying to read them, but for my first night home he told me he'd hidden them. I wasn't allowed to read them until tomorrow. "Tonight is my time."

When I walked past the office and saw the desk my heart sank. A farm plus a fishing business means lots of mail. Mail, and most of the letters that I could see had windows, poured off the desk top. On the floor were stacks which had arrived on different maildays, and he'd even kept all the junk mail. I had only two days to spend at home, and already I knew where most of that time was going to be spent. For tonight I pulled the door shut on it all.

But I still wanted to see my own mail. Of course I did. At last I wore Joe down, and we spent the next two hours reading letters from people who had read my book. To say I was so touched by the many comments is to be quite inadequate. Never, ever, could I have imagined such a situation, or my emotions. So many people, strangers, were reaching out to me in these letters. Some said they wanted to write and thank me for speaking of suicide as I had. Distant relatives, guests from Heberley's Guesthouse in Oyster Bay, people I didn't know but who loved the Marlborough Sounds - the book had touched many memories.

One letter in particular from Auckland brought me to tears. It began: 'A real book, about real people in real surroundings and real situations, real problems, real family and friends, real answers, real battles won and some lost, real feelings expressed, real laughter.' Then it went on to say: 'I knew your mother. We worked together at Tanner Couch. I was there at her presentation for her long service with this company. Through your mother I heard of you in loving terms, and I remember you. My son too worked with your mother and held her in high regard. It is with pride that we recall you were a Northcote lass and your parents well respected yachties.' It finished with the words, 'I hope there will be another book,' and it was signed, Phyllis Batty.

Some letters I read out loud to Joe. Often I couldn't finish reading aloud because of the lump that would build up in my throat. When I'd finished we sat in silence, the pile of letters covering the lounge floor. We were stunned by the love, and support, that had come from so many strangers, and by the amount of enjoyment my book seemed to have given so many people.

Bed would have been a great place to stay on my first morning home but the thought of having only two days to wash and iron my clothes and repack my suitcase, as well as pack Joe's, drove me out and up. And I knew I had to open that office door because accounts, wages and PAYE were just some of the things that had to be attended to. In the office I worked on until late on the Sunday afternoon. I finished off with the thought that anything else could wait for the next two weeks.

Joe and I were to drive to Christchurch on the first day of the South Island author-tour. We left Okukari at 6.30am as my first appointment in Christchurch was with a radio station mid-afternoon, followed by a newspaper interview. Then it was into bookstores for book signings, and in the evening my first live television interview, with George Balani on Canterbury Television.

That day, Monday 13 May, was a mailday I'll never forget. We collected our mail in Picton before driving south. There was one very official-looking enveloped addressed to Joe. It came from Government House. I had an idea what it was going to say because for months I'd been aware of the secret discussions and planning centring on my husband, but for Joe it was just another letter. He was driving and told me to open it. "I can't. It's for you." I wanted him to open it but nothing would make him. I tore open the envelope, taking care to keep the golden crown in one piece, and with hands shaking I took out the letter and glanced over it. It was as I thought. Joe's name had gone forward for an honour, and his work in all the search and rescues he has been involved with over the years was to be recognised if he accepted it.

"Read it out." Joe's impatient voice reminded me it was his letter. He drove on, and I began.

In the shocked silence when I'd finished, all Joe said was, "I never expected that. Imagine what people will say."

"They'll all say it's no more than you deserve."

Joe felt that he shouldn't be honoured. It wasn't just for him, I said. I knew many local people had spent a lot of time gathering information and making a case so his name could be considered and the work of search and rescue.

We drove for some time in silence. Finally Joe said that he'd accept it. Not just for him, but for our sons, his Uncle Joe, who drowned while trying to rescue a fisherman, and his father and grandfather who'd always been involved with sea rescues and searches over the years. "Because of them," he said.

Joe, I, and Christchurch with its one-way traffic system do not mix at all well, and it was two extremely tense people who finally pulled into the motel where we were to stay for the night. If it hadn't been so cold the half-hour walk into the city to sign books would have been pleasant but I don't think Joe enjoyed the experience of my making myself known in bookshops any more than I did myself. Most of the shops had already sold out of my books, and there weren't any to sign. I felt embarrassed every time I walked into a shop and made myself known. I imagined they were all thinking who does she think she is. Joe and I wondered if the shops hadn't wanted my book and only bought in one or two or were they selling so fast they couldn't keep up with the demand. I still didn't have the courage to ask. I was glad when we headed back to our motel.

I didn't have time to worry about my live television debut. By the time I'd tried to eat my meal which by then was sticking in a throat beginning to constrict with fear, and freshened up and carefully put on my make-up and changed my clothes, it was time to head for the studio. "Leave the vehicle where it is," Joe said. "Ring for a taxi." The thought of getting in the wrong lane or going the opposite way in the one-way system in the dark had me ringing promptly, and I left Joe stretched out on the couch in front of a television set already tuned to the channel that I was to be on.

I passed the instructions I'd been given to the driver, who knew the way - down a drive at the side of the Canterbury Television building in Manchester Street, to the double glass doors. I was to ring the doorbell and a Lee Howden would meet me. I didn't quite believe it would happen, but it did. I was whisked away to the make-up room, and told to lie back in the chair. A completely different face greeted me when I next looked in the mirror. Lee came back and took me to the waiting room. From here, I was told, I'd be taken in to the studio.

There was a coffee table with coffee, milk, sugar and cups sitting on it. As much as I thought I'd have liked a cup I doubt if I could have lifted it to my mouth, let alone swallow it, I was shaking so much.

Two other guests of George Balani's were waiting. I was to be the last. I sat trying not to let the two men see how nervous I was. Deep breaths and pretending to myself that I'd done it all a thousand times didn't seem to be helping. I watched the two men. They seemed to know each other and obviously television interviews were common-place for them. Then one asked me why I was here. When I told him

I'd written a book there was a spark of interest until he found out it was my first, and the story of my life. I cringed as I felt his eyes slide over me. Of no consequence, I felt he was thinking. I was thankful when he disappeared through the heavy door with the red light over the top. I could watch his performance on the television set in the waitingroom. George Balani introduced him and I realised why he was slightly familiar. He was a politician.

So soon the soundproofed door closed behind me. I wondered if condemned prisoners felt as bad as I did as they were led back to their lonely cells. Cables were lying all about the room and there seemed to be hundreds of small screens, lights and people. George came and introduced himself and his charming manner soon put me at ease. At the close of the show I was surprised when he told me we'd been talking for more than ten minutes. I arrived back at our motel knowing it had gone well and I could turn over another page of my itinerary.

Next morning we knew a phone call was coming through from an Invercargill radio station on my cellphone. Joe wanted to be out of the city with all its traffic by 9am, before the call came through. Memories of Christchurch still haunt me - speeding cars, traffic lights and that one-way system - but we did finally find our way out of the city, and on the main highway south we relaxed. The phone interview with the radio station was nothing compared with driving in Christchurch.

I had appointments in Ashburton and then Timaru; more interviews with newspapers and radio stations and calls on bookshops. I was becoming more confident but I still had to overcome nervous shakes that left me feeling sick until I actually met the interviewer.

It was in the offices of the *Timaru Herald* that I was to learn how much the book was being read. Peter O'Neill, the feature writer, introduced himself and congratulated me. He must have read the book and liked it, I thought. His next words stunned me.

"You haven't seen the latest bestseller list? It's just come out. You're number two in the New Zealand books."

I had no idea there was such a list. And if I had known, I'd never have dreamt that my book would find its way there. All sorts of feelings coursed through me. Excitement. Disbelief … and also the realisation that although I'd written it, it was our family and our lifestyle that had put it second on the list.

The best part was that Joe had come to the newspaper with me and could share in my news. I floated out of that interview and floated out to our car. I felt it would have started without my even turning the key. I was on cloud nine.

After that I noticed a subtle change in Joe. Where he'd been hesitant about bookshops before, often waiting outside while I went in to sign or speak with the staff, now he would stride in and become quite indignant if he couldn't see my book. I knew that at last he believed in it and he was proud. And I found myself picking up the number one bestseller, Alison Holst's latest recipe book, and admiring it.

Our first appointment in Dunedin was in Port Chalmers to look at fishing boats. Then it was back to the city for a radio interview and later in the evening my last live television interview which was to be with Southern Television.

I sat and waited for my time on air, listening to the busy noise around me. Voices drifted in through the door, never any faces but lots of different conversations. In all the noise and bustle there was no sign of panic, apart from me. By now I'd been told the format of the show. I'd met the interviewer, Robert Freeman, who had told me how he'd made one of the fish dishes from my book. He assured me he'd followed it exactly and on camera he was going to introduce me then ask me to try some of the Akaroa Oven Fried Fish he'd made. I was told to say how delicious it was.

I knew I'd fluff this show. I just knew it. I'd dribble, I'd find it too hot, perhaps I'd choke. All these thoughts kept leaping in my head as I waited.

They brought me into the studio and sat me at a table opposite Robert. The usual cameras and leads were draped over the room and I giggled to myself when I found myself thinking showbiz jargon - the sooner these cameras roll the sooner I'll be out of here. I realised I'd travelled a long way down this part of my life and couldn't help wondering what might be next.

Right now I had to try to be calm and composed on television. After meeting so many different faces over the last month I had a real fear that one of these times I'd say "Good evening," when it wasn't, and use a wrong name. Next, Robert's reheated fish was brought in. His words, "I cooked it 20 minutes, just as you said," had me worried when he added that he'd cut the fish into bite-sized pieces before cooking, to make it easier to manage.

The pieces were coated with beautifully browned breadcrumbs. I took a piece, and put it in my mouth. I knew I had to tell Dunedin how lovely Robert's fish was but I just couldn't swallow it. My cooking time was given for full-sized fish fillets. These tiny pieces were mummified. It was time for me to speak but the dry fish stuck around my teeth and there was a ball of rubbery fish at the back of my tongue. I longed to stick my little finger in my mouth and hook the dry fish off my teeth and away from the back of my mouth. I kept my eyes lowered as I knew if I'd looked up at Robert or caught sight of myself in one of the television screens I'd start giggling. I could feel giggles building inside. Just in time I managed to discreetly remove it from my teeth with my tongue and push the ball into the side of my mouth to deal with when I was off the air. Then I could be loud in my praises of the cook but I declined the offer of more fish. And at the end of the interview I was able to laugh with Robert.

One of the reasons Joe had come south with me was to visit Gough Brothers. They had built our last fishing vessel, *Te Wai*, in 1994 and Joe reasoned that if I had a new book, he'd have a new boat. I honestly thought he was joking until he told me he wasn't coming to Stewart Island with me. This trip had been arranged with Margaret and Colin Hopkins at the fishing conference in Nelson and Joe had been as keen as I was to go over to the island. Now my pleading went unheeded. Joe was spending the time with Tony Gough, and I was travelling alone to Stewart Island on the *Southern Express*. This was the newest addition to the Foveaux Strait run, an aluminium catamaran, 65 feet long and also built by Gough Brothers. I was to speak to a group on Stewart Island, the highlight of my tour.

The *Southern Express* pulled away from Bluff wharf at 9.30am. As we steamed down the harbour and past the red lights, I felt again the same excitement mixed with fear of the unknown that I'd felt the day I'd sailed out of Bluff Harbour aboard the *Te Wai* on her maiden voyage up the east coast. Today off Stirling Head the sea was jobbly, and sheets of spray picked up from the ferry's bow wave were flying past us. Further out, three and a half metre-swells rose from a dull green sea, their white tops curled down into the troughs. The skipper informed us we were travelling at 22 knots. I felt the boat lift on a big wave then crash down into a hollow as the wave disappeared from under us. One woman screamed and I noticed a couple of strapping young men looking very green as they stood in the doorway.

For me it was an exhilarating ride as we skimmed with the seabirds over the crests. Bluff was only a chimney - from the Tiwai aluminium smelter - on the horizon when Stewart Island came into view. The colour of the sea had changed to dark green trimmed with white foam as the wind whipped the tops off the waves. We left the strong winds of Foveaux Strait outside Half Moon Bay and the shining waters of the harbour lapped against golden sand. A hotel, post office, shop and school were at the centre of the bay. Higher up, to the right and left of these buildings I could see some houses nestled in the trees, and many larger houses sprawled in the mid-day sunshine, their windows overlooking the water.

The *Southern Express* shuddered to a halt alongside the wharf and as I waited for the gangplank to be lowered to the deck I could see butterfish swimming among the waving kelp as they searched for the tender portions of the kelp fronds to eat. As my eyes became accustomed to the clear blue depths I could see an occasional paua clinging to the rocky bottom. Already I could feel the magic of Stewart Island.

Margaret met me in her car and whisked me to one of the larger houses that had caught my eye as we had steamed in to the bay. On the way she told me about the trouble they'd had getting their car to the island, how it had been damaged as it was lifted off the freight ferry and how it had to be returned to the mainland for repairs before being shipped out for the second time. An affinity with Stewart Island was born as I thought back to the dramas we've had over the years, getting things to Arapawa Island. My piano jamming in the door once it was on the island always stands out in my mind, as does the bringing in of generating plants, household appliances and groceries. Some needed sheer backbreaking strength, others the tender care of a new-born babe, but whatever was brought to the island was, and still is, hard work, needing two or three times the handling that town dwellers give their possessions.

That afternoon Margaret took me to their source of power. She told me how they too had to fight for their electricity which has been on the island since 1988. The three Caterpillar engines generate a total capacity of 600 kilowatts. The station is computerised and, depending on the draw of electricity, two or three of the engines run, cutting in and out when needed. A building stood in a clearing. This housed the engines, Margaret told me, and the three smaller buildings standing apart from it were the cooling towers. The exhausts of the generators are fitted with mufflers. The silence was so profound I could hear the birds calling in the bush and the leaves of the trees rustled in the light air.

Just as with us, the privilege of having electricity on Stewart Island is expensive. All consumers had to pay $2500 up front, and $25 has to be paid monthly towards engine replacement and a line charge. Electricity costs 40 cents per unit. But like us Margaret agrees the joy of being able to turn on a light without having to start a generator is worth every cent they pay.

By evening the weather had changed dramatically and it was raining and blowing. I doubted if people would come out on such a dreadful night but this was Stewart Island, I was reminded, and people would come to hear an author speak, especially one from another island.

Stewart Island is a very close-knit community and as I listened to the conversations around the room I was intrigued by all the diverse groups on the island. There were groups for make-up, reading, a local paper, school groups, a theatrical society, and by the end of the evening the possibility of a writers' group. After I'd spoken and answered questions it was my turn to hear some of their stories. One face I recognised from a Country Calendar programme on television. It belonged to the youngest 70-year-old I have ever met. I'd watched her shear sheep and manage the isolated farm on Stewart Island with her husband but I hadn't realised how slight a person she was until I met her. "It's the rhubarb wine I make," she laughed when I remarked how young and spry she was.

Her story about her false teeth sent Margaret and me home still laughing. Her family, she'd told us, demanded she had her plate fixed. "Two front teeth had fallen out and I lost the flaming things," she said. "I was told to get it done for Christmas."

I imagined what a dental trip would mean for this elderly woman. Not just a trip in her small boat to Half Moon Bay, but across on the ferry to Bluff and then into Invercargill. Couldn't do it, I heard her saying. What she did say I'll never forget.

"I've always collected sheep's teeth. Clean them up and keep them in a jar. Poked around and found two that fitted the gaps." Our mouths dropped open as she went on to explain how she'd filed them down before she glued them in. "Took me over two hours. You know," she mused, "my family were really pleased I'd had my teeth fixed."

My return trip in the *Southern Express* was the complete opposite from the day before. Foveaux Strait was flat calm and the one-hour trip was soon over and we were pulling into the wharf at Bluff. The author-tour was over. The remainder of our time away was Joe's and mine.

And Joe was to have his new boat. This one was to be three feet longer than *Te Wai* and one foot wider. I thought of all those trips up and down the country while the building was in progress, to say nothing of the horrendous toll bills that would be in our mail every month until the boat was completed. I started to dread the next six months but then I thought back to the wonderful trip we'd had up the coast from Bluff to Okukari with *Te Wai* after her launching, and I perked up. It could be another chapter for my next book.

But what was I thinking of? Next book? Wherever I'd spoken in New Zealand, one question I was always asked. "Will there be a sequel?" My answer had been a definite no. Now, driving on the Bluff to Invercargill highway, I suddenly realised how wrong I'd been. Book number two was under way - throughout the tour it had been writing itself. All the places I had been, the new experiences and the people I had met. These things in themselves only had to be written down and I'd have half a book, while all the time back home in Okukari Bay, because of our way of life and living on the edge of Cook Strait, new chapters just keep on building.

CHAPTER THREE

It Depends On How You Look At It

EVERY farming family and every fishing family gets used to emergencies big or small, and finding ways of handling them. As we both farm and fish, we have twice the opportunities for crises to arise. Actually we have three times the usual opportunities because of where we live and because Joe heads Search and Rescue for the area. We have become adept at dropping whatever we're doing if someone is in trouble on the sea. But we are lucky. We are three families here in Okukari Bay, so we cope with things together.

Joe and I have the top house in our bay, the one which makes our address 'First house on the right, the South Island', that's if you're coming south from Wellington. Our two sons and their families live close together, and close to us: Young Joe and Joy, with Rachael, 14, and Angela, 12, except that Rachael these days is home only at weekends from boarding school at Marlborough Girls' College; and James and Lisa, with Haydn, 6, and Danielle, 4.

Until recently both our daughters, Helen and Pauline, lived in Picton, but early in 1996 Helen and her partner Peter and children Amanda, 10, Carl, 9, and Glen, 6 - their ages now - moved to Maruia. There they lease land to graze stock while they build up their own stock numbers of deer and cattle. Now when I come to Picton, instead of sharing a quick visit with two daughters I see more of Pauline and her husband, Dene Wilson - Pauline at the veterinary clinic where she works.

I suppose, when I think of the different things we do, that something out of the ordinary happens so often. I don't mean just something that seems big to other people. It depends on how you look at it. Take my word processor and how much I've relied on it when doing my writing. It has loomed very large in my life. First of all there's the pressure that comes from working to a deadline. I'd get so frustrated if I couldn't be working on my book. Times when we were busy on the farm I'd find myself writing in my head, and then getting angry when I didn't have the time to write the words down. But the very worst time of all was when my word processor packed up.

As I went along, my publisher had been editing the first part of my book, and I had set myself a date on which to have it retyped, incorporating the changes. I wanted to see it on nice clean paper and then sit down and try to read it as if I was someone else. Suddenly my machine started to print partial letters and munch up the ribbon. When I took the ribbon cartridge out I could see that the used ribbon was like a bird's nest within the cartridge, and some had twisted around the printwheel, stopping the ribbon advancing. Faulty ribbon, I told myself. I always keep spare ribbons on hand so I replaced it. Two pages printed out well and then it started to play up again. The same thing happened. By now the inside of my machine was covered in black shavings and wherever they touched there was a black greasy mark. Instead of a clean white tidy manuscript it was beginning to look like pages that had been dragged from a grubby school-bag.

Black fingerprints covered the operator manual when I searched for the cause. As I didn't know the names of the different parts, I studied the pictures to try to decide what were the ribbon guides, the ribbon sensor and carrier. I understood my machine when it was going well. I could type in the words, store them and recall them. I could open up any part I wanted and either add to it or delete - but with anything else I was stumped.

I put ribbon number three in place, and before long I was in strife once more. This time one typed page was condensed into one-third of the paper. I found a reason for this in my instruction book. 'Reflective strips on the back of the printwheel may be dirty. Gently wipe them with a tissue or cloth.' Following the instructions and aided by the pictures I cleaned my machine. As I removed the parts I laid them on the desk precisely in the position I'd found them. When I put the last part back I felt a wonderful sense of achievement. I was the master of my machine.

I found the page of the chapter that I'd been working on and turned on my machine. A message came up on the screen. 'Check printwheel.' Nothing I did would remove those words. In desperation I called on Joy, the typist in our family. Could she fathom it out? Nothing she did made any difference.

The next morning I rang the agents in Nelson. "Clean the machine where the printwheel sits," I was told. "It obviously isn't making contact."

A short time later the last three pages were printed and I noticed the sun was shining. It was going to be a lovely day. I set myself a goal. I was going to complete one chapter before I stopped for the day.

While dinner was cooking I set my machine to print out the work I'd completed. I was relieved it was finished as it was a chapter that had needed quite a lot of editing and I had added to it. All day I'd been sitting in one position and concentrating, and now I had a headache, my neck was stiff and I had a sore back. Suddenly I heard a change in the typing noise the machine usually makes. I ran in, only to find nothing was being printed on the paper. This was the last straw.

"That's it," I told Joe. "I'm going to town tomorrow to buy a new machine." Even as I said the words I thought how ridiculous that would be. I'd written more than 100 pages and the thought of having to rewrite them or try to transfer them on to a new disk if I bought a different type of machine changed my mind. "Well, I'm taking it to Nelson to get it looked at."

At 7am the next day we were steaming out of the bay, the screen in a carton and the keyboard wrapped in a cotsheet. Just 50 minutes with an expert and I had a machine that worked again. Worn-out parts had been replaced and I was told it should go for another few years.

I couldn't wait to get back home and start writing once more, but Joe planned the first part of my day. "Seeing I was so good to you and took you to Nelson, you've got to be nice to me. Cook me one of your sultana cakes and a sponge."

I was enjoying writing, and in the next two days I completed all the changes from the first editing. The last chapter was nearly done when Joe arrived inside. We had a cup of tea, and, as I hadn't finished mine when Joe left the house again, I took it in to drink as I worked. I don't know how it happened, but the cup slid out of my hand and fell over the keyboard. I was using memory and my writing was coming up on the screen but the tea made my machine type out letters without me touching a thing. When it got to the edge of the page there were three or four 'beeps' instead of the usual single beep. I sprang into action, not feeling the heat of the tea where it had landed on my legs. I flicked out the disk in case I lost what I had been working on, and sat in horror until the involuntary typing stopped. Then I pressed some of the keys and found there were many that wouldn't work. Somehow, I thought, I'd have to remove the cover to dry the keys.

Trusting that Joe wouldn't come inside and find me attacking my newly fixed machine - when he'd threatened that if I fiddled with it again he wouldn't help me get it to Nelson - I lifted the top cover. There were four screws that I'd have to remove. Two came out easily but I couldn't unscrew the others. Still lots of keys wouldn't print. I tore up strips of newspaper and slipped them down in between the keys, trying to soak up the tea. "Knock knock." It was Lisa with Haydn and Danielle, bringing up mail for the mailbag. By now I was on the verge of tears. How could I have been so stupid? I was terrified to tell Joe. I could just imagine his reaction. "He won't take me to Nelson to get it fixed again," I told Lisa.

"Get out your hairdryer. That will dry the inside," Lisa suggested. So while Lisa held the hairdryer with the hot air driving down between the keys I put in another disk and kept trying the keys. Slowly slowly they all came back to life. Now I could confess to Joe - and get on with my writing.

Then there are the days when all the men are away, fishing, and I have all the time in the world to do my writing. If I want to write all day there is nothing to stop me - that is until something goes wrong on the farm.

On this occasion I had five lovely days with nothing to do but write. No interruptions - just me and the dog. Five days shrank to four when I remembered my dental appointment on one of those days. But still - lovely.

To do essential jobs, I had to make the best use of any time taken away from my writing, so I let all the farm dogs off for a run at once. As we had two pups I knew I shouldn't do this as two off together are likely to chase sheep, but I'd seen Joe doing it when he was at home and I thought I could keep an eye on them as I worked on my book. After lunch the dogs were tied up and the chooks let out, and it was then I noticed a ewe running around the fence that surrounds our house, frantically maa-ing. I knew she must have lost her lamb, and went outside to see if I could find it. At the back of my mind was the thought that two playful puppies may have chased the lamb and separated it from its mother. Other lambs answered the ewe's bleating but she bunted them all away. They weren't hers.

A bleat came from over in Maori creek, the steep gully that runs along the side of our house on the seaward side. Perched on a narrow ledge 15 feet below me was the lost lamb.

The shiny clay bank had no footholds or anything growing out of it to hang on to. I peered over the edge, trying to think what to do.

Marcia Rowe, my friend from Aotea, was over for the day, working in my garden.

"Let's sit down and plan this," she told me. "I haven't a head for heights and you make me nervous standing on the edge like that."

First we tied a rope around a post. Then our plan was for me to go further up the edge of the bank where I knew I could clamber down into the creekbed. "When I get below the lamb, throw me the other end of the rope and I'll try to climb up the 12 feet or so to reach it. Then throw me another rope and I'll tie the lamb up. All you'll have to do is pull it up."

This sounded so easy. But during the winter Joe had felled a lot of old pine trees that had been part of our shelter belt. The pine needles had been filling up our spouting and causing problems with overflowing guttering, so the trees were cut down and a different species planted in their place. Most of the trees had tumbled down into Maori creek and I crawled through branches and over limbs as I tried to reach the lamb.

In places the creek had gouged out deep pools, and as I slid down waterfalls I had visions of hitting my head, being knocked out and drowning before Marcia could reach me.

I edged along a foot-wide ledge above one of these deep pools, trusting in the rooting system of rather spindly-looking five fingers, and tried to control my shaking legs. My clothes were sticking to me. When the ledge ran out I slid down into the creek once more. The thick canopy of trees blocked out all the light, and only the sound of Marcia's voice somewhere above me kept me going.

When I thought I was immediately beneath the lamb I climbed through the trees so I could grab the rope when Marcia threw it. Then, when I saw the steep bank in front of me, I knew I couldn't do it. I also knew I couldn't get back the way I'd come. I'd never be able to climb up the steep bank that I'd slid down at the last waterfall. I couldn't see through the trees ahead and I impatiently wiped away tears. Marcia came from a logging family, and her shouted warning to me that it was dangerous beneath fallen trees made me more nervous.

I dropped to my knees, and could see a faint glimmer of light ahead. Slowly I slithered along the creekbed, breaking off branches that tried to block my way. The sight of the beach made me feel like singing. I was like a prisoner just released from jail, and I wanted to run along the white sand but I couldn't. My legs felt like jelly.

The lamb would have to stay there. I decided my life was more valuable than one lamb. It sounded sensible but that didn't blot out the plaintive maa-ing of the ewe or the answering bleats of the lamb. How would I sleep if I had to listen to that all night?

When Marcia was about to leave I walked over to the edge of the bank to check that the lamb was still there. It wasn't. It had moved further along the ledge to a more accessible place. If I used a rope, I thought, now I might be able to climb down and get it. Rachael had other ideas.

"I'll do it, Grandma. I can climb down to that first ledge. See? It's only a little way down, and then I'll drop down to the ledge where the lamb is."

I felt my muscles tightening as I watched Rachael swing down over the first ledge and then again over to the next. She walked the lamb around until it could go no further, when it stood as if it knew that Rachael was there to help. We threw another rope down to her to tie up the lamb, but she couldn't let go her line to do this. This time Joy climbed down with a rope and I threw a woolpack to them. The lamb was bundled into the pack, a rope was tied around it, and Marcia and I pulled it up. What we'd been through that afternoon was forgotten as we watched the mother lick her baby while it pushed her nearly off her feet as it sucked from her bursting udder.

The next day was going to be my day. No doubt about it. All I was going to do was eat and write. I told myself I must make up for the time I had lost in the lamb rescue.

I woke up to no water. Without water the bait freezer at the end of our wharf shuts down. Already it had come up from minus 12 degrees to zero, and it wouldn't take long before the cartons of bait were ruined.

Joy and Rachael were already trying to fix things. They located the problem up the paddock - cows had trampled on the 33mm polythene hose and it had pulled apart at a join. Rachael came inside to ask if I had some tools they could use to unscrew the joiner as it was cross-threaded. Nothing I could find held the pipe tightly so we took the joiner right off the hose, rode down from the paddock and put it in the vice.

Up at the paddock we tried to join it together once again. It was easy to push one end of the hose into the joiner, but every time we tried to push the other end of the hose in, the force of the water burst our first join. We finally managed it. Hurray. But our relief was short-lived. The hose exploded from the join and danced its way down the hill, drenching Joy and me.

"Never never again am I fixing this water," Joy stated as we tried to unscrew the joiner again. Another trip down to the vice, but this time we couldn't undo it. Our hands were too sore.

Lisa had been away with her two children. Just then we saw the *Felix* - a catamaran of 45 feet owned by the new owners of Te Pangu - coming in the bay, bringing Lisa home. I ran down to the wharf. Sam Edwards, the skipper, managed to unscrew the joiner with tools he carried on his boat. A cup of tea, a change of clothes, and now with Lisa we went back up the paddock to try again.

This time we pulled the hose apart further along the line, and screwed the faulty joiner together without any water flowing through. While Joy watched that join, Lisa and I managed to get the other one together. I had to push my dripping hair from my eyes before I could see Joy's hand signals which told us that her join was holding together.

From there the hose runs around the side of a hill before filling up a concrete holding-tank behind our houses. A check at the tank showed us that was filling. The hose running into Joy's house had to be bled to get rid of airlocks, and then it was only the freezer that had to be restarted.

There is a little brass button on the motor that drives the compressor that has to be pushed down whenever the freezer stops. Coming out of the bright sunlight into the little room that houses the compressor blinded me, but I'd done it dozens of times before so my hand automatically reached out to press the button. It was stuck down. All this water - and now it wouldn't start. I could have screamed with frustration. All this time the temperature was creeping up. Ruby had often told me the story about Joe when he was little, dressed in his best town clothes, lying down in a Picton street, and screaming and yelling because he wanted an icecream and she'd said to him, "Later." Right then I felt like Joe must have felt that day.

Cellphones either on the boat or in the car have changed our way of life. The instant communication makes it easier when all the men are away. I was able to ring Joe and find out what to do. Lisa came down and held the torch while I read his instructions which I'd jotted down. Put main off. Stand on compressor bed. Reach up to grey box on wall. Take out two screws. Make sure it's got a plastic handle (I was told the box was alive as it was above the main). Lift off the box, and, using the screwdriver, press the little blue switch.

I wiped my hands dry and took the screwdriver from Lisa. "Love you," I laughed at her as I tried to make light of it. Taking a deep breath I followed the last instruction. The freezer came on.

Even though I told Lisa that I was going home to bed so I could get up once more to start my writing day again, I felt the familiar rush of pride that we'd coped without our men. It might take us longer and the cost of a few cellphone calls but on these occasions the victory is sweet. With the freezer running again, Joe's phone call, "We knew you'd cope," was the best of all. It made me forget that I hadn't managed to do any writing, but unless something else went wrong I could look forward to the next day.

Writing days that I lose when I have to help on the farm, do running repairs, tend sick animals or rescue lambs are accountable. The days I waste when I've done stupid things aren't - like the time I locked myself in the chookhouse.

Six years after my dog Quita and Lisa's cat Nuffy had killed our chooks, Joe and I were offered 14 hens and a rooster by our neighbours, Katherine and Peter McPherson. They were leaving Whekenui where they had been farm managers for the past three years but because they had three days of travelling to their new farm they decided to leave the poultry.

When Joe began to build a new chookhouse the weather was so wet and windy he set up the frame in our shed which had housed the generator before Arapawa Island was reticulated. Joe's intention was to finish the frame, then slide it outside before he put on the iron. It was still windy, too windy to handle sheets of iron, so Joe finished off our new chookhouse, completely, in our shed. All we had to do was slide it outside, along the front of the shed, down the side between pine stumps and roots that looked like clumps of varicose veins, back along the other end of the shed and into position. He nailed skids beneath it and with him towing it with the four-wheel motorbike and me slipping timber beneath to slide on, and both of us pushing at each corner and every tree root, three hours later our chookhouse was in place.

It was close to where our old chookhouse had been and I reminded Joe of the time his mother had been inside feeding the chooks when it had lifted in the wind and shifted three or four feet. She'd had to shuffle along with it. I didn't want that happening to me so it was well wired down before Joe built the run. With the rooster Joe imagined we'd soon be having chickens, and then he'd build a coop to keep them separate. This was to be his egg factory.

Joe rode over to the McPhersons to collect the chooks and rooster just on dark, and they arrived at our place in one big cardboard carton tied on the back carrier of the bike. Our chooks were in residence.

The rooster crowed at 5.38am the first morning. I liked the sound.

Our grandchildren loved to come up and collect the eggs and I'd be handed warm, brown eggs throughout the day. Angela asked if she could be in charge of feeding so there was very little left for me to do.

The first strong winds tested the chookhouse and proved that Joe had built a strong building, a fact he kept proudly reminding me of. It was during these winds that Angela came to see if I'd fed the chooks and collected the eggs. When I told her I'd already done it she closed the door with a bright, "Bye, Grandma. See you in the morning."

A short time later Rachael rang. "Have you seen Angela?"

Joe told her that she'd been here but must be on her way home. The rest we heard the next morning. Angela didn't arrive and after about 30 minutes or more had gone by Joy jokingly remarked that she hoped she wasn't locked in the chookhouse. Rachael ran up and found her in with the chooks, not able to squeeze out the small hole Joe had made for the chooks to pass through into their run. The latch had fallen down on the outside of the door. Joe and I never heard her screams above the noise of the wind.

Joy told me she was a very distressed little girl and everyone laughing didn't help. It took a few days before Angela could laugh about it, while all the time Joe kept reminding us he'd built a strong chookhouse.

The following week I had plenty of time to remember Joe's bragging words and our laughter at Angela's expense. The chooks had been cackling all morning and in the end it got the better of me and I went outside to collect the eggs. The door slammed behind me. Three eggs had been laid and I placed them carefully in my bowl before turning to leave. I pushed on the door and it remained shut. I pushed harder. The latch had dropped down and I was locked in this well-built edifice with 14 chooks and one large rooster.

A quick look at my watch and I saw it was 11.15am. I knew Joy and Lisa would be inside teaching school, and Joe and the boys were away fishing, but I balanced on the perches anyway, and yelled "Help!" through the six-inch gap below the roof on one side. I called out to everyone. The sheep on the skyline stopped eating and lifted their heads but no-one came.

I flopped down in one of the lower nests to wait. Surely one of my grandchildren will come up around lunchtime to see if there are any eggs, I thought.

After a few minutes I yelled again, and then knelt amongst the chooks and poked my head through the small hole that leads to their run and yelled. The chooks on the outside seemed intrigued by the strange head that filled up their doorway. Their inquisitive eyes stared unblinkingly into mine. One pecked at my nose and I giggled as I pulled back. I felt like a turtle pulling his head back inside his shell.

I looked at my watch. Only 30 minutes had passed! It seemed an age. More yells for help. Still no-one came. I sat down in my nest and watched the antics of the chooks. I was intrigued how flexible a chook's neck is. It can bend it into an S-shape to peck at a last grain of wheat under the bottom plate of the chookhouse, and nearly right around to preen under each wing and the tail feathers. Their jerky movements fascinated me as they edged closer to check the intruder. I laughed as they tried to walk along the edge of their plastic nesting boxes. They were too slippery and too thin and the chooks kept overbalancing but once their claws reached the wooden rails that held the boxes they had no trouble running pigeon-toed to the end before they jumped down to the floor. I became an expert on chook behaviour.

After a while they became used to me. One chook fluffed up her feathers, and wriggled herself into the dirt. Her top and bottom eyelids joined in the middle and she dozed. Three more chooks laid eggs and I loved watching them begin their cackling at the base of their necks. Then their beaks would begin to move and a quiet chuckling noise slowly built up into the satisfying cackling I usually hear. Others joined in, even though they hadn't laid an egg.

Now I know that our chooks don't like potato peelings, my herbal tea bags or lemon and orange skins, but they love raw pumpkin, especially the piece where I'd cut away the stem of the pumpkin we'd had for the previous night's dinner.

Three hours and twelve minutes after I'd first called for help, Rachael heard my cries. She said she knew where she'd find me. I was getting to the panicking stage. What if no-one comes near all day? Joe was away until tomorrow, and worst of all was the time I was wasting. And - I'd have to agree - Joe's chookhouse was built to last. I'd tried in vain to batter the door down with my feet.

Rachael's face was very concerned when she opened the door. I could see she wanted to laugh but it wasn't until I laughed that she laughed with me. My throat was so hoarse I couldn't speak for a while. A long cool gin and tonic helped. Joy came to see if Rachael had found me and we laughed some more over a cup of coffee. Later that same afternoon Lisa came up with the solution. "Saw a hole in the door near the latch so it can be opened from the inside."

Joe was disgusted when he saw the hole Lisa and I had sawn in his strong door, but when I suggested he sat inside for three hours to see what it was like he agreed the hole was probably a good idea.

National Radio broadcast the news on 1 March 1996. Stock on Arapawa Island was infected with true hydatids (*Echinococcus granulosus*), and 700 sheep from the island had been slaughtered.

We were returning from Nelson and when we arrived in Picton later that afternoon the first three people we saw raced over to us wanting to know if all the stock on the island would be slaughtered. Was it safe for them to visit the island? And some even wondered if we should change our shoes before we stepped on Picton's streets. I felt like telling them that we don't usually wear our gumboots or farm shoes when we come to town and remind them that it wasn't foot and mouth disease.

By the end of that afternoon Pauline's phone at the vet clinic was ringing continuously with similar questions and one person even thought there was rabies on the island. While I was buying my groceries an elderly lady who always comes from Picton to our church services anxiously asked me if they'd have to be cancelled now our island was "contaminated with hydatids".

Eight weeks earlier some of our old ewes, that we'd sold two years previously, had been put through the works by their owner and two had been found to have true hydatids. Immediately, under the Biosecurity Act 1993, the whole island became a controlled area. This meant that all stock coming off the island had to be slaughtered and MAF had to be notified of all stock movement on the island. All our ewe lambs and culled ewes which we always sold in the Blenheim saleyards had to go to the works. The news item was correct when it stated that 700 sheep had been slaughtered, but the impression it gave was that 700 sheep, all with true hydatids, had to be killed. In reality only three of these sheep were found to have the disease.

In both Joe and me, anger boiled. In 1989 sheep on another farm on the island had been found to have true hydatids, but this hadn't been publicised. We felt if there had been a tighter control at that time, the disease mightn't be a problem today. Most farmers have a responsible attitude to their dogs and dose them regularly at six-weekly intervals, but with the rise of the pig population on Arapawa and the huge influx of pig hunters to the island with their dogs, it is a continuing concern, especially when we are often rung up to be asked if we have seen a stray dog which the hunter has lost a few days ago. These dogs have to eat something and most probably it is a dead sheep or goat - the life cycle of true hydatids could begin. But it is not only pig dogs that can spread the disease. Holidaymakers have also lost their dogs for a number of days, and a hungry dog will scavenge or kill.

Nailed to the door of our boatshed is one of the 70 Biosecurity Notices, Declaration of a Controlled Area, that MAF erected on wharves, jetties and beaches where dog owners would have access to Arapawa Island. They are also near the wharves and launching ramps in Picton and Waikawa. Clause number seven states: 'All dogs aged three months and over coming into the controlled area (including those from within the Marlborough district) must have a valid treatment certificate indicating that they have been treated for hydatids in the previous 42 days.' The notice ends with clause nine: 'All dogs aged three months and over leaving the controlled area shall be accompanied by a valid treatment certificate showing that the dog has been treated for hydatids within the previous 42 days, and after leaving the controlled area such dogs shall be treated again for hydatids no later than 42 days after the date of the last treatment within the controlled area.'

All the farmers on Arapawa can only hope that dog-owners read and act on the notice.

But the farmers too are aware of their part in eradicating the disease with the building of offal pits and dog-proof home-killing facilities, and being responsible for dosing dogs at six-weekly intervals with a tablet containing praziquantel. This treatment will kill the tapeworm, no eggs will be dropped in the dogs' faeces, sheep, goats, cattle, pigs and deer will not eat contaminated grass - the life cycle is broken.

Because of movement control after that scare in 1996, all the cattle we sold had to go to the works, so we opted to send out a mixed age load of steers and bulls. We don't have cattle yards on the beach at Okukari but Joe had supplied some of the timber for the new cattleyards built at Whekenui, with the proviso that we could use them when we shipped out cattle. Rather than yards built on the breastworks as had happened previously, a race was built to allow the cattle to be loaded on to a truck and trailer which would come up on the barge. The truck would drive down a ramp off the barge up to the race, fill up the truck with cattle and drive back on to the waiting barge. Here the cattle were transferred to the trailer and then the truck went through the same procedure.

This method was a first for Arapawa, and as I watched the operation going so smoothly I thought back to the hilarity we'd had when we'd shipped cattle from Okukari using temporary yards erected from pine trees felled especially for that purpose, and taken down straight after. The constant movement of the sand in the wind and seas on the beach prevented us from building permanent yards. We could get the cattle into the yards but there was no way they were going to climb up the ramp from the beach and on to the barge so we brought Trudi, our house-cow, down to the beach and tied her up on the barge to entice the cattle up the ramp that lifted gently in the slight swell. We'd managed to get two or three on to the barge when they broke out. As I sat watching the driver back his truck up the ramp to join the trailer I remembered Pauline's hysterical shrieks of laughter mixed with fear as she high-stepped it through waist-high water with a mob of frightened cattle chasing her until they ran past in their flight for freedom. Once again they were rounded up into the yards where they circled round and round, pawing up the wet sand and tossing their heads as they snorted the salt water from their nostrils. When at last we were watching the boat and barge pulling out of the bay and were congratulating ourselves on a job well done, we glanced along the beach and at the far end saw three black and white heads peering through the scrub. I imagined I could catch the glint from their smiling eyes from where I'd stood.

As our modern shipment of cattle steamed out of the bay I carefully pulled myself up from where I'd been watching. My body hurt all over. Our cattle drama this time had taken place the day before, as we drove the cattle over the hill from our place to Whekenui.

They hadn't wanted to go, and some of the younger bulls kept trying to cut back and run to the flat to the yards where our cows were. From the road I watched, horrified, as Joy tried to stop one that broke from the mob. She was below it as it skidded towards her down the steep face. She side-stepped just in time but it gave us all a fright. Five minutes later when the bull was back with the mob and Joy had recovered her stick and herself, I could tell by the laughter that this was going to be one of those stories to be related at a later date.

Suddenly another big bull dived up off the road and headed in the opposite direction. Lisa was on the four-wheel-drive farm bike with Danielle and Haydn. As she leapt off the bike she yelled out to me that she'd bring that one back. When I reached the bike I thought I'd better shift it from the middle of the road as the two children were still sitting on it and I had visions of them letting off the handbrake, and the bike running down the hill.

I climbed on, turned the key and started it up. I let off the handbrake and as I turned the handle bars to reverse it into the bank, Haydn, who always sits up in front, jammed his knee against the throttle. The bike shot in reverse and backed up the bank before flipping over. In retrospect I asked myself why I didn't turn the key off but it all happened so quickly. I was pinned to the ground, my left leg jammed beneath the bike. Fear gave me the strength to hold the bike up and stop it rolling down on me completely. Fear for my three-year-old granddaughter. I knew Haydn was all right. I'd seen him fly off the bike and he was now sitting on the road crying, "My bike. My bike."

But Danielle. She is such a slight little girl and I had visions of her crushed under the weight of the bike. I twisted around and kept holding up the bike until I pulled her clear. I didn't feel the pain when I could no longer hold up the bike and it fell down on me. Both children were crying at the sight of their bike upside down but with everyone intent on getting the cattle up the hill and through the boundary gate no-one heard.

Slowly I managed to slide myself out. Somewhere I'd read how if you fall off a horse you must get back on it straight away so I figured if I intended to keep on riding a four-wheeler around the farm I'd better do the same. I rolled the bike over on to its wheels and climbed back on but it was flooded and wouldn't start. All I could do was fall back on to the road and wait until we were missed, and amidst black curtains of pain that kept sweeping over me I thanked God that I hadn't seriously hurt the two children cuddled up to me, so early into their journey of life. Haydn had a sore thumb and Danielle had some grazes to her face.

Over the next few days my body came out in massive bruises, and I nursed a wricked neck, grazed shoulder and a swollen leg that I couldn't bear to touch. But it was the nights that were the worst as every time I'd shut my eyes wanting sleep I'd relive it all over again and the thought of what could have happened had me going to the bathroom to wipe my face with a cold flannel as I tried to control my shaking body. I live with it still on sleepless nights.

I still ride and enjoy the four-wheelers. They have made mustering much easier and quicker although some still claim it's safer on foot. I suppose it depends on how you look at it.

CHAPTER FOUR

Being a Vet

WHEN our children where young, my subconscious was tuned to their cries. Now it's the ringing of the phone that has me wide awake, wondering who is in trouble. When I stay in Picton and Pauline is on call, I always wake up if the phone rings, and as I'm awake I go with her to keep her company.

One night I found myself in a paddock holding the torch over a cow that looked to me as if it was dead. "Downer," Pauline had told me as we left her house. "It's a colloquial term. Basically, the cow is down although it's usually associated with metabolic diseases. Often happens around calving," she explained.

This cow needed an injection into a vein, and a flutter valve was used to let the drug run in more slowly. I stood and watched Pauline monitor its heartbeat, but once the farmer had a spare set of hands to hold the torch I ran back to the warmth of the car. I pressed into the seat-back, and sat chafing my hands between my knees. The car doors had been left open and in the glow of light from the nearby shed I watched as my breath fogged up the windows and I felt as if I was in a cocoon.

It made me think of the five years Pauline was at Massey University when she'd wrapped herself totally in a world of study. There was nothing else in her life until she emerged with her degree in veterinary science. I'll never forget the trauma before every exam. We always heard from her that she'd fail. I sat all of Pauline's exams. I'd watch the clock knowing she was on her way to the exam, in the room, reading the paper, and then the start. I'd whisper a prayer under my breath to keep her calm. She'd done the work, surely help from above wasn't too much to ask, I'd reason with myself. After each exam the phone call, and I could always tell from her voice how it went. Pauline often referred to those years as her 'agony and ecstasy'. Was it really worth it, I wondered, as I held my fingers against my lips and tried to stop my chattering teeth.

Another night I found myself sitting in a parked car in a yard with cattle trucks pulling up all around me while Pauline attended a cow that had gashed its leg in transit. The cattle rattled the steel ramps as they left the confines of the pens on the trucks and headed for the open paddocks where they'd overnight before travelling further down the South Island.

Late one evening Pauline was called out to Rarangi to see a Welsh pony. As we drove along the empty road Pauline asked me to keep an eye out for the side street we had to turn down. A four-wheeler with an adult and child waited on the corner to show Pauline the way to the horse. We stopped in front of a house where a group of children stood quietly while Pauline gathered up what she'd need. I dozed until the laughter and talking that followed Pauline to her car woke me. The joy and relief on the children's faces as they waved goodbye, and Pauline's words as she described the miniature horse, made me understand a little better why she'd chosen to become a vet.

Then there was Toby. Toby was about eight years old when he came to live in Picton with Sue and Max Edwards in 1993. The first time I heard about Toby was when Pauline told me about a lovely rottweiler which came to the clinic. I shuddered when I thought of this dog she was treating. These were the dogs I read about. The ones that attacked for no reason and tore chunks of flesh from their victims. "He's not like that," Pauline laughed at my fears. "He's a gentle giant."

I looked at the coloured photo taken in the clinic, of Toby sitting between Pauline, and Kerry her vet nurse. Weighing in at 50 kilograms, the giant, yes. But gentle?

When Toby became listless and began to pick at his food, his owner, Sue Edwards, said she thought it was the ageing process, especially when she noticed a bluey haze covering his pupils and the whites of his eyes very bloodshot. But when he stopped eating and started to vomit, Sue took him to see Pauline. These symptoms, combined with his rapid and shallow breathing, made Pauline give an initial diagnosis of heart and liver problems. Toby had an ultrasound scan which eliminated the heart as the cause of the liver congestion.

The thought of a dog having an ultrasound seemed incredible to me, more so when I thought of all the water that I'd had to drink before I had an ultrasound. Pauline explained that as Toby was having his heart scanned he didn't need to drink but his chest would be shaved, and the picture I had in my mind of a huge dog lying back on a table with legs spread apart was dispelled when Pauline explained that the ultrasound was taken with the dog standing.

Toby's condition deteriorated. "At this stage Max and I thought we might lose him," Sue told me. "One evening he was so bad when we went to bed that I got up in the early hours to check on him." Sue recalled the time she'd spent looking in the pouring rain before finding him and carrying him inside and putting him in a bed with an electric blanket, and the cat snuggled up between his paws.

The results of Toby's ultrasound showed that he had only a mild heart problem but by now he was presenting liver failure, so on 10 July 1996 Pauline opened up his abdomen for exploratory surgery. She found a primary tumour that had totally disintegrated his spleen, with secondary growths in his liver. Pauline removed the spleen to de-bulk the tumour which weighed two kilograms and three-quarters filled a plastic bucket, and sent a biopsy away to confirm it was a malignant tumour.

Pauline has often called on one of Cedric Stewart's pig-hunting dogs when she has needed to give a blood transfusion. In an emergency a dog can be given one blood transfusion without cross-matching, preferably with blood taken from a large male dog which has been vaccinated. Toby needed blood so a call went out. Maureen Stewart brought Buck to the clinic and 500mls of Buck's blood was transfused into a transfer pack before being given to Toby during the operation. Later Pauline admitted that she had her doubts if Toby would even wake up. He was so sick with his liver failure and he wasn't a young dog. But that same evening he went outside, tubes and all, to urinate. Two days later he went home.

The tumour was cancerous. His options weren't good. He could be put down now or he could live for approximately six weeks. One other option was chemotherapy.

"This was our only option," Sue told me later. "We felt he'd come through the op so well. He wasn't ready to go."

Pauline admitted to more guarded feelings. "He'd been through so much." She wondered if it was fair putting him through any more. But he went ahead in leaps and bounds, and one week after his operation Toby became one of the first dogs in Picton to go on chemotherapy.

For the first eight weeks he was taken to the clinic once a week and injected with the drug through a vein in his neck as his leg veins had collapsed. His blood cell count was monitored weekly and Sue kept a daily check of his temperature, faeces and urine as well as giving him oral chemo-drugs, including steroids. Now Toby is on a maintenance level of chemotherapy and visits the clinic for this once every three weeks where he is weighed and checked, and his blood is now monitored at six to nine-week intervals.

It was on one of these early visits that I met Toby for the first time. By now I had heard so much about this dog having chemotherapy. Pauline was so excited that she was able to give Toby this chance that she'd told me about it.

"Will he lose his hair?" I asked as I tried to visualise a hairless dog. He didn't lose his hair because chemotherapy affects only cells that are multiplying. Toby's hair had stopped growing so it didn't fall out as it does in a human. But where Toby had been shaven for his scan, operation, and drip, no hair had regrown.

Sue parked her truck outside the clinic and came in to check with Pauline if she was ready for Toby. Her invalid mother was in the cab, and, as Sue was helping her, Pauline asked me if I'd go and bring Toby in. I looked through the window and saw the back seat filled with dog, and fear brought on by the news media alone made me shake my head. I saw disappointment in Pauline's eyes so I went outside. I couldn't help my feelings and I didn't want my throat ripped out by a savage dog. Sue was struggling with her mother's wheelchair and without thinking I offered to give her a hand. With a "Great," Toby's lead was passed over to me, and he docilely led me into the clinic. A packet of chocolate bites was pushed into my free hand. I was Toby's friend, and he wolfed them down as I enticed him on to the scales. He weighed in at 45.4kg.

Looking back in my diary I saw I'd written "impressive dog, impressive treatment," on that day. It was easy to see Toby adored Pauline and she him as she checked his gums, to see if he was pale, and his lymph nodes for enlargements. He sat at the nurse's feet and let Pauline insert the catheter into the vein in his neck. It was all over in a few minutes and he didn't need to come back for another three weeks.

I was so impressed that I wanted to know Toby better, so two months later I visited him at his home. A notice at the gate telling me to 'Beware of the dog' made me wonder for a moment if Toby no longer lived here. I went inside and was greeted by joyous wagging of his stumpy tail and then he lay on the floor with his legs in the air, being a dead beetle, but with a coat that shone from his diet of cottage cheese and vegetables, and boiled chook and rice. Sue showed me the diary she was keeping, "to help others who may find themselves in the same situation as we did", and, as well as his diet, sleep, and exercise patterns, an almost daily entry was, 'happy dog'.

I couldn't begin to imagine the cost of the drugs and I asked Sue why she and Max had chosen the option of chemotherapy. "So far,"

Sue replied, "it's cost us $2000 but fortunately we are now in a position to afford it." As if he knew Sue was discussing him, Toby came up and pushed his head up under her arm and as Sue went on she rubbed his ears. "He is a special family member and proof that a dog responds to love. He's so gentle." I understood Sue when she said that he's helped many people overcome fears of this particular breed. It was easy to picture this dog asleep on the floor with one or two young children using him as a pillow as they watched television. "My goddaughter used to be terrified of dogs but she adores Toby."

Sue and Max said they weren't dwelling on what might happen when Toby came off his medication. "We have him now. His liver is functioning. He knows he is loved and he gives us love in return. Perhaps he'll stay in remission - who knows?"

A few weeks later Pauline thought Toby was coming out of remission. He was depressed, didn't want to do anything and was vomiting with loss of appetite and abdominal pain. Sue had to drag him into the clinic.

Pauline administered pain relief and took blood. His red and white blood cell count was extremely low - Pauline thought a side-effect of the chemotherapy. Toby was given supportive therapy which included drugs for pain and drugs to stop him vomiting. Further blood tests confirmed Pauline's suspicions that it was the chemotherapy, and although Toby was still very sick she said she was relieved it wasn't her initial fear that Toby was coming out of remission.

With alterations to his chemotherapy regime Toby made a slow but steady improvement over the next two weeks, and one month after the scare he led Sue into the clinic, eager for his chocolate bites from Pauline. Routine blood tests showed that Toby was entering 1997 in the best shape ever.

Toby came off his chemotherapy in March 1997. Eight weeks later a blood test showed no sign of leukaemic cells in his blood circulation.

My island world grows bigger. I've discovered not all rottweilers are savage, and I've had a glimpse of Pauline's joy as Toby has responded to the drugs she has administered to him. I understand why she chose to become a vet.

As if it were only yesterday I can shut my eyes and I see her in her black gown with its purple hood depicting veterinary science, her quick embrace as she told me that she felt as excited as she had on her wedding day. "Except," I reminded her, "today, your hard work is behind you. In marriage, it's still ahead."

The opera house in Palmerston North was crowded with people who undoubtedly had supported and encouraged those they'd come to see capped. I loved the pomp and splendour of the ceremony, beginning with the academic and official procession followed by the singing of Gaudeamus.

Each graduate had the stage to his or herself. Pauline stopped at the top of the steps at the righthand side of the stage until her name was read out. "Pauline Louise Heberley - with distinction." I wept for my parents, wishing they could have shared my joy at seeing our youngest walking across the stage to be capped and handed her degree. Joe reached out and took my hand in his and I knew he felt my pain but at the same time our hearts were filled with pride. I saw something of all Pauline's siblings in her. Her compassion from Young Joe, her sense of humour from James, and her perseverance from Helen. I was proud of all my children.

Going out on calls with Pauline, even giving her a very small hand at the clinic - that's easy. Trying to take her place in a major animal emergency is something else again.

Until 1997 I'd never calved a cow. In my 34 years of living at Okukari I could count the times on one hand when assistance had been required, and I'd always managed to stay right away, leaving it to the men. But when a cow cannot get rid of her calf and the calf is obviously dead, and our men are away fishing, and Joy, Lisa and I are the only ones in the bay, there comes a first time for us all.

My day had started with a run along the beach. Back at the house I'd flopped in a chair at the table and as I'd sipped a long glass of cold water the usual euphoric feeling after a run slowly spread through my body. I watched the line of sun as it crept along the sand lighting up my footprints. The two oyster catchers with their sleek black plumage and red beaks and legs, that had taken off with indignant squawks as I ran past, were already back foraging in the wet sand at the water's edge. I sang my way through the shower and after breakfast settled down to spend the next six hours that I'd promised myself working on my book.

Later that morning Rachael came inside and told me that she could see a cow from my kitchen window and she thought it didn't seem well. Through binoculars I could see she was giving birth. Her contractions were so strong that each wave seemed to be nearly lifting her off the ground.

I rang Pauline. "Leave it for an hour," I was told, "and if she's still the same ring me back."

From the house I watched her futile attempts at trying to expel her foetus. The contractions seemed to be more savage and when I could stand it no longer I climbed up the side of the hill for a closer look. The calf was dead. Its head and one hoof were presented, and I could see the cow would never get rid of it without help.

As I slid down the hill to ring Pauline I was glad that she'd persevered through her 'agony and ecstacy' and was now a vet. Her voice on the other end of the phone as I panted out my message calmed me slightly until she said, "You'll have to calve it, Mum."

"No!" My eyes lifted to the huge beast lying on the hillside and I knew I couldn't do it.

"Mum?" I heard Pauline's voice asking me if I was still there. "Listen to me."

Slowly I was given instructions, punctuated by her insistence that I could do it. But not on my own. An SOS was sent out firstly to Joy and Lisa to help walk the cow down the hill and into the yards, but she was too weak. She wouldn't move. Another call to Pauline told us we'd have to calve her where she was but she suggested we rang our neighbour, Mike Radon, a commercial fisherman who dived for sea-urchins - kinas - in California and who was in New Zealand for a few weeks. Maureen Stewart's husband, Cedric, was painting for Mike so he also came over as Pauline thought we'd probably need their strength.

I glanced at the group of us as we trudged back up the hill with ropes, a bucket of water with a liberal amount of dish-washing liquid in it to use as lubrication of the birth canal, and the cellphone - my link with Pauline - and I couldn't help but laugh inside. I felt like the intrepid men in the television programme, Dad's Army, who came from all walks of life to save Britain from the Germans in World War Two, except today there was a painter, a diver, and three nervous women attempting to save a cow.

With each contraction Cedric and Mike tried to pull the calf but it wouldn't budge. In over an hour there were only five more centimetres of calf lying on the ground to show for all the hard work. Memories of the sheep with Siamese twins that I'd tried to deliver a few years ago had me sliding my hand into the vagina in an attempt to feel any abnormalities and endeavouring to find what had stopped the normal birth. But I'm not a vet. She was at the end of the telephone.

"You'll have to open up the calf along the belly wall mid-line and pull out its organs."

Silently I passed the phone to Cedric. I turned away as he brought out his sharp pocketknife, and the sight of the calf's tiny organs, and the lungs that hadn't even had a chance to take a first breath, made me gag as they lay scattered on the grass.

"Pauline, Pauline," I whispered under my breath, "why aren't you just down the road instead of 18 miles away by sea?"

Still the calf would not budge. On the cow's next contraction we tried once more. The bellow that burst from the cow made me contract all my stomach muscles as I felt her pain. The body of the calf slithered out.

Pauline was worried the cow's vulva or vaginal walls could be ripped but from what we could see she appeared to be all right. But worse was to come. Pauline asked me to feel up inside her uterus to check it wasn't torn but when I cried that I couldn't, the vet at the end of the phone told me I had to do it and she explained what I had to feel for. My arm up to my shoulder disappeared into the cow as my hand groped around in the hot, quivering, jellied mass. It seemed intact. My arm came out with a loud burp and it hung down at my side not wanting to belong to my body until it had been scrubbed at least two or three times.

The cow was weak and it needed drugs urgently. Our speedboat was out of action but Mike suggested that his wife Antonia take me into Picton to collect the drugs from Pauline as he wanted her to have some practice using their speedboat without his sitting in it with her. Two hours later our cow had been injected with a pain relief and an antibiotic.

All this time she was sitting on a wide track and I hoped she'd make a miraculous recovery and walk away before she rolled off the edge and down the hill to the creek at the bottom, with its steep banks on either side. That evening, as she struggled to get up, she rolled part way down. Once again I called on Lisa and Joy but this time we were on our own as Mike and Cedric were out hunting. The three of us dragged, pushed and rolled the cow down the hill, using ropes to keep her from rolling too fast. We edged her away from the steep creek but we still had to drag her across a swamp where her 350-400 kilograms soon started sinking. My fear was growing as fast as the darkness. Pauline had told us she had to be kept warm and now we had her in a swamp, creating a mini-dam as water built up against her.

It was too dangerous to bring the tractor to her, so Lisa suggested we attempt to pull her out with their four-wheel motorbike. We tied a rope around the cow, immediately behind her front legs, and one around her neck, which acted like a bridle beneath her chin. Gradually, with lots of rests for the cow, we managed to heave her out up on to the flat, where we covered her up using old woolpacks and fleece-wool. Then we positioned Lisa's and my motorbikes between her and the edge of the creek. Surely she wouldn't move any further than the length of the bikes, we decided.

We all felt stretched and exhausted from our efforts but as we sat around the table talking over a cup of coffee we all agreed it was a satisfying exhaustion. We had done our best for the cow and now it was only time which would tell.

When I rang Joe, his words, "You all did a great job," made us feel proud of what we'd achieved, and Joy's comment, "Well, girls can do anything," had Lisa and me laughing in agreement.

At first light I was outside checking the cow again and the sight made my heart sink. She had moved past the two parked bikes and was now sitting on the edge of the bank. I could see that if she rolled over the edge we'd lose her. Another SOS and Joy and Lisa were with me to help, and with ropes tied to her four legs and around her neck we managed to pull her out of danger and form a barrier with the bikes again. During the day I went outside quite a few times and shifted the bikes, so keeping her away from the edge.

At 3.45pm it was time for her antibiotic injection but when I reached her she was hanging half way over the bank. This time the girls heard the urgency in my voice and they ran. To lose her now would be dreadful. We used one bike as an anchor and tied her back legs to it. We put a loop over her head and tied another rope to her front legs to hold them up and gradually went ahead on Lisa's bike. At one stage we nearly lost her over the bank but with the bike holding her back legs while Joy and I pulled her front legs we finally managed to pull her up to the flat again.

Worried that she might stumble down the bank during the night, we knew we'd have to tow her down to a safer position. Using two woolpacks tied together with old crayfish-pot rope we slowly towed her to a better place where we left her with water and a huge pile of grass and foliage from some of the trees the cattle eat around the farm.

That night we were too exhausted even to feel elation at our achievement. I just looked at her and wondered if she'd ever get up, or after all this she might still die or have to be shot. And that seemed so terrible after what we'd put her through.

All that was forgotten when I opened my bedroom curtains in the morning. The cow was gone. She was better. Then my heart plummeted. She'd probably dragged herself over to the high bank that overlooked the beach and fallen 20-30 feet on to the sand. I raced out of the house still in my nightgown, scared of what I might find. But she'd walked over to a creek and was standing in it while she drank. My sore back was forgotten as I tore down to Joy's and then on to Lisa's to shout the news. I wanted to sing and laugh out loud. This was our victory to savour.

Later as I sat in the quiet of my kitchen, pictures of the last two days flashed through my mind. Without Joy's and Lisa's help we'd have lost that cow. I cringed as I remembered the bellows of pain and the soothing way Lisa had spoken to the cow and Joy's strength as we'd heaved her up the bank. My girls never gave up. Even when all our energy had been sapped from our bodies I'd hear their words of encouragement to the cow, "One more go, old girl. You can do it." And the laughter when a rope slipped and someone tumbled into the bog or fell in a thistle or gorse bush. The laughter lightened our load.

I thought again of Pauline's graduation day when I'd realised how she shares so many of her siblings' qualities, and in the morning stillness it came to me that those same qualities are in Joy and Lisa. Without their compassion, sense of humour, and perseverance we wouldn't have saved the cow. I was just as proud of my daughters-in-law.

CHAPTER FIVE

The Sea Is Our Road

MY CAR is a 14.6ft Haines Hunter fibreglass runabout with a 90HP out-board motor. Joe had bought the speedboat in 1983 when he was elected to the Maritime Parks Board. "It'll make it easier for me to attend meetings," I was told. No longer teaching school I found myself using it more than Joe did. What joy in my independence. I wouldn't have minded had it taken me two hours to reach Picton instead of the actual 40 minutes. Just being able to leave the bay, if I wanted to, opened up new doors for me. But many times since then I've wished my car had four wheels and was parked in a garage so that when I wanted to go out I'd only have to jump in, turn the ignition key and go. I have to admit some people are never satisfied. But there it is. My boat is not a car, and I am governed by a list of considerations.

The most important is the weather. There have been incidents when the wind has got underneath small boats as they've come off a big sea, and overturned them. Only once have I really thought we might flip as I felt the speedboat lift in the wind when we came off the waves before crashing down in the troughs. But I wasn't scared. Not even when Joe told me to crawl up underneath the for'ard deck and lie flat on the bunk so my weight would help keep the bow down did I feel fear. I was with Joe. So I jammed my feet against the roof to stop myself being thrown around, and each time the boat lifted off the waves the screaming of the propeller spinning in the air warned me to brace myself for the thump that would follow when we hit the sea and slid down a wave into a hollow.

That was one trip when I arrived in Picton needing a shower, a hair dryer and a complete change of clothes. Once we were in Picton and I looked back up the Sounds to where we had come from, and saw the white water lifting off the tops of the waves as they scudded over the harbour, I attacked Joe for bringing me through such weather. His, "Well, we're here, aren't we?" reply only made me more furious. It took a withering glance from a stranger as he walked past us in the marina where Joe was tying up the boat - just listen to that fishwife of a woman - that shut me up. It's always the same whenever I've been really worried or scared. I try not to do it, but the moment the pressure comes off and I know things are going to be fine I have to take it out on the one I love. And knowing about it doesn't make me feel any better.

When I take the speedboat out myself I choose my days with care. A westerly wind is deceptive. At Okukari it can be flat calm but at Dieffenbach, where Queen Charlotte Sound and Tory Channel meet, the tides plus the westerly wind blowing straight across the Sound and into Tory Channel turn it into one of the worst stretches of water in the Sounds. Thirty-four years of living here have made me weather-wise. I have learnt to gauge the strength of the westerly by looking out my kitchen or lounge windows, down Tory Channel as far as Wirikarapa, where the channel turns and disappears from view. The westerly wind can build up a huge sea in the stretch of channel from Dieffenbach to Wirikarapa and when I look through the binoculars and see white-topped waves I stay at Okukari. I know what it will be like at Dieffenbach.

When it blows a strong southerly it is not only the wind that keeps me from using the speedboat. A southerly swell built up by the wind rolls in the bay and crashes up the beach. Any attempt to launch the speedboat would fill it with water or wreck it as it sat on its trailer on the beach.

And nothing in this world would put me in the speedboat in fog.

If I'm thinking of going into Picton, any sign of fog in the channel keeps me with my feet firmly on my island ground, and my mind floods with memories of that particular trip, early in the morning, when I was going in to play the organ for the 8am and 10am services at Picton's Holy Trinity church. I can still taste the fog, and shiver as I relive the coldness of that day, when my face ached as if I had severe toothache. I can still feel the numbing pain in my hands, even more intense when they began to warm up, and I can feel again the cold tentacles of fog as they slid beneath my Swanndri and sank down in my gumboots.

On that day the first shafts of light were beginning to fan across the sky as I skimmed down the channel in the speedboat. The grey waters of the Sounds melted into the shoreline. Stands of pine trees and native bush not yet emerged from night shadows grew blackly against the hillsides and on the skyline the tops of the trees stood out in sharp relief against the grey sky. There was no one to hear me and I laughed out loud with the sheer joy of being alive and the feel of the wind as it rushed past my face.

Closer to Dieffenbach I noticed pockets of fog in the gullies, and low cloud flattened the hilltops. "She'll be right," I told myself as I turned the wheel and swung around Dieffenbach into Queen Charlotte Sound. Here the fog was lower on the water, swirling around in patches, but I could still see occasional stretches of land. I'll steam from point to point, I imagined. Then without warning I was enveloped in thick fog.

No way was I going to attempt to go any further so I turned around to head back to Chum and Mavis Thomas's home near the power line crossing. From there I could phone the vicar and tell him I wasn't going to make the 8am service but I'd try for the 10am one.

When Dieffenbach didn't come into view I realised that I couldn't be heading in the right direction, and I felt panic. Then there was a lift in the fog and I was able to get my bearings again, and turn into Tory Channel, and reach the Thomas's home. I phoned to explain why I would have to try for the 10am service.

I waited an hour and once the sun started to shine through the clouds a lot of the lowlying fog lifted. "I'll give it another crack," I told Chum. "Surely it'll be better down the Sounds by now." Once out of their bay I was soon passing Dieffenbach for the third time that morning. Ahead I could see the fog had thinned, but the land on my starboard side was still shrouded in it. Again without warning the fog bank rolled over the water and for the second time that morning I couldn't see a thing. This time there'd be no turning back. There wasn't enough petrol to reach home. Picton would have to be my next stop.

I kept steaming in the same direction but then I remembered how disoriented I'd become earlier, so I slowed down. All I could see was the boat I was on and the ripples that fanned out from the bow on the water's surface. I stopped. I was scared I might run ashore or might be going round in circles, and I reasoned with myself that if I stayed in one place I'd burn less fuel and be more likely to hear any boats coming towards me.

I was wrapped in silence. The years peeled away and I remembered the deafening silence of my early days at Okukari when the quietness was so loud it sang in my ears before it built up to a crescendo that had me screwing up my eyes and covering my ears with my hands, in pain.

Imagination had me rushing to the side of the boat to see who or what was making the heavy breathing I could hear, only to see the tail feathers of a shag sink beneath the water. Then I heard what I'd been dreading - the muffled thump of the Interisland ferry. I strained my ears to try to catch which direction it was coming from. A trickle of perspiration felt warm as it ran down my back, and as I turned the key to start up the boat again I looked at my wristwatch - no ferry was due at this time. This was my imagination playing tricks, making sounds in the silence of my mind. I left the motor running. At least with that going, I thought, I'd have more of a chance to get out of the way of any boats.

While my heart thumped, slowly fragments of the shoreline appeared and as I recognised them I was able to head towards Picton. After tying up the boat I walked to my friend Mary's place where I could change my clothes. Each step echoed in my head and when I spoke it sounded to me as if I were talking through a long tunnel. I stood, dripping with water, letting Mary bustle around and strip off my clothes. As I sat with my feet in a bowl of hot water she chafed my hands to bring them back to life and pain. A hot drink warmed me inside.

By 10am I felt human although for the first two hymns my fingers fumbled over the keyboard. By the end of the service I was feeling myself again and when I saw a friend in the congregation who had recently had a hysterectomy I waved out to her. I hadn't seen her since the previous month when I'd been playing the organ and afterwards we'd discussed hormone replacement therapy. Then I'd laughingly told her if she wasn't on it she might grow hairs on her chest.

As soon as the service was over I packed up my music and hurried outside. I could only see her husband and I thought she must have already left. I tapped him on the shoulder and asked him if his wife had a hairy chest yet? A stranger turned around with a stunned expression on his face. Oh my God, I thought, I've done it again. Muttering an apology I rushed back inside the church where I saw my friend. When I told her what I'd done she said no, her chest was fine, but after hearing my story her stomach was sore from laughing.

All the way home laughter kept bubbling up when I thought of how I'd asked a stranger about the state of his wife's chest. No wonder my father so often used to quote to me that 'Fools rush in where angels fear to tread'.

The sparkling sea and cloudless blue sky made it hard to believe how inhospitable the Sounds had been less than four hours ago. It wasn't only the cold that had seeped into my innermost self that day, but fear. The fear of not knowing where I was and not knowing where I was going.

Mechanical problems make me realise my car is a boat after all. When it breaks down in the middle of Tory Channel I can't step out and ring up the garage for a tow. The trouble has to be fixed on the spot or perhaps a passing boat can be flagged down.

Joy with her two girls, and Lisa with Haydn were taking themselves out for the day with me to Dryden Bay. Fifteen minutes from our bay there was a clacking noise in the engine and as I stopped it I turned the boat in out of the tide towards the shore. My first thought was that we'd wound something around our propeller but when we lifted it out of the water it was clear. Next check was the fuel but there was plenty in the tank and I could see there was fuel to the motor. We wriggled the battery terminals before trying to start it again, but the engine was dead. Rather than put the anchor down we tied on to a thick piece of kelp to stop us drifting.

We weren't too concerned. The day was perfect with little wind and the sun was shining. We all agreed with Joy's comment, "Surely someone will see us and offer us a tow," so we sat back and waited for a boat to pass. Everyone complained we'd run out of things to look for in 'I spy' before a boat came in view and we all waved out. They steamed past, all waving back to us. A memory from my days of sitting my skipper's ticket jostled to the surface of my mind. "We should wave something orange" - and so when we saw the next boat we waved a spare lifejacket. They didn't notice our distress signal.

"You could let off the smoke flare, Grandma." But unless we were in serious trouble I'd already decided to leave it where it was. For me serious trouble would have been if Joy, with her diabetes, needed food. The weather and sea conditions were good and sooner or later our men would miss us.

Another boat steamed up the channel. Joy jumped up on the cabin roof, waving our international distress signal while the rest waved and yelled from the cockpit. They turned in, and came alongside. A call on their VHF marine radio explained to Joe where we were. I asked him if he could come and tow us home, but our rescuers told us they were passing our place and didn't mind doing for us what Joe so often does for other people.

The breakdown was serious, so when the big boat next went to Picton the speedboat was towed in and a new motor installed.

Thank goodness it's not as serious as that every time the motor stops. Coming home from town one day I heard the new motor cough and splutter. Then it kept losing its revs until finally it stopped altogether. Surely it can't have died already, I thought, as I quickly checked what I could. No fuel was getting from the petrol tank to the hose that led to the motor. It didn't take much figuring out that if I wanted to get home the motor needed fuel, so I ripped off the fitting on the end of the hose that clips on to the fuel tank, unscrewed the cap on the tank, and pushed the hose down into the petrol. Then I stuffed a piece of rag around the hose where it went into the tank, to stop petrol slopping out. It got me home, perhaps not safely, but at least soundly.

Fuel, in one way or the other, is the most common cause when the motor stops. I haven't forgiven Joe for the time he sent me off to Picton with only a part-tank of fuel.

It was summertime. As well as all the usual visitors we'd had in the house during the holidays, we'd employed two university students to cut scrub. I'd reached the stage where I felt as if I were running a boarding establishment. My life revolved around cooking, cleaning and washing, all essential jobs. One of the scrubcutting machines had broken down and Joe wanted me to go into Picton then drive through to Blenheim to pick up a replacement part. I didn't want to go. There was just so much to do. I told him I'd much rather stay at home. "Go yourself!" I yelled as I picked up the clothes basket and headed out for the clothes line. "He doesn't have to come home and cook dinner," I muttered to myself as I plucked the pegs off the line and threw the dry clothes into the basket.

"Please, love," I heard through the open window. It was when he said he'd cook the dinner for me that I began to listen. "You get changed," I was told, "and I'll go and bring the boat in to the wharf."

The last words Joe yelled out as I pulled away from the wharf were that he'd checked the fuel and oil.

The stiff nor'westerly wind blew my cobwebs away, and as I neared Picton the wind veered more to the west and blew straight on shore. The waves hitting the boat broadside on made it uncomfortable and I had to brace myself at the wheel. Then the engine stopped. "Damn! Damn!" I said half to myself and half to an unhearing Joe as I slithered over the wet cockpit floor to change the tanks over. When he'd told me he'd checked the fuel I presumed he'd meant he'd connected the motor up to the full tank. I unplugged the fuel hose from the empty tank and pulled the other tank closer to make it easier to clip the hose on. It was empty. "Bloody hell!" I cursed to myself.

I took a quick look around. There were no boats nearby and these waves would soon have me rolling around on the weather shore. We always carry a spare oar - our auxiliary motor - and I bent down to remove it from the shelf where it is always kept. It wasn't there. I scrambled in the cabin and lifted up a squab to drag out the anchor which I knew was in a locker underneath the bunk. As I put my finger in the hole of the lid covering the locker I realised that I had a good paddle right in front of me. I left the anchor where it was and tried my hand paddling with my makeshift oar. It was only about four feet long and ten inches wide, but as long as I hung over the lee side of the boat and took long deep strokes, I managed to keep heading in the general direction of Picton.

My back was stretched, my knees hurt from jamming them against the inside of the boat, I was hot, my arms ached and I could feel a blister on my finger where I'd hooked it through the hole in the piece of wood. With every dig I made in the water I called Joe a few more names. My 20 minutes' paddling seemed more like an hour when a runabout came close and told me they were going in to Waikawa and if I wanted a tow to throw them a line. I was able to fuel up there, and soon I was on my way to Picton.

Picton to Blenheim was nothing compared with what I'd been through but all the time the words I was going to say to Joe were building in my mind. By the time I arrived home in the bay I had a full head of steam and I knew exactly how I'd greet that husband of mine for sending me off with not enough fuel for the journey. A strange boat was tied off the end of the wharf and I wondered who was visiting. I saw Joe strolling down the track with someone each side of him and I recognised his aunt and uncle. "You look like you've got a body-guard!" I called out, trying to be lighthearted about my trip. He needed one. Words I wanted to say would have to keep until later.

Picton is a small town and news of my running out of fuel had already reached Joe. Before I could say anything he told me he'd thought there'd be heaps of fuel, he was sorry, and he'd invited Rex and Eileen for dinner. By the time they left, my fury had evaporated. How could I stay angry when everyone laughed about it? But it taught me two things. I have a very devious husband (one who could make sure we had visitors around), and now I always check the fuel for myself.

It took a midwinter swim to teach me about tying a boat up. Once again I'd been in Picton playing the church organ, and I was bringing out some friends for a few days. Instead of tying up the boat I threw the bow-line up on the wharf while we unloaded the gear. I decided to tie the boat off the end of the wharf and come back down after lunch and put it out on a mooring in the bay. As I climbed up the tyre I reached out and grabbed the rope. Visitors are always struck by our beautiful white sandy beach and we all stood looking at it as I explained how the currents make it so cold you can't even swim. I pointed out places where the bank had fallen away, exposing indentations in the fresh soil where there had been Maori pits. Okukari was once the site of a fortified Maori pa, and over the years we've picked up many adzes both in greenstone and obsidian.

History was forgotten when we noticed our boat drifting out of the bay. I'd picked up the wrong piece of rope. The dinghy was out on the mooring, there was no one else at home, and I'd let the speedboat float away.

The first thing to come off was the string of Mikimoto pearls that Joe had recently given me, followed by my town clothes, stockings and petticoat. The gap between the wharf and the speedboat was widening rapidly with the nor'westerly blowing out of the bay.

A big gulp of air and I leapt off the far end of the wharf. The cold took my breath away and I was still trying to catch it when I reached the speedboat and clambered up the ladder over the stern.

My humiliation wasn't over yet. As I brought the boat alongside the wharf to climb up on the tyre again, another launch came in and tied up on the other side. I had to greet them in my now see-through underwear as if I did this sort of thing all the time. I was delighted when I discovered they were friends arriving for a Sunday visit. A hessian sack found in the boatshed sheltered me until I got up to the house and warmed up under the shower before getting dressed in my usual Okukari clothes.

Over the years I might not have learnt the technical terms to use to describe a problem with the motor but I can often tell what is wrong with it. Not long after Joe and I had arrived home after being away for a fortnight on my South Island author-tour, Joe had to go in to Picton for a meeting. The boat hadn't been used for more than a month and so Joe had put the battery on the charger the day before in case it was flat.

He backed the trailer down the beach but before the boat was launched Joe thought he'd better make sure it would start. There was only a clunk. He tried again but every time he turned the key he got only this clunking noise. The battery terminals were checked and I watched Joe fiddle with all the fuel lines before tearing off the cover of the motor. I peered into the motor with him because these are the times I learn about it. Another turn of the key and the same noise. I remembered hearing that same sound once before and although I couldn't describe the cause I suggested to Joe that it sounded as if "that little wheel that goes up the rod and engages the bigger wheel at the top is stuck". An exasperated husband told me to mind my own business but he looked at my 'wheels' anyway. That was in fact the problem, and when Joe freed them up the motor started. He got to his meeting in time and at the back of my mind I stored away the correct description for my 'stuck wheels' - the starter motor is not engaging.

Today, if both our boats are fishing and I want to get to Picton and I can't use the speedboat because of one or another of the conditions on my list, we have another boat we can call upon. The Edwards family who own the *Felix* use it as a charter boat and for a reasonable charge we can get into Picton. Once a week we now have a Sounds town day, and the return trip costs us $35. As I grow older I am finding I enjoy the day so much more without having the responsibility of the speedboat in town and worrying if the wind is getting up. I can bring much more home, and the pleasure of stepping off a boat at our wharf without the hassle of having to pull it up or put it on the moorings far outweighs the cost.

There have been many times when I've been organised to go to Picton and haven't been able to start the tractor which we use to tow the speedboat to put it in the water or pull it out. Twice the tow bar on the tractor has broken, or the ground has been too greasy to back the tractor down to the beach or the boat hasn't started. I've become quite philosophical about it after all these years and I just walk back up to my house, change, unpack my bag and leave my list handy so I can keep adding to it.

Rachael and Angela, two of the seventh generation Heberleys, have often asked me why I'm not angry or disappointed at not getting out. Their comments turn the clocks back in my mind to stories that Charlie, a fourth generation Heberley, has told me. His Uncle John, Arthur Heberley's oldest brother, used to row a 14ft dinghy 16 miles from Oyster Bay in Tory Channel to Picton. He'd play his game of rugby and row home in good time to start work first thing on Sunday morning and if he was lucky he would be able to hoist a sail and sail part of the way.

And only one generation back from us - with our speedboat and two fishing boats, or being able to call on the *Felix* - Charlie's three older brothers rowed four miles from Oyster Bay to Te Weka Bay for school lessons. A Mr Baxter who had been a schoolteacher before coming to the Sounds taught school from his home. As Charlie was the youngest, he began school lessons with his mother in Oyster Bay, and when a school opened up in Te Pangu Bay he walked the two miles there and back every day.

Weather that keeps me at home didn't keep those earlier generations of Heberleys off the sea, and I am left in no doubt as to why these Heberley men are still men of the sea today.

CHAPTER SIX

Out Fishing

WHEN a storm cut short my tuna fishing trip out of Westport in March 1995 I didn't know if I'd ever go tuna fishing again. The golden promises that I'd been enticed out with hadn't eventuated on the trip. The hot sunny days when all I'd have to wear were shorts and a T-shirt, the smooth seas and the fish waiting to take my lures - these didn't happen. My trip was cold and windy with a big ocean swell. I'd felt seasick and I'd struggled to keep my balance because of the wet weather gear I had to wear over my clothes, and when there was a tuna on my line I found it extremely difficult to pull it aboard. As for the ominous forecasts with the stormy-looking sky and the sea that quietly built up, sending us over the Westport bar at midnight, they didn't leave me at all keen to go tuna fishing again. At least not for another year.

But this time I was going to cover a part of the New Zealand coast I hadn't yet experienced. From Okukari, we'd sail up the west coast as far north as Manukau, a distance of approximately 290 nautical miles. I'd studied the map carefully before committing myself, and it seemed minor in comparison with my voyage up the east coast from Bluff to Okukari, when we'd steamed 467 nautical miles to bring the newly built *Te Wai* home. It seemed easy.

All the omens were good the day we left Okukari. Both the *Fugitive* and *Te Wai* were loaded up and the last of the gear stowed aboard. Because I was coming there were many comments about how low in the water *Te Wai* was sitting, but I was going prepared for the hot summer days I remembered from my Auckland childhood, away out on my parents' yacht, *Mangawai*.

About 8am the lines were let go and we pulled away from the wharf. I felt strange waving goodbye to our family, seeing tears in the eyes of our grandchildren as they waved goodbye to their fathers. Joy and Lisa were stoic in front of their children, and I felt a tight squeeze in my chest as I thought of that first burst of loneliness I always feel when I arrive back at the house after saying goodbye to Joe and wander through the quiet rooms. None of Joe's favourite magazines will be lying around. They are always the first things to be packed. No sunglasses sitting on the fridge waiting to be picked up, no toothbrush, electric razor, old comfortable pillow, his cigarettes that I always moan about, or coats and hats that hang inside the back door - everything's on the boat. No one to expect home for meals for at least eight weeks - 56 nights - if it's tuna fishing.

For the first half hour it's always easy to sit in the silence at the kitchen table, gazing out at the view and watching the changing patterns made by the sun and tide on the water. Then one makes oneself get going so with a sigh I'd push the chair away from the table and gather up the cups of our half-drunk cups of tea - a drink neither of us wanted what with Joe wanting to get to sea while I didn't want him to go. I'd wish he'd just leave and I could begin to get used to living on my own again. Oh yes. I knew how my daughters-in-law felt as they walked back to their loneliness.

Before heading north we were calling in at Picton to ice-up, top up the gas bottles, fill up with diesel and buy the last of our stores. It could be a week before we came into a port again. A heat haze blunted the bare skyline and the stacks of cumulus clouds in the azure sky agreed with the latest weather fax that we'd received as we left the wharf. New Zealand was in the middle of highs.

At 2pm the fish freezers were both full, each with three tonnes of flaked ice. The inner insulated lids were slid in place and the top hatch covers fastened. The boat engines were started up and we were off. I could feel the tight excitement of the fishermen as we headed to sea. I noticed they kept looking up at the tuna poles, still sitting snugly against the yoke near the top of the mast, and their anticipation of the future catch hung in the air.

We cleared the northern entrance of Queen Charlotte Sound at 3.30pm and an hour later the tuna gear was lowered into the sea - just in case. Nothing came near the lures that day, but 25 miles out and 12 miles off Stephens Island Joe was a whaler once again when he spotted a 50ft sei whale. I was surprised when Joe told me the spout was only vapour, not the water it had gulped in as it fed on the krill and other small surface organisms. As we came closer it sank beneath the surface, leaving only a smooth patch of water and a few sea birds hovering overhead.

Both boats steamed in company and as darkness fell it was a good feeling to look out on an otherwise empty sea to the lights of the *Fugitive* nearby. A chat between boats on a ship to ship radio frequency helped ease the solitude at the wheel.

I felt the boat lift in the long ocean swell that tucked itself under the stern of the boat before we'd run down the sea. It brought back alarming memories of my tuna fishing trip out of Westport, but James assured me it was nothing. "Always the same out here," he reassured me with a grin. "You'll soon get used to it." Nevertheless I took myself to bed and slept until 11.30pm. I could make out the shape of one body in one of the other bunks as I clambered out of mine and climbed up the steps into the wheelhouse. Joe's face was in green shadows from the electronic light of the navigation equipment, and Nick, one of the crewmen, was making coffee before he took over from Joe. James was the sleeping body I'd left below.

In front of us the sky was lit up. Eyes and mind still in sleep mode told me it was the moon rising. Then I looked again. The light seemed to take in the whole horizon, bright and white, and it wasn't until Joe told me it would most probably be a New Zealand joint-venture fishing vessel drifting with a sea anchor that I realised it was a boat. He told me he was going to stay on the wheel until we passed it, then he'd catch up on some sleep. As we drew closer we could see it was about 100ft long and I tried to imagine the size of its generator which could light up the huge bulbs that were draped from bow to stern. We steamed close enough to see each bulb but there was no sign of life aboard. When it lay astern of us Joe disappeared below, for a sleep.

The monotonous sound of the engine and the regular bleep from the scanner on the radar soon made my eyes heavy too and I dozed in the wheelhouse. At 3.30am I was wide awake watching the lights of Opunake sink below our stern, while inland, and a little further north, the towers with their gas burn-offs from the Maui pipeline lit up the sky.

Cape Egmont light had been visible for the last 20 miles and it was a relief when we at last left the flashing light behind us. I'd found myself becoming mesmerised as I counted the three quick flashes and then counted the 30 seconds in between. Once we were around the Cape a new course was set on the GPS and it was my shift at the wheel.

The shift before dawn is called the graveyard shift. I sat in the darkness watching the GPS - Global Positioning System - as it showed our speed, distance travelled and the distance until we reached our next weigh point, or the place when another course would be plotted in. It was cold in the pre-dawn light and I sat with my hands buried in my jacket pockets, trying to keep warm. The last stars still hung brightly in the black sky and I could only imagine where it met the sea out to the west, while the lights of New Plymouth twinkled on our eastern side. Slowly golden streaks appeared in the sky, lighting the land from black to dark blue. Strings of light clung to the land as the sun rose until at last it broke free to show a sea completely calm. The new day blackened the *Fugitive* as she steamed near us on our port side. Her curling white bow wave was the only thing to break the surface.

Young Joe's voice burst over the VHF. "We've had our first strike! Only cokes, but it feels great." I was told later that cokes are small tuna. James heard the message, leapt out of bed and put the lines out. We had strikes immediately and the flapping of the fish on the deck had Joe and Nick out of their beds. I felt sad watching the blackish-blue colour on the tunas' backs and their silvery-coloured bellies fading as they died. But these fish were great for me to practise on, using the overarm strokes I'd been shown last year to pull them in, and I soon had the knack and was able to land my share of the catch - even the bigger ones weighing anything from seven to ten kilograms.

In the middle of the day the heat was almost unbearable and we all kept looking for a cool spot on the boat. If the tuna were striking we wouldn't be noticing the heat but it was too hot even for the fish. The stern deck, sheltered from any breeze, was hot to walk on and we kept the hose running over it all day. Nothing stirred the surface of the water and fragments of the *Rime Of The Ancient Mariner* kept drifting across my mind. It was as if we too were that 'painted ship upon a painted ocean'.

I stretched out on the for'ard deck, trying to catch the moving air, and peered over the bow down into the sea. Shafts of sunlight splintered the navy blue world below, reminding me of the patterns the children used to make with their Spirograph set. Each shaft was like a centre pivot and beams of refracted light from its base burst back to the surface, forming hundreds of symmetrical patterns. Looking through my sunglasses I saw a different world with a myriad plankton, chain jellyfish, and the pelagic barrel-salps which were no doubt trying to keep out of the way of the shrimp known as the barrel-shrimp, as these eat out the inside of the salps and then move in. I couldn't see any of the sardines, pilchards or squid that the tuna feed off as they were down too deep. I'd spent the last hour watching the echo-sounder screen for tuna signs. The red seagull shapes that passed across the screen were fascinating. "Tuna marks," I was told but they were down

35-40 fathoms. "Too deep," Joe told me. Then swirls of yellow drifted across the screen and I was told this was feed, but though it came up close to the surface the elusive red seagulls stayed down too deep. "If they'd only lift a few fathoms we'd have them," Joe muttered as he stared into the screen. When Joe told me they could lift the fish from 25-30 fathoms I did some hasty arithmetic and was amazed when I worked out that the fish would take the lures from a depth of 150-180 feet.

"Yes!" came from Joe. Then "Full house!" This had me running to pull tuna aboard. A full house meant there was a fish on every line and everyone had to work quickly to clear the fish and get the lines back in the water. Once the tuna are in a feeding frenzy and taking the lures they will often keep following the boat and keep being caught. The heat was forgotten as our catch tally grew and when that flurry of fish was over another 37 were added to our total catch for the day.

As soon as possible after it is caught each fish has to be spiked. We use a Phillips screw driver, pushing it into the head between the eyes, through the brain and driving it into the base of the backbone, killing the tuna quickly. I hated watching it being done but I was told it is much more humane and the fish are not stressed. But the bottom line is that most of the tuna go to overseas markets in America, mainly for canning, and the better the quality of fish we sell to the processor the more we are paid. Then the tuna are placed in a plastic bin filled with a slurry of ice and salt water to cool them quickly before they are packed in the freezer.

Our days began at 4.45am with a cup of tea and toast. Early morning and late evening are the best times to catch the fish as these are their natural feeding times. Quite often a strike would have us all out on the deck in the semi-light to pull in fish, our cups of tea forgotten. Breakfast was a big meal usually around 9am, after the fish caught in the early morning were away in the freezer. Except for one morning, the day James caught his first yellowfin tuna. Then plates with congealing eggs and bacon on them were left on the table and the toast forgotten under the griller.

By the way the black rubber was stretched out we knew it was a big fish. As James pulled in the line Joe reached for the gaff ready to hook the fish and help James lift it aboard. A fish weighing in around 35 kilos lay threshing on the deck until Nick spiked it. James held it up for a photograph. With its head on the deck of the boat, the tail reached James's shoulders.

This fish had to be handled in a different way as it was more valuable and would be sold whole. Unlike the tuna which were not gutted, this fish had to be gutted by pulling the guts through the gills before the fish was put in the slurry and down in the freezer. Everyone laughed and was excited as we waited expectantly for more yellowfin. But we trolled for hours without a single fish taking a lure. Tempers became frayed. We trolled north and we trolled south and for variation east and west. No one seemed to be catching fish around us and the fishermen were discussing why they were not biting. I heard, "Too calm, too hot, wrong type of feed." There were other reasons and most of them we could do nothing about. Then Joe thought it could be the hooks as we had been steaming through masses of chain jellyfish. We pulled the lines aboard one by one and cleared them of the jellyfish. When I asked what difference it makes if the hooks are covered in the jelly-like mass I received a withering glance and the reply that the tuna can see the hooks.

Frustration leads to playing pranks. When the fish are slow in the middle of the day it's a good time to have a shower as by the time everything is cleaned up at night and the engine stopped it is after 10pm and the only thing on anyone's minds is sleep. *Te Wai* has a two-inch hose to pump salt water and it is this that keeps the water washing across the stern deck to keep it cool. The shower opens out on to the stern deck. There is a draining hole below the door to let the shower water run away and it's great fun for the people on the outside to jam the deck hose in the hole and fill the shower with salt water. This is a cross between an initiation ceremony and slow torture but I told them if they wanted a meal cooked each night they'd better not try it on me.

Instead James caught his father out. While Joe was sitting on the toilet James reached out over the side of the boat and pulled on a line and started yelling. The toilet door burst open and Joe raced out on deck, still pulling up his shorts. When he recovered his sense of humour he told us he'd looked out the window and seen the length of the stretched rubber so he was positive we must have hooked another yellowfin.

Fifty miles west of the Manukau Heads we were in another world. We were outside the coverage area of the cellular phones and couldn't pick up any radio or television. Our only communication for two days, apart from talking on a ship to ship frequency between our own two boats, was with Kevin McBrydie of Marlborough Marine Radio when we called in at 8.30pm each day on the SSB (single side-band radio). I knew if there was anything wrong at home the girls would get a message through to us via Kevin but I found myself frequently checking the cellphone to see if we had entered the coverage area. Sometimes we'd be in it and I'd reach out to use the phone, only to find the signal had gone again. I knew how Joy and Lisa would be feeling without the daily voice contact and knowing everything was OK on the boats. When you're alone at home the imagination grows until it's easy to think one of the boats has blown up with a gas explosion, or sunk for some only too imaginable reason, or perhaps been run down by a ship as they've drifted during the night. At sea I realise how stupid those thoughts are but at home they're real.

I thought again how time has changed things. When Joe had our first boat built in 1966 she had only a radio-telephone. Ruby, my mother-in-law, had a large radio that was powered by eight torch batteries. She could tune in to the marine radio station and pick up Joe but couldn't reply. When Joe went away fishing he'd make a time to call me each evening and I'd go across the lawn to my in-laws' home and wait to hear from Joe. The radio had to be tuned in perfectly or Joe's message wouldn't be heard. Sometimes the interference due to the atmosphere would blot out the voice I longed to hear - just to let me know he was all right. And of course once the boat was out of range I just had to believe in his commonsense as I wouldn't hear from him for days. In those early years, I spent many sleepless nights wondering if he was still on top of the ocean.

Once again Joe was on the receiving end of a practical joke. A can of tuna had been brought aboard, no doubt with the joke in mind. A hole was made in the top and a hook on one of the lines was pushed in before the line was thrown back over the side. When the tin hit the water the black rubber at the top of the pole stretched out as if a fish were on it. "Yes!" yelled James, and Joe, who had been lying out in the sun, leapt up and started to pull in the line. Everyone waited for his reaction when he got it to the surface and flicked it aboard. Faces fell when Joe just pulled the can off the hook and tossed it back over the side with the words, "Foul-hooked some rubbish."

Further north there are always more shark around. Occasionally the boys set a line up at night to target the blue or mako shark. The line is made up with six feet of chain with a breaking strain of two tonne. At one end there is a galvanised steel hook 12 inches long while the other end has a length of rope attached to it. The chain and hook, with half a tuna on it for bait, is then lowered into the sea over the bow and the end of the rope is threaded through a deck chair or the handle of an empty plastic fish-case before being tied to a bollard. The chair or fish-case is left on the wheelhouse roof and when there is a strike it crashes down on the for'ard deck, waking up the fishermen. There isn't a market for these sharks. This is sport for the younger crew members.

As we were coming in towards the Manukau Bar near the end of my trip, James put out his shark hook. A mako took the bait of a small tuna and James managed to bring the shark alongside the boat. I looked down into its mouth of sharp pointed teeth and as it flung itself around I could easily count its five large gill slits. Joe was about to gaff it aboard when it gave one last great twist and heave of its body and it was free, its erect dorsal fin slicing through the water as it swam away.

A few days later Young Joe's crewman fell overboard and I heard he was nearly walking on water by the time he climbed back aboard the *Fugitive*, no doubt remembering the size of that mako. Young Joe said it was very rough and his crewman had been sitting on the bait table which itself sits over the fish freezer. One of the shorties at the stern had a tuna and his crew jumped off the table to go and pull in the line. At the same time the bow of the boat dropped into a trough, causing the stern to lift, and the crew was catapulted into the sea.

I'll never get used to the idea of drifting around the ocean at night. Visions of a coastal boat or a container ship running us down make me nervous about sleeping below decks. Instead I curl up on a narrow seat built around the table, trying to hang on while the boat rolls, and unable to sleep with the noise of everything crashing from side to side. We had some calm nights and I became quite good at sleeping with my knees braced against the table-top. Any sleep I missed out on during the night I usually managed to catch up with in the slack periods during the day. My worst time on this trip was the night we spent just outside the Manukau Bar. I'd seen a few big ships during the day and I didn't intend to be listed as missing, presumed drowned, after a collision at sea. This was one night I spent on anchor watch, listening to the snores of exhausted bodies but too nervous to join them in sleep. Everyone on the boat thought I was mad and when I asked Joe if he wasn't nervous about being run down by a ship he assured me he felt very safe with me up in the wheelhouse keeping watch.

Joe was up at 4am and started the engine and turned on the GPS to check our position. Daylight was just breaking as we crossed the bar and as it grew lighter and we slid past Cornwallis, Laingholme and Titirangi I couldn't believe the changes. The baches I remembered from my youth now seemed to be the permanent homes of affluent people.

At 7am we pulled into the wharf at Onehunga where we waited for the truck so we could unload the catch from both boats, then refuel, and fill up with both ice and water. I couldn't wait to stand on an unmoving surface but when I first stood on the wharf I felt as if it were coming up to meet me. By the time the shops had opened I'd begun to feel normal so I walked up to Mangere Bridge with two lists of supplies for the two boats. It felt strange being around a lot of people again, and hearing traffic noises instead of the boat engine, and I was glad when I'd finished and was able to catch a taxi back to the wharf with the stores.

Before I'd left home I'd told my family I'd travel down the North Island visiting relatives on the way. It seems my family knew their mother better than I knew myself as they'd told one another that once I hit Auckland I'd go straight home. Now my trip was over. I was leaving the boat but I found that all I wanted to do was go home to Okukari. A flight out of Auckland was soon arranged.

Those golden promises I'd been enticed out with in the previous year had come true this time. The weather had been perfect with calm sunny days and I'd lived in shorts, T-shirts, sunhats and bare feet. I'd seen sunsets as vivid as those I'd seen in Hawaii and watched as a perfectly rounded sun hung on the edge of the ocean, slowly flattening before it disappeared. The sky would change from a light grey with a strip of orange cloud above the bright light until sudden darkness swept over the sea.

I also had my answer about why these men go tuna fishing. I had been told that it is the last open-access fishery. Anyone can fish for tuna, and they have to build a catch history for when it becomes a quota species. But I could see it was like a summer holiday - most of the time. A chance to get away from home and have the cobwebs blown away in the warm sea breeze, a time for meeting up with the friends made last year, swapping fish stories, and yarning on the wharf while they waited for fuel and ice. I could understand Joe's saying, "There is no other fishing quite like it." I feel the same way when I arrive home after being away for a few days and walk into my kitchen and take in the view from my window - there is no other painting quite like it.

Once tuna fishing is over the following two or three months are spent lining for grey shark. After the men's long periods away from home during the tuna season those at home find the weekly trips away catching shark much easier to endure.

During May to September we catch crayfish. This is the cream of our fishing business when large amounts of money can be made in a short space of time. It is only because the ITQ (Individual Transferable Quota) scheme was put in place in 1986 that we have such a lucrative crayfish fishery today. Crayfish stocks had dropped alarmingly, causing many fishermen to drop out of the industry. Well before 1986, responsible fishermen had urged the government to take steps to control the quantity of fish being taken, either by limiting the number of crayfish pots each fisherman could use or by having some months closed for crayfishing. Although the ITQs meant massive cuts in the quantity of fish permitted to be caught and a great deal of paper work for the fishermen - or more often their wives - they have proved to be highly successful in most New Zealand areas.

After a day out in the boat craying I feel exhausted from bracing myself against the continual movement of the boat, plus the speed with which you have to work. Some pots have to be pulled at slack water, others when it's flood tide, and some on the ebb.

I enjoy getting out on the boat and if one of the crew is away or sick I occasionally find myself filling in. At such times I can't pick my weather. The night before I toss and turn, worrying about what it will be like.

This particular day James and Lisa were away, the crays were biting and so I found myself walking down to the wharf, waiting for Joe. He rowed out to *Te Wai*, swinging from her moorings in the corner of the bay, let go the rope and brought her in to the wharf.

At 7.30am the sun still hadn't reached our bay and the water was a dull metallic green except for around the mouth of the lagoon. There a large semi-circle of muddy water, brought down the creek from the heavy rain the night before, flowed into the bay. Kelp, and logs washed down from flooding rivers, were strewn along the top of the beach from the last southerly storm of three or four days ago, and as I jumped aboard the boat I caught a whiff of the distinctive sulphur smell of rotting kelp. I'd heard the weather forecast and the nor'westerly wind was expected to increase during the day but right now it was only about 10 to 15 knots with just enough wind to push smooth ripples out of the bay.

We were starting at the channel entrance today as slack water was at 8am, and so less than five minutes after leaving the wharf we were at the first pot. I could see at least five of our red or yellow crayfish floats all marked with our vessel registration number, 62861, and the name *Te Wai*.

Joe came up alongside the first float and pulled the boat in reverse to slow it down, and I stretched out to hook the rope beneath the float before pulling it back into the boat where Joe could grab hold of the rope, lift it over the davit and take a turn around the line hauler. These are some of our deeper pots, some as deep as 80 fathoms, and while the rope was being coiled in a heap on the deck I gathered up three or four gurnard frames, supplied by the fishing company we fish for, ready to put in the bait bag. I always think of it as recycling as we are using the remains of the fish after the fillets have been cut off. Crayfish love the fish factory's remains. The bait bags are made out of fine mesh plastic netting, the size of a woman's handbag, with an opening at the top to put the bait in.

As I watched, a small red buoy came to the surface. This was the down buoy so I knew the pot must show up shortly as this buoy is about one-third of the way up from the bottom of the line, and is held in place by a simple knot in the rope on the top side of the buoy. Its job is to hold the slack rope up from the sea bed, so it doesn't chafe or hook on rocks, especially at slack water when the excess rope is not held taut in the tide.

For a minute I couldn't help thinking of the hot summer days when we went catching the tuna out of Auckland, but here I was on this early August morning, freezing and getting soaking wet from the water flicking off the rope as it came through the davit.

The pot came to the surface and swung in to the side of the boat. As it landed on the top of the bulwarks Joe stopped the line hauler and flicked out the rope from it. The sight of the crays flapping about, all a good size, made me forget my discomfort. Then came a busy few minutes clearing away the old bait and replacing it with the fresh while Joe quickly checked that the pot had no holes. The trawl mesh which covers the steel frame can develop holes big enough to lose crays if it rubs against a rock. Holes must be repaired before the pot is put back into the water. Joe measured crays that were on the borderline for size. They were either thrown back or they joined the others in a white plastic bin which had water from the deck hose circulating through it. Usually very small crays fall out through the escape gaps before the pot lands on the deck. Now, by law, there are gaps built into all pots.

Joe always works the wheel at the back of the wheelhouse where he can control the line hauler and keep an eye on the echo sounder. Once the pot was ready to be set I could see him studying the sounder, searching for the foul on the seabed, maybe a rock pinnacle, all places where crays might be living. "Chuck it in!" he called. I pushed the pot overboard and soon the only sign we'd pulled that pot was a mass of seething bubbles and the scavenging sea-birds, fighting over scraps of old bait washed from the pot as it sank to the bottom.

Another quick circle and we rounded up on the next pot. This time, once I'd hooked in the buoy and passed it over to Joe, I had time to contemplate the weather. So far the signs were good although the thin cloud streaks high in the sky were a warning that the wind would probably increase later. North of us, Wellington Bay still lay in shadow although it was easy to pick out the floats marking the pots as they bobbed on the surface. My eyes followed the curve of the bay around to Perano Head. Its stark cliffs stood out in the early morning sunlight but it was the indigo sky above the sun that held my attention. Two rays of the sun shimmered like jewels on rich velvet.

"Keep your damned feet out of the rope! You'll be over the side!" Joe's angry words snapped me out of my daydreams. Charlie had drummed those same words into me the very first time I'd gone crayfishing. He'd told me about the time he'd nearly gone over the side during a whale chase because of a rope around his foot. He'd harpooned the whale and it had taken off. The rope was snaking out through a two-inch fairlead, with a pin over the top to hold the rope in, when a loop in the rope caught his foot. Fortunately for my father-in-law, he'd been wearing short gumboots instead of the usual thigh gumboots. He'd fallen on his back, grabbed hold of the gunpost and managed to free his foot before his boot reached the fairlead. I wriggled my toes in my boots as I tried to imagine the pain. A 50-tonne whale could pull a boat under. I had no doubt the two-inch fairlead would not have saved Charlie. His foot would have been mangled before the pin broke and he went over the side tied fast to the whale.

I certainly didn't want to go over the side attached to a crayfish pot, and Joe didn't really need to tell me I was out here to work, not daydream.

We'd finished the pots at the channel entrance and took off over to Perano Head. "Keep an eye out for the floats," I was told. "There should be four out here in the deep." As the tide slackened the floats started to break the surface and we worked flat out to get them before the tide started to run and took the floats under. There was no time to measure any borderline crays so we put them in a separate case on the deck.

After the frenzy of pulling gear in the changing tide it was a pleasure working the gear in the shallows along the shore. Some of these pots were set in only three fathoms of water, and they could be seen from the surface. Suddenly we landed a pot filled up entirely with a conger eel. These can grow up to a length of two metres and about 15 kilos in weight. I looked at Joe in amazement when he yelled at me to keep my hands away from it. "It'll tear your finger off!" he warned, but I'd already stepped well back. There'd be no chance of losing a finger, I thought to myself, and I watched anxiously as Joe picked up a knife and made lunges at the threshing eel. I could see he was trying to stab it at the base of the head and it kept twisting around in an effort to attack its tormentor. Even after it lay still and the pot was tipped on its side to let it slide out, Joe told me to keep well clear because it would attack anything that came close.

The last of our pots to be pulled were off Cape Koamaru. We steamed up to them in the face of a stiff nor'westerly. It was enough to lift the tops of the waves and keep the back deck awash. I could feel the water defying gravity and seeping up the inside of my waterproof leggings. My legs grew colder by the minute. I knew I was working sluggishly, and tempers became rather frayed when I missed the odd float.

This is the time of day when I've had enough crayfishing. Eight hours of constant motion, working non-stop, takes its toll. I find myself counting how many pots we have left to pull, and don't care about our catch numbers. Dried salt makes my face feel tight and itchy and all I can think of is arriving home and having a hot shower. Once the last pot has been pulled I can collapse on the seat in the wheelhouse and steer for Okukari Bay, in sheer relief, leaving Joe outside to scrub down the boat.

This day only one job remained, to drain out the white bin so we

First generation.
James (Worser)
and Te Wai.
Photo taken before 1877.

Second generation. John Heberley.

Third generation. Arthur Heberley.

*Fourth generation.Charles Heberley. Charlie is holding the Heberley
Memorial Shield. Around his neck he wears his taonga (treasured
possession). The central figure represents Charlie. On one side the figure
holds a mere depicting Charlie as the head of his whanau or family group.
On the reverse side it holds a harpoon representing his years as a whaler.
The two shoulders represent the slopes of Mt Egmont (Taranaki) as Worser
was the first European to climb the mountain. The two whales on each side
are Te Wai and Worser, and the eight twirls engraved on the taonga are their
eight children.*

*This group of Campbell Island whalers in 1909 was led by John Thomas
Heberley. Back row from left: Harry McKegney, Charlie Heberley, Charlie
Jackson, Willy Thoms, Dick Norton. Middle row: Harry Heberley, Jack
Norton, John Thomas Heberley, Arthur Jackson. Front row: Tim Norton,
Andrew Anderson, Harry Norton. (Photo Alexander Turnbull Library)*

Joe Heberley in 1927. Joe, aged about 18, is about to shoot a whale.

Herbert Heberley in 1927. Herbert, aged 16, cuts the body fat from a whale. Note the sacking bowyangs to protect his legs.

Jim Heberley, aged 14, at work at the Tipi Bay station, in 1927. He wears sacking bowyangs and lace-up leather shoes.

Tipi Bay station with two whales waiting to be processed.

Men from Tipi Bay whaling station scan the waters of Cook Strait on the western side of Tory Channel in 1927.

Senior Constable Bill Gibb.

Tranz Rail Rescue. The day of her dedication 1996.

could put the crayfish we'd caught into the holding tank moored in our bay. This is a wooden slatted crate measuring 7x7x3 feet, with a hinged lid on the top. Our crays are all exported live so they have to be kept in the tank until we ship them to Picton.

Joe took over the wheel and brought the boat alongside the holding tank. I picked up one rope attached to the tank and took a turn around a bollard on *Te Wai* while Joe picked up the other. I was furious with him as I'd just discovered he hadn't kept the two blue cod we'd caught in a crayfish pot, when all the way home I'd been sitting at the wheel thinking about the fresh fish I'd cook for our dinner. I felt like telling him to tie his own tank up and put the crays in himself. Still grumbling about how mean he was, and if he wanted a meal he could get it himself, I watched his balancing act on the capping rail as he leaned over the side and reached across the holding tank to lift up the lid. It was sticking and he stretched out a little further. The lid broke free with a rush and Joe lost his balance. He slid, head first, right into the tank of flapping crayfish. When he reappeared I ran to the side to give him a hand up, trying to keep from laughing.

After the crays were all in the tank and Joe was securing the lid I had to go into the wheelhouse out of his sight and hearing. Hot tears were sliding down my face when I felt his fingers tapping my heaving shoulder. I turned to face him then he also dissolved in laughter. "Never seen so many of the buggers before my eyes," was all Joe could say. I forgot all about my anger of a few moments before.

A few days later the holding tank was full and we organised a day to unload. The tank is towed in to the beach with the boat and pulled up out of the water with the tractor. The crayfish can be worth up to $30,000. I can imagine the worst - the bottom bursting open and our losing the lot, or an octopus having eased its way into the tank and killed a lot of the crays. Only once have we lost our catch, when the tank rolled as we were towing it ashore. That time we didn't have many crays, and the days of high prices for export fish hadn't arrived. All the same it was a week's work in the winter months, and hard to come to terms with.

The men always work quickly to empty the holding tank and transfer the crayfish to big plastic tubs. These are carted along the wharf on the transport tray behind the tractor, and lifted aboard the boat. Water is circulated through the tubs to keep the fish alive, and once in Picton they are packed in plastic fish tubs between layers of woodwool. Each lid is tied down so the live fish cannot escape. All our crayfish go to Oamaru by road where they are unpacked and placed in salt water, usually around 12 degrees Celsius, to perk them up after their eight hours out of water. Later they are shifted to another holding tank with colder water where they are kept for a minimum of three days to purge them.

Our crays are exported mostly to Taiwan and China, and to survive the 38-hour journey they are packed in woodwool in 40-litre polystyrene bins. On average, 10 of our fish fit in one bin. A plastic pack of ice goes on top of the fish, and before the lid is sealed a temperature recorder is placed in with the fish as an insurance policy.

Our responsibility is over once the fish leave the boat in Picton. All we have to do is head back to Okukari, unload the bait and begin another week of crayfishing. Our cray season, beginning in May, is short as we usually have our quota caught within four months but it means we sell our fish when the prices are high, as once the crayfish from Australia and South America come on the market, prices drop.

During the months we catch our crayfish we keep only the bucks (males) as the hens (females) have eggs and must be left in the water. Joe agrees that this is essential to conserve fish stocks. He is positive that unless this fishery is continually monitored in the years ahead, it won't be sustainable. And we both like to think that there will be a place for our grandchildren in the industry if they wish to carry on the Heberley tradition of making a living from the sea.

CHAPTER SEVEN

Questions

THE FIRST official day of winter, Saturday 1 June 1996, had begun for me at 4.30am. I struggled into cold clothes to get to Picton's ferry terminal by 5am, thinking I must be crazy.

I had to be at Broadcasting House in Wellington at 10.45am in time to speak by phone with Brian Edwards on his Top Of The Morning programme. My slot was to begin at 11.10am. Rather than depend on getting in to Picton from Okukari Bay at that time in the morning I'd chosen to stay with Pauline and her husband Dene, in Picton. At least I wasn't freezing coming down the Sounds in my speedboat, I kept telling myself. All the same a little voice chipped in, telling me I had to be mad.

The Interisland ferry *Arahura* shuddered as she pulled out of her berth. I gazed at the sheer beauty of the reflections from the town lights shimmering on the smooth waters of the harbour. Beneath the stern the propellers churned up a mass of seething water, and hundreds of bright shafts stabbed the blackness as the lights were held in the lifting spray. The cold seeped into my bones and it had me remembering the very first trip I'd made up the Sounds just after I'd married 33 years ago. That day I'd watched Picton grow smaller and further away in the wake of our boat and I was homesick. I'd longed to feel my parents' loving arms. Auckland had seemed so far away. Tears pricked the back of my eyes now, so I turned my back on those long ago memories and strode into the warm light of the aft lounge.

Sitting in the quiet darkness, I knew just where we were as I felt each gentle turn the *Arahura* made in Tory Channel. An hour after departure we passed Okukari, and as always I found myself on the deck watching our still sleeping bay, as we slipped past and out into Cook Strait.

The rise and fall of the ferry out in the Strait reminded me of the weather forecast I'd heard on television the night before. Strong to gale southerly winds were predicted by lunchtime. Now in the first light of dawn the sea looked cold and inhospitable. There was no end or beginning to where the sea and sky met.

During the hour-long trip across the open Strait the wind slowly freshened. I overheard a child asking his mother where the porpoises were today and why he couldn't see any birds? The sea appeared dead. Not even seabirds skimmed the tops of the waves. A freshening 35-40 knot southerly followed us up Wellington harbour, and, as I came off the ship to find my cousin, Jean, I felt relieved that at least I'd managed to get to Wellington for my interview. If the ferries stopped running now, it wouldn't be the end of the world.

Unknown to anyone then, it was to become the end of the world for the crew of the 14.6-metre fishing vessel, *Chance*. About this time they made the decision to leave Port Underwood, and head for Picton where they would discharge their catch.

By 11am the wind in Wellington was gusting up to 50 knots, and driving rain sent my already lowered temperature lower. Added to this was the usual malaise that hit me before every interview, and the pounding of my heart made me shake as much as the cold.

Inside Broadcasting House I found the same friendliness I'd met throughout New Zealand. I began to feel slightly better and by the time I was talking to Brian I felt as if I were in control of my shaking body. This time I was speaking to a voice only, as Brian is based in Auckland, and although the idea of this had made me extremely nervous, I found it the easiest of all my interviews. I wondered if this was because I didn't have the distraction of a person on the other side of a desk, smiling and urging me along with a smile and head noddings. Or was it because this was the last of my scheduled radio interviews? Anyway I relaxed completely as the air time ticked down.

I don't have to be at Okukari to be in the middle of an earthquake. This time I was so intent on the questions Brian was asking and the answers I was giving that I didn't feel the jolt. The table in front of me was rocking, and I noticed the microphones shaking. Thinking I'd knocked a leg of the table, I told myself to watch out where I put my feet. It wasn't until I came out of the studio and was congratulated for the way I'd kept on talking throughout the earthquake that I realised what had happened. I felt stupid, confessing that I thought I had been responsible.

Outside the studio the weather was worse. Southerly-driven rain and the force of the wind made me decide to try to catch the earlier freight ferry home rather than hang around waiting for the 2.30pm ferry on which I was booked. Already 50-knot winds buffeted the harbour and I was thrilled to find myself able to leave Wellington earlier, especially when I was told that the next ferry might be a non-event.

About the time we left Wellington, I was told later, the last contact with the fishing boat *Chance* was made. The skipper had called up on his marine radio and told Marlborough Marine Radio that he was off Lucky Point, three miles south of the channel entrance, where Joe and I had once capsized our dinghy when collecting firewood. By then the southerly wind was gusting up to 70 knots and the seas were rising.

On the ferry it was obvious we were going to have a rough crossing. The seas in the harbour were beginning to heap up and white foam from breaking waves was being blown along in streaks. A voice on the intercom advised us not to leave our seats. I'd called Joe on our cellphone to let him know I was on my way home, and now, watching the sea, I felt relief that both our sons were in from crayfishing.

When we reached the entrance of Wellington harbour, higher waves with long overhanging crests met us. The resulting foam was blowing in thick streaks in the direction of the wind. The sea looked as if a giant hand had drawn its fingers through the surface, leaving it a white seething mass.

The boat rolled heavily to port, shuddered, then righted herself. From down below there was a loud crash and I was pleased that I didn't have a vehicle on board. From the smashing sounds from the cafeteria, I wondered if any dishes would be left unbroken. Water washed over the deck and as she rolled to starboard it smashed against the windows. Suddenly a rush of water hit me as it found a crack in the glass, and came squirting through, soaking my going-to-town clothes. A call for the electrician to go down to the train deck made us all wonder what had happened. Car owners all heaved a sigh of relief when they were told no cars were damaged. As the ferry lined up the leading lights in Whekenui before it came in the channel entrance, another couple of seas tossed us around as if we were no more than a cork bobbing on the water. I thought of the many times I'd sat on the heads overlooking these very waters. I knew how rough it could be, and I was grateful I was on a ship the size of the *Arahunga*.

Inside Tory Channel the waters were smooth compared with Cook Strait. I looked across at my home and settled back to enjoy the last of my trip to Picton. A waiting boat picked me up from the ferry terminal and I arrived back in Okukari Bay just on dark.

At that time someone picked up a lifebuoy from Jackson's Bay just inside Tory Channel. It had the name, *Chance*, on it. It was not reported. No one realised the *Chance* was overdue and as the night wore on and the wind howled around the house no one had any idea that somewhere, possibly just outside the channel entrance, the sea had claimed more lives.

The southerly raged all the next day. Our fishing boats remained on their moorings. The following day the *Chance* was reported overdue. All morning I heard Marlborough Marine Radio calling the missing boat but it was not until Picton's Senior Constable Bill Gibb phoned later in the day that we learned the whole story.

That a boat was missing and nothing had been done about it for nearly 48 hours was unbelievable. Two men, in their late 20s and 30s respectively, were aboard. The fact that we were so close to where she most probably went down made it worse.

A search was mounted, and many fish tubs, presumed to be off the missing boat, told a story that we didn't want to hear. A pond board, used to hold fish in place on the deck of a fishing vessel, was picked up on Te Awaiti beach further down Tory Channel. Our boys, Joe and James, searched the coastline from Cape Koamaru to the channel entrance. They found nothing. Joe was busy assisting the police with the search.

And it was on this day that the Queen's Birthday Honours were publicly announced. Joe was awarded the Queen's Service Medal for his work in Search and Rescue.

That evening, when it was too dark to search any longer and the men had come home, friends and family gathered and we celebrated with Joe. But the main topic of conversation was the missing boat. All the hows, wheres, ifs and whens … I felt the sadness all mothers feel for a son lost at sea. I gazed across the table at my two sons, so happy about the honour which had been bestowed on their father, and I realised once again how vulnerable are all those who make a living from the sea. How easily it could be my family who were missing. It brought home to me the main reason Joe is always so willing to go and search in any weather. "If I was in trouble out there I'd like to think someone would rescue me."

Early next morning I walked along the beach in case anything had been washed ashore. As I came across the usual high piles of bull kelp that are always washed ashore after such a storm I felt sick prodding at them with a stick, not knowing what I might find. I was thankful that only fish tubs had been washed up on the sand. When Bill Gibb arrived aboard the *Interisland Rescue* to pick up Joe and begin a shore search, I went with them.

Seas at the channel entrance were still too high for a small boat to attempt to go outside but a helicopter as well as a fixed wing plane were searching the outside coast, as were the local fishing boats in the vicinity. A climb up the hill on the opposite side of the channel was a different experience for Joe, different from his early whaling days when this led to the look-out. Now there was no adrenalin rush with the thought of whales being spotted in the Strait. Instead there was apprehension about what the sea might have thrown up on the coastline overnight. There was nothing.

A walk along a beach usually brings me so much pleasure, but not a walk searching for clues from a missing boat. Now an orange, its skin covered with sand from rolling around in the heavy surf, a half-cabbage wrapped in clingfilm, a cigarette lighter - all took on new meanings. Normally I'd kick them along the sand and think nothing of them. But could these have come off the *Chance*? Perhaps they'd intended to eat cabbage the night they went missing. Plastic containers, rope, a diver's knife ... Flotsam took on a new importance.

At the end of our search there was very little lying in the bottom of the police boat to help the families in their grief. And as the next day dawned and the seas were flat calm I found it hard to come to terms with this sea and the cruel way it keeps its secrets to itself.

For the next few weeks I found myself walking the beach, wanting but not wanting to find something that would help in the puzzle. I hugged the shoreline when I took myself to Picton in the speedboat, in case there was something, but there never was. The families searched with a plane for six more days. The sea remained empty of what they wanted to find.

Two weeks later the families of the missing men came to the channel entrance in a charter-boat. Slack water held our yellow buoys marking our crayfish pots on the surface, and the wreaths thrown by the families drifted amongst them, aimlessly. Once the ebb tide picked up, the flowers would be carried out to sea. It seemed to me, as a mother, that the aimless drifting of the wreaths must have been like the parents' lives since the *Chance* went missing.

Later that same day I took myself along our beach for a walk. My head was full of questions. Although I hadn't known those young men off the *Chance* it still affected me as I thought of my own two sons, also fishing. I needed to be near the sea.

Above the high water mark, sand was still heaped up, a legacy from the storm when the *Chance* went missing, and I plonked myself down. The water in the bay was flat calm, but, as always happens with the first of the flood, a surge was building up. Waves lifted from the smooth sea and dumped themselves on to the sand. With my hands wrapped around my shins and my head resting on my knees I watched as the water trickled a little higher up the beach with each wave. Debris on the beach disappeared as the fingers of the flood tide reached into all the nooks and crannies. I sat there a long time. Familiar faces lost at sea shimmered through the ripples.

The sea now covered the sand and I stood up stiffly. Gone were the driftwood, seaweed and debris. To me it was like a rebirth. As I stood drinking in the lonely beauty of the place, the understanding I'd been searching for came to me. Life was like the sea. People speak of life ebbing away, and the ebb tide did take away the wreaths. But it is the flood tide's strength and power that brings a renewal of life. The realisation made me punch my hands in the air and run along the top of the beach, skipping away from the waves as they washed over the dry sand. Again the sea had lightened my heavy heart.

Meanwhile promotion for *Weather Permitting* went on. I simply hadn't expected anything like this. A growing confidence was letting me begin to enjoy public speaking. The nerves were still there but they seemed to affect me in numerous ways. I discovered my hands sweated.

The Friends of the Nelson Library had invited me to speak during Nelson's National Library Week. More than 80 people came and questions flowed. Then an elderly man asked me if I would hold out my left palm. I thought he was going to read my fortune.

My palm was bright blue. In shock I looked at my other hand. It matched. Loud laughter erupted from the group. It seemed many had noticed my blue hands while I was speaking. I was baffled. Then someone noticed the blue cloth over the lectern, and one very apologetic woman realised it should have been washed before they'd used it.

Book signings are another ordeal and I doubt if I'll ever feel confident at these. I hate sitting in a store waiting for customers. Some drift past, pick up a book, flick through the pages, look at me as if I am a being from another planet, and stride off without saying one word. Then the men. "I'm buying this for the wife, you know." I get the impression that they are embarrassed to be seen buying a book with a picture of a woman on the cover. Many have picked up the book, studied the cover and said in surprise, "Is this you? It's a lovely photo." This has me struggling for an answer when I'm feeling quite posh in my best clothes, with hair tidy, and make-up. But the positives - who have come into the store especially to buy a book as they have known I was in town, or to get me to sign their already purchased book - far outweigh the negatives.

And funny things happen. An elegant woman came up and asked me to sign a book she'd purchased some time ago for her daughter. It was still in the store's wrapping paper. I don't know who got the biggest surprise when I unwrapped it. It was John Grisham's *The Rainmaker*.

People turned to see what we were laughing at. She told me she'd bought two books at different times, one for her son and my book for her daughter. She'd taken the wrong book out of her drawer. "If you write another book you can put this in it."

A special luncheon in Masterton had both Chris and me on the early morning ferry. By now I was becoming cunning and I took a duvet and pillow aboard with me. We were in Wellington at 8.30am, picked up by car and driven to the Wairarapa where we visited Catriona McEwan, Neil Bennett and their charming baby, Jamie.

On to Masterton where we swept up a drive lined with tall trees, their gnarled branches stark against the blue sky, and came to a stop at the main entrance of St Matthew's Collegiate. The scene could have been England in the 19th century.

Watery sunshine mellowed the red bricks and reflected off the white-trimmed windows. Ivy clung to the walls and as I walked towards the building autumn leaves caught in the breeze swirled in the air. I came back to the 20th century when a group of girls dressed in uniform poured across the lawn

This luncheon was organised by the Ladies' Auxiliary of the Wairarapa Cancer Society. The school donates the use of its diningroom and kitchen facilities, all food is prepared by members of the Auxiliary, and Hedleys, Masterton's bookshop, provides wine and supplies the books to be sold. Today 120 people had paid for the luncheon and all the money raised would go to the local branch of the Cancer Society.

Our time in Masterton was soon over and we caught the railcar to Wellington and the 5.30pm *Arahura*. I was exhausted but as we reflected on our day I began to feel much better. It seemed to us that this cooperation by different groups is a great idea.

Presumably there's a big range of speakers, and local people get to hear about other ways of life while doing something worthwhile. I had met many more good people and I was thrilled to have had the chance to speak and help raise funds for the Cancer Society. Most of the women I had spoken to had been involved in one way or another with the disease. Far too many had seen loved ones die with it. No, the tiredness I was feeling was nothing compared with the tiredness many of those people would have experienced. It reminded me of something else my father used to say. "There but for the grace of God go I."

My memory slid back seven years to the times when I'd thought those words so often. My friend Bev had cancer. Over the past five years she had battled breast cancer and we all believed she had beaten it. Then visual disturbances and headaches sent Bev to the doctor. A brain tumour was diagnosed. There was also a shadow on her lung.

I went through a period of denial. Bev can't die. She is a year younger than I am. That isn't the order of life. She doesn't smoke, and drinks very little. I kept asking myself, how or why Bev?

As I saw her gradually deteriorate I accepted there was no order in life. Death wasn't only for the elderly. It took young people too. It was only in the last week of her life that Bev appeared to accept defeat.

She and I had met in January 1959 when we began working for Berlei NZ Ltd in Auckland. From the first day we had worked together, and our friendship grew. She spent many holidays with my parents and me on our yacht, and we were always mapping out our lives and loves as we lay on the deck watching the stars through the rigging. Dying was never thought of. That was something our grandparents did. There were far more important things happening around us. The Auckland Harbour bridge, opened in 1959, was already said to be not big enough. We had a geothermal power station at Wairakei, only the second in the world, and now natural gas from the Kapuni oilfield. Our world was changing and we were going to be there with it. Then I met Joe, and Bev travelled to Motueka to work in the orchards and it was there she met her future husband, Bill.

Although not far as the crow flies, the distance kept us apart but we kept in touch with letters. Bill worked for Charlie, my father-in-law, for a while and it was a special time in my life having Bev in the bay. A new baby on the way made them decide to move back to Motueka.

A burning behind my eyes had me shutting them to try to stop the tears my memory was evoking. I saw Bev, so thin and ill, standing in the bathroom, toothpaste spread along a comb and asking me what she'd done wrong. I heard the laughter as I took the comb from her hand and showed her the toothbrush. Bev's loud voice of disgust telling the woman from the hospital that she didn't need a wheelchair, and, towards the end, how Maureen Stewart, my special Picton friend, and I shared our time with Bev to allow Bill to go to work, while their son Scott could concentrate on his first year of an apprenticeship, and their daughter Marissa on her school certificate year.

The last time I saw Bev, six days before she died, she gave me some verse and asked me to read it aloud at her funeral. Her eyes brimmed with tears and without a word being spoken we both knew her time was near.

So close to death - yet she could still laugh at herself. I was giving Bev a bed bath and she told me at least there was only one breast to dry under, and then in the next breath she told me life was a bugger. I felt clumsy and hated seeing her wince as I tried to move her in the bed. She grimaced with pain as she said, "Bet you never thought you'd be doing this all those years ago." It was at these times my father's words ran through my mind.

A floor to ceiling window the width of Bev's lounge overlooked the Mt Arthur Ranges. The hospital bed they'd brought in for Bev faced this window so she could look out at Mt Arthur framed in the centre of the picture window. She called it her mountain. I was pleased when Maureen, who was with Bev when she died, told me it was a beautiful fine day. I was glad to think that as Bev closed her eyes for the last time she would have seen her mountain standing out clearly in the morning sunlight.

Bill asked me to play the organ for Bev's funeral. "Please - no." I felt that was asking too much.

I knew Joe was disappointed in me but my pain was too raw. I hurt with a pain that made me feel sick. Joe finally talked me into playing and one hour before her funeral I was at the church running through the music and getting the feel of the instrument.

The hymn, 'What a friend we have in Jesus,' was easy to get through but when it was time to play the song, 'The place where I worship is the wide open spaces', I struggled. It was so much Bev. The words, 'Mountains are altars of God', broke me up. I doubt if anyone noticed. Everyone felt the same.

There was one last thing I had to do for Bev. Read out the verse as she had asked me to. My first reaction when I read it over again after Bev had died was that I wouldn't tell anyone about it, but deep down I knew I couldn't do that and live with myself. With the minister standing next to me in case I couldn't go on, I read out Bev's message.

> I have not died
> I have just lain down from life's journey
> My loves are now your loves
> My dreams are your dreams
> I will not look back to see
> If you are following me
> Instead I want you to look forward
> To where I will be waiting for you
> Cherish my love and friendship
> In your hearts.

CHAPTER EIGHT

The Creatures of Okukari

WHEN I arrived back in the bay after Bev's funeral, I'd found it hard to feel any love or friendship for Quita, my little dog. That's when I'd discovered that, between her and Nuffy, Lisa's black and white cat, they'd killed eight chooks, the first I'd ever had. The remaining three were perched in the chookhouse preening their very wet and ruffled feathers. Occasionally I'd noticed the dog and cat stalking the free-ranging chooks though I'd never dreamt the pair would run them to ground. But it was hard to put all the blame on Quita as I'm sure she thought the brown hens were wekas.

There were no wekas on Arapawa Island until a group of Victoria University students removed them from an island in the Queen Charlotte Sounds, to protect the native kauri snail, and liberated them on Arapawa. No one heeded the fact that Arapawa Island is also the home of the native snail. Now wekas run all over our island. They tear off the young leaves from our vegetables and scratch up freshly grown plants. When Quita started chasing wekas from the garden I praised her, never thinking she'd chase my chooks as well.

Whenever I've been away for a day or more, Quita is always down at the wharf to meet me, and when I arrive up at the house on the motorbike my cats greet me at the gate.

Tiger is a handsome grey tabby. When his 19-year-old body is showing his age, a steroid injection gives him a new burst of life. Recently he disappeared for a week and I spent hours searching for a body, crawling through the shrubs, scared about what I might stumble on. Just when I was accepting the fact that he must be dead, there was a bang against the lounge window. I looked up and there was Tiger, sitting on the windowsill. He had leapt eight feet. It was as if he'd been raised from the dead and I wondered if I should rename him Lazarus.

Marmaduke is a 17-year-old overweight ginger tabby with a distinctive bend in his tail. With Tiger in the house I didn't need another cat. Helen and Pauline had other ideas. Helen had brought home a stray cat she'd found in Blenheim. Before it died it had four kittens - Marmaduke was one. I put my foot down when I was told we had to keep these four kittens. I insisted homes had to be found for them - and it wasn't going to be Okukari. I closed my ears to the crying and pleading. "But Mum, these are the most beautiful kittens," didn't change my mind.

It was Christmas morning and a big brown carton was smuggled inside and placed under the Christmas tree. Amidst lots of giggling I was told it was my special present. I loved the special presents I'd been given over the years. They were always something the children had made - a clay dish in the shape of a sunflower and painted yellow, a pegbag from a cloth flourbag, and I'd even been given a treasured green bottle still filled with dirt but sparking clean on the outside. The unwrapping of presents had begun when I heard strange noises coming from inside the box and it started to move. My special present was four kittens. Helen and Pauline had decided if they made me a present of them I'd have to keep them.

We found homes for three, and Marmaduke stayed at Okukari. Two years ago he developed diabetes and now I have to inject him twice daily with insulin, before each meal. Visitors are amazed when they see me drawing up his two types of insulin, but his doses of .07mls of both Actrapid and Monotard have changed him from an ungroomed and dull-coated obese cat spending all his time sitting at the fridge door, or gulping copious amounts of water, to a much slimmer cat with a healthy coat. I was horrified when I was told he must either have injections or be put down, but he doesn't mind the injections as he knows that straight after his shots he gets fed.

George was a Picton cat no one wanted. I heard about this lovely white cat with the most glorious blue eyes, and when I met him it was love at first sight - even though he's deaf and has a dry eye which needs drops daily.

After all, I have a daughter who is a vet.

Three cats should keep the mice down but mine are either too well fed or too old and every year when it starts to get cold we are invaded by mice. They come in the back door and we've even seen them running up the rough Summerhill stone walls of our house, and through any open windows. When Joe and I arrived home from my South Island author-tour we had plagues of mice in our ceiling. In desperation I bought some rat poison in the shape of eggs, pushed open the manhole with the head of a broom, stood back, and threw three eggs up through the hole. Then I remembered that the header tank for the hot water cylinder wasn't far away from the manhole. I had this awful feeling that Joe might have left the lid off when he'd been cleaning it out before we'd recently replaced our hot water cylinder.

Pauline was at home for the weekend and when I mentioned to her that I might have thrown rat poison in our water tank she offered to climb up and see if she could find the three eggs. With a "Mum, Mum," and a sigh of exasperation, her legs disappeared through the manhole. She found two, and the lid was indeed off the tank. When Pauline clambered back down and told me that she'd tried to feel if it was in the tank but it was too deep, I was frantic. I could imagine Joe's comments when he arrived up at the house for morning tea. I'd turn the water off, drain the hot water cylinder, and scrub out the header tank, I thought. I tried not to think of the cost of heating the water.

"It mightn't be in the water, anyway."

"I reckon you'd have heard it plop. You're probably worrying about nothing." But when Pauline went on to tell me we'd know if it was in the water if we started to get nosebleeds and our hair fell out, I felt more worried than ever.

I heard the motorbike stopping at the gate and I imagined Joe's scathing comments, and then I realised that if he hadn't left the top off in the first place this wouldn't have happened. Before he reached the back door he got an ear full. It was all his fault. While I went and bailed some water out of the nearby creek to made a cup of tea, Joe swung himself through the manhole. His loud yells that he'd found the third egg, and it wasn't in the water, made me breathe again. We wouldn't die of arsenic poisoning after all.

I can't remember a time when we haven't had a pet of some description. Mandy, our first house dog - as distinct from the farm dogs - was part fox terrier and part 'something else'. The fox terrier gave her a white body and brown and black markings but the 'something else' gave her short legs, floppy ears, a square nose and quite a long body. I hadn't thought about having a small dog until one day when we were in Picton and four young children arrived back at the boat, complete with dog, basket, and a crocheted blanket. I was taken to meet the ex-owners who assured me they were pleased to give Mandy to my children. As I said an embarrassed goodbye to the elderly couple, I wondered what sort of sob story my children had put across.

Mandy loved the life on the island. She tore around, always joining in the children's games, but her favourite sport was to be her downfall. Whenever it was time to muster the cattle, a yapping ball of energy would charge in around the hooves, nipping at their hocks. It was a game and nothing would stop her. An irate cow turned on her, and chased her along the front of the woolshed and down to the beach. There was nowhere for her to hide and as she raced past the upturned dinghy she tried to squeeze underneath. The cow's horns pushed her the last little way. Screaming kids raced down and lifted up the dinghy to find a muddy splodge with two bright eyes and quivering whiskers. She whimpered when she was picked up but after a warm bath she seemed fine and charged around the lounge playing with four relieved children.

It wasn't until we were out mustering again a few weeks later that we noticed something was amiss with Mandy. She'd be running and then suddenly stiffen and fall over. This happened two or three times but once we arrived home she was fine. The following winter she developed arthritis in her spine and she fell over more often. A visit to a vet and an X-ray told us that she'd damaged her spine when she'd tried to escape from the cow.

One night she didn't arrive home for her tea. It was dark and I could only reassure my miserable children that she'd probably be home later when she got really hungry. The next day four anxious faces sat at the breakfast table and as soon as they'd eaten they took off to look for their little dog. Their crying confirmed my fears. She must have gone stiff and fallen in a puddle and drowned. They brought her home and I wiped their tear-stained faces and my own while they all had turns at cuddling Mandy for the last time.

We put school lessons aside and wrapped her in her special blanket before placing her carefully in her grave. The children had selected this place, behind our house, where they would be close to her and where she could see down the channel. Their grief hurt me but I sat apart from them and watched as they covered her with soil and patted it down firmly but gently. They picked flowers and arranged them over the brown mound. At last they were happy with their handiwork and although they were still sad I felt they would accept her death much better because they had done those final things for Mandy.

But our house needed another dog. People thought that because we lived on a farm we should have a big dog. But with five or six farm dogs on the place, I had no ambition to own another large dog. It had to be a small one.

Cedric Stewart found the right one for us. He'd seen its brother and thought it was just what we were looking for.

Midget arrived in a shoebox. She was golden-brown, and a cross between a short-haired chihuahua and a Japanese poodle. At first she

The original homestead. (Photo supplied by the Kenny family)

Midget, my little dog, adopted these guinea pigs.

James with two 40-kilogram groper

The tractor pulls the holding tank ashore where the crays are transferred into the big plastic bins before being taken along the wharf to the fishing boat.

Seawater is circulated through the bins during the trip into Picton where they are packed in smaller blue and white bins with the wood wool stacked against the side of the wheelhouse.

The cattle truck drives off the barge to collect our cattle from the yards.

Doing running repairs on our television aerial.
(Photo Ian Garrod)

Scruff hitches a ride on my four-wheeled ATV. (Photo, Ian Garrod)

Te Awa, 1 February 1997. Being prepared for her launching in Bluff Harbour.

With the words, "I name this boat Te Awa. May God bless her and all who sail on her," Helen smashes a bottle of champagne.

was so tiny I was terrified that the cats might eat her, thinking she was a mouse, or she might be walked on, or jammed in the kitchen door when it slammed shut in the wind. In spite of my worries nothing happened to her and she survived another 15 years. She eased the pain of Mandy's death but Mandy was never forgotten and her grave was always kept clean and free of dead flowers.

Midget never knew if she was a dog which should have been a cat, or a cat which should have been a dog. The dog in her loved to go out with James and Helen chasing goats. I'd watch them disappear over the top of the hill with a brown dot bobbing behind. It was probably just as well I didn't know what went on once they were out of my sight. I have since been told how Midget would run the goats down in a creekbed and then James would cut their throats. Only once, as he was threading the knife pouch on to his belt, was I told anything more. I had given him words of warning about not taking the knife out of its pouch and running with it, when back came the reply that kept me from asking any more questions.

"I don't take the knife out until we've caught the goat. Then I sit on the goat and sharpen my knife before I kill it."

I couldn't believe this was my James speaking. I pressed my fingers to my temples in horror and tried to shut out the bloodthirsty scene. Helen, trying to appease me and no doubt seeing their hunting days as coming to an end, quickly reminded me that, "There's hundreds out there and they eat grass that a sheep could be eating."

The cat part of Midget loved stretching out in front of the fire or cuddling up in a bed. She'd sneak right to the bottom and hide. She was so small there was no tell-tale lump in the bed. Another favourite game was to go along the rocks at the end of our beach with the children. As they waded through the rock pools and overturned the rocks I'd hear her frenzied barks as she played with the crabs that scuttled away. She'd bite at them and give them a good shake before tossing them in the air. A yelp would tell me one had latched on to her nose.

Night brought a new game. The children caught the moths which fluttered around the lights and put them in a preserving jar with a lid on. Midget would roll it around the floor, trying to bite at the moths through the jar. The words, "Motha motha," had her forgetting the jar and she'd be leaping three or four feet in the air, trying to catch another flying moth.

We never mated Midget. Until we had her spayed we kept a close watch on her when she came into season, as we didn't want her mating with a large farm dog.

At this time Helen and Pauline had guinea pigs. I was told they were two females but before long we had more than 20. Every afternoon when school was finished, the girls would let them out of their cage and play with them. If the lawns had just been mown they'd make tracks and tunnels from the cut grass. The guinea pigs loved it. Midget also joined in the games.

The guinea pig population had increased again. It happened to be six weeks after Midget had been in season, and, if she'd been mated, it would have been time for her puppies to be born. She started lactating.

At first we didn't understand what was wrong with her, as she'd tear through the house, jump up on any bed and look out the windows to where the guinea pigs lived. Once outside, she'd be up at the cage, whining and trying to get inside the netting. No amount of growling or smacking would keep her away. Unable to stand her behaviour any longer, the two girls let her in with the guinea pigs, whereupon one very contented chihuahua soon had three baby guinea pigs tucked in close. We watched in amazement as one crawled away, and, as if she'd done it all her life, Midget reached out, picked it up in her mouth and soon had it snuggled in and suckling from her once more.

Then our problems started. Midget whined when the girls took her out, and nothing would make her leave the cage. She lay on the top of it, watching. When the girls carried her inside and shut the door she barked and howled until we opened the door and she could run outside and back to her babies. As the guinea pigs grew and the girls let them outside to play on the lawn, Midget would take her babies away from the others, tuck them underneath her and let them feed as long as they wanted.

This episode was her only experience of motherhood.

Midget shared our lives for 15 years and her death was like a death in the family. She hadn't been well for some time and she'd been treated for failing kidneys. An injection would improve her for a short time and I told myself that when her quality of life was gone I'd have her put down. Brave words when she seemed all right, but cruel words when I knew her time was up.

Midget had deteriorated over the weekend and I knew it was the end for her. I'd carried her in and out to her toilet all weekend and early on the Monday morning she lay whimpering in her basket. Joe and the boys had left to go fishing and I was taking Lisa to Picton so she could drive to Nelson. Pauline was studying at Massey. In fact we were alone in the bay. We both burst into tears as I filled Midget's hot water bottle for the last time and tried to make her comfortable.

The trip down the Sounds held no joy for either of us. It was taking Midget nearer to the end of her life. In Picton Lisa left for Nelson and I waited with a friend until I could ring the vet and make an appointment.

The smell of the surgery, the hot sun shining through the window on my back, and my wee dog whimpering in my arms, made me vow that I'd never have another pet dog as long as I lived. I held her as a line was put in her front leg and I watched as the drug passed through before it put her to sleep. I was told that as she was so near death it took very little of the drug, and I was grateful that I never once felt her body wince, or react to pain. It was truly a merciful death.

The words of the vet followed me out the door and all the way back to Okukari.

"You will get another dog. People like you always do." But I knew better. I carried her up from the wharf and more tears washed down my face because she wasn't there to meet me. It started to rain and I brought her body inside as I couldn't bear the thought of her getting wet.

When Joe arrived in from fishing we buried her in the garden, and a pohutukawa tree was grown over her. It has flourished over the years, and every summer, when the red flowers shine through the dark green leaves, I remember our Midget.

Two months later Pauline was back from Massey for her summer holidays and we read in the paper that a litter of long-haired chihuahuas was for sale. We phoned but were told there was only one left, the runt of the litter. She was held for us, and, on the next trip to Picton, Pauline and I went to view the puppy. Chiquita, or as we call her, Quita, stole our hearts and we brought her to Okukari. Our house came alive once more.

As well as these animals there have been many other different pets over the years. A baby pukeko lying in a paddock was carried home nestled in two grubby cupped hands. A constantly open beak and raucous shrieks had me feeding him tinned babyfood that I kept in the cupboard in case someone arrived unexpectedly with a baby. In vain I tried to see, in the wee scrap I held in my hands, the future handsome adult, indigo-blue and black with white tail, red beak and legs.

He was named Starshine and he lived in a box in the hot water cupboard between feeds until some over-affectionate children picked him up squeezed him to death. They dug another grave, and Starshine was buried, with full honours, next to Mandy.

Pop, Squeak, Whistle, Bang, Prince and Princess were ducklings. My children were adamant that the ducklings had no mother. When I ordered them to take the ducklings to the paddock and to let them go I was told that the mother wouldn't want them now they'd been handled. My round plastic basin disappeared. The next time I spotted this basin there were six ducklings swimming around in it. I told Helen and Pauline these ducklings were their responsibility. I wanted nothing to do with them. Five of the ducklings survived and grew into adult grey ducks.

Often we'd see the two girls running along the beach with the five ducks waddling after them. I'd laugh at the looks on the faces of passengers aboard the mailboat when they spied five ducks following me along the wharf. I worried that the ducks, soon to be fully grown, had made no attempt to fly.

"It's because no one has shown them," Pauline told me. During the next southerly gale, when the wind was blowing in the bay, I was staggered to see a duck being carried high in the air by the wind although it didn't seem to be flying. Then I noticed Pauline and Helen standing on the edge of the bank, facing into the wind, and throwing the ducks aloft. They'd be blown a short distance, before crashing to the ground. I don't know if it was fright or natural instinct that made them fly, but shortly after that they flew away. I breathed a sigh of relief because the ducks were making a mess on the paths and I was forever washing down the concrete around the house.

The next year an adult grey duck arrived at our front gate. Helen and Pauline were positive it was Bang. Then he took off and as he soared into the sky I recalled words I'd read long ago, about how, if you love something, let it go. I knew he wouldn't be back as I remembered the last line: if it flies away, it wasn't yours to keep. There was no sadness, this time. Helen and Pauline were both aware that these pets had only ever been on loan.

For many years there was one particular grey duck that, when it arrived in the bay with all the other ducks, seemed to take an interest in

Helen and Pauline. It would swim up to them with its mate and later its ducklings. Although I couldn't tell if it was Bang, the girls were convinced.

Throughout the years there have been the pet pigs. These were wild ones Joe has brought home when out hunting, the descendants of the pigs Captain Cook brought to the island in the 1700s. As well as Isabelle, the pig who refused to eat my steamed pudding, and Charlie Brown, who wallowed in Ruby's garden and loved to come inside and make his bed from the lounge cushions, we've had several other pigs. Each one of them has been irresistible as I've held their trembling bodies in my hands and they've looked at me through their long curling lashes. When they've reached full size I've wished I'd said no to another pet pig.

A young boy who was working for us couldn't pass this one particular pet pig without the pig tearing out and taking a sideways munch at his leg. He'd kick out and the pig would bite the other leg. The pig would froth at the mouth at the sight of me carrying his bucket of food. I reached the stage where I was too scared to get in the pen with this pig. He was a big pig. The eyes that I'd fallen in love with when he was young now were mean, as he eyed up those who went near him. I told Joe that he would have to go before he got one of the children down.

Not long after I'd made this statement I was outside when I heard my mother-in-law's shrieking. The sound was coming from her house. I could tell she was terrified and ran to help. Her mop, minus its handle, lay near the back door. I could hear hysterical screams coming from the kitchen and I imagined all sorts of things. When I arrived at the door I was met by an enraged pig which skidded on the polished floor and knocked me off my feet as he shot past me.

"He met me in the kitchen," panted Ruby. "I shooed him with the mop but he ripped it out of my hands. Shook it to bits."

We tried to calm each other but with our men out fishing we knew we'd have to try and entice the pig back into his pen somehow. A bucket of scraps seemed the best answer. I began the trip to his pen, trying to be brave and speaking kindly to the menacing hulk that stood outside, his head pulled right back into his shoulders, glaring at me with those piggy eyes. One piece of bread didn't work. He gobbled that up on the run and came at the bucket, hitting at it with his nose, trying to reach the food inside. I tipped a heap on the lawn and took off.

This time I managed to open the front gate before he caught up with me. I calculated I'd have to give him what was left in the bucket and I hoped that I'd have time to reach his pen. To the sounds of his chomping I raced down to his pen and got the gate open just in time. He still had his eye on the bucket. I heaved it into his pen and as he chased the bucket inside I slammed the gate.

That was the last time I saw the animal. With my mother-in-law to back me up, he was removed from Okukari and was one pig no one was sorry to see the end of.

Oscar was a dachshund. He belonged to Charlie and he was a one-man dog. Like Quita, he too had a penchant for chooks. The problem was, they weren't our chooks. They belonged to our neighbours on the island, Nan and Gilbert Perano. Joe's parents were away when Gilbert phoned to say he'd caught Oscar chasing their chooks and that the dog had killed two. "I'll bring him up to the boundary gate if you or Joe like to come and meet him," he added.

An apologetic Joe met up with Gilbert and took Oscar's lead. Once over on our side of the hill, Joe let go of the lead and chased the dog all the way home, yelling and pulling faces at him. A hate formed between Oscar and Joe, as strong as the hate between me and the pig.

Charlie and Joe were both fishing at that time and Oscar always went out on the boat with Charlie. Oscar hated Joe to such an extent that he'd bark and snarl whenever Joe's boat came in sight. Charlie often told us how he wouldn't see Joe in the distance until Oscar ran up the bow and stood with his front paws on the bulwarks and barked.

If Oscar could, he'd race in and nip at Joe's ankles at every opportunity. One evening Joe had to fetch some papers off his father's boat. When he jumped aboard he woke up Oscar, who must have sneaked aboard as the boat lay alongside the wharf. The dog panicked when he realised it was Joe and messed in the wheelhouse. Joe arrived back up at our house in fits of laughter and told me the story. I couldn't believe that Joe had left the dog there and didn't even clean up the mess, or tell his father.

The next day Charlie told us about his dirty, stinking dog and what he'd done.

"Can't make it out," he said. "He's never done that before."

It was many years before Joe confessed to being the cause of Oscar's behaviour. The relationship between Joe and Oscar steadily grew worse. In Oscar's last days, when he could barely lift his head, Joe would bend down to pat him and the dog would still manage a growl. Dogs do remember.

Helen and Pauline had a flock of pet sheep. Any lambs they'd raised joined their flock as well as the occasional black lamb. Over the years the numbers increased. Every year, when all the other lambs went to the sale, the girls would hide their pet lambs until the barge was leaving the bay. They all grew up to be a menace on the farm. We always had a fight to get them through the race or into the dip as they never believed they were sheep. They'd hang back and each one would have to be personally pushed to where it had to go. But when they wanted to eat some of my garden they'd find their way through shut gates and solid fences.

Helen and Pauline spent hours playing with their sheep. Their play taught me that sheep aren't dumb, and, like most animals, they can be taught almost anything. All that is needed is patience.

They had names like Billy, Frisky, Marge, Lamb Chops, Whisky and Soda (twins), Rhian, Fonz, and of course Lucky, who thought he was a Heberley.

The girls would muster their pets in, and line them up to clean their teeth - it took me a long time to work out why the toothpaste never lasted long - and measure around their middles. The wool would be examined and notes written down. I'd be invited to see new tricks and over the years I've seen adult sheep grin as their bellies have been scratched, jump over hurdles on command, roll over on their backs and kick their legs in the air, and paw at the ground as "please" for a biscuit. Some days the sheep would be dressed up and they'd be married. I was invited to Sammy's and Rosie's wedding. The girls had cleaned Rosie's teeth, brushed out her wool and cut the brushed-out wool around her face into a bob. They also put flowers in her wool. The wedding breakfast was lollies, biscuits and freshly picked grass.

All the pets had to pass tests, and they'd receive badges. There was the cliff-climbing badge and the swimming badge. I'd see a flock of sheep running along the beach, Helen and Pauline leading the way. To obtain their cliff-climbing badge the sheep had to climb the steep bank at the end of our beach. They all managed to swim enough to obtain their swimming badge.

Looking back over the years, I believe the rapport that all four children have with animals developed because there were no other children close by to play with. The animals responded to the love they were given, and gave their trust.

Tucked away on a shelf in a wardrobe I found a book that the two girls had begun in 1977.

> *Lucky*
>
> *Is very fat has a lovely fleece and is a nice romney.*
>
> *Littleone*
>
> *Had a very sore tummy when he was small. He has picked up now and I think he had an excellent face and fleece.*
>
> *Blackboy*
>
> *Has a nice black fleece. Needs marking. He is a nice wild breed. Runs very good, needs drenching. Is getting horns and I feel he will be dangerous.*
>
> *Sammy*
>
> *Sammy is very sweet and loves grandma's clover. I am getting him a dog collar so I can tie him up.*
>
> *Lamb Chops*
>
> *Lamb Chops is fat. He is bigger than the rams. His main fat places are on his head and backside. His nose is 15 inches long, his tum is 57 inches round. He is getting old and he is white.*

Tears came to my eyes when I read two lines entered under the month of April: *Pets got worried. Lucky died. It was very sad. Not much news.*

I've forgiven Quita for killing the chooks. The remaining three were given away so they could survive. Our new chooks have settled in their new house very well. Quita has left them alone and so far I've been their only intruder when I was locked in their house for three hours. Now our family has left home, Quita is my only companion in the house when Joe is away fishing. She has grown very possessive and won't let anyone touch me while she is sitting on my lap. It has become a game for Joe to put his hand on my arm or leg and say "I'm touching Mum." Quita then flies at him, teeth bared, and, for such a small dog, gives a ferocious bark.

Writing, I have discovered, is extremely lonely. There are times when, frustrated at not finding the right words, or finding no words at all, I've felt like tearing my hair out. My little dog lies at my feet and when I speak her fluffy tail thumps on the floor in support.

The motorbike is her favourite mode of travelling. She races around it whenever I climb on, waiting to be picked up. Then at times I'll make her run. I'll start the bike, rev it up and with a "Ready steady go," she takes off. I love to let her run in front of the bike and I'll laugh out loud as I watch her streaking out like a hare, stretching out both her front and back legs simultaneously. At the shed I'll jump off the bike and while still caught up in our game, I'll run and try to beat her inside. If one of my granddaughters see me, I'm told off for speeding.

That's when I try to put my age in perspective. I don't feel 55 and, I ask myself, how is one supposed to act when they are in their mid-fifties? I think back to my mother who was 55 when her grandson, Young Joe, was born. I always thought I had a young-looking mother in comparison with my friends' mothers, but I doubt that she'd do some of the things that I do. She would definitely not 'hoon' on a motorbike as I'm told I do. I don't think she would have tried skiing for the first time on her 54th birthday.

A trip up to Rainbow skifield with our friends Marcia and Roy Rowe was my birthday present. It was to be a whole day's skiing. We drove up to St Arnaud, the village at the northern end of Lake Rotoiti in the Nelson Lakes district, in the afternoon and stayed in the lodge so we could be on the skifield as soon as it opened next morning. To ensure an early start we'd paid our account the night before, and instead of waiting for breakfast we decided we'd eat the breadstick spread with smoked salmon and cream cheese which we'd brought with us. The only problem was, when I took it out of the fridge everything was frozen.

We had been told there would be someone at the chain hut just after 7.30am. There we'd be fitted with chains before driving any further up the mountain. On the 30-minute drive to the hut I put our frozen food over the heater vents on the dashboard. Nobody was at the hut so Joe pulled off the road to wait. We peered in the windows and saw chains of different sizes hanging up so knew we were in the right place. "Must have slept in," Roy decided.

"Could've had breakfast." My Joe always thinks of his stomach. But it didn't alter the fact that we had to sit right where we were until our vehicle was fitted with chains.

As four-wheel-drive cars whizzed past us and other cars stopped to put on their own chains, we waited. Our salmon, cream cheese and bread had thawed. In the crisp mountain air, surrounded with beech trees and the tantalising glimpses of the snow-covered peaks, we ate our epicurean breakfast.

Finally the waiting got too much and when the next car pulled over to fit chains Joe asked them what the story was with hiring chains. "You have to go to the next hut, mate. Just five minutes up the road."

The streams, filled with ice and tumbling over boulders, and the clarity of the mountains against the sky brought back the words of the song that had been sung at my friend Bev's funeral: 'Mountains are altars of God.' At the carpark I stood and gazed at the circle of altars. I understood why primitive man worshipped things of beauty.

At first I was scared that I might hurt my knee which had been operated on for a torn cartilage but once I'd fallen over and found it was still OK, I didn't worry. At least I didn't until our instructor told us to meet at a place which was on a rise, and then we were told to ski down the slope and stand in line to use the ski tow. "I won't be able to stop," I warned our instructor.

"Do as I've shown you. Ski-plough."

It's so easy for you, I thought, as I tried to remember how to turn the front ends of my skis in. I ran right into the middle of the group and more than 20 people landed on top of me.

Next winter I'm going back. I'll practise my ski-ploughing and maybe graduate to the intermediate slope.

And thinking of my mother and remembering her fear of the sea, I know she would never have gone fishing, or out on any searches and rescues in Cook Strait.

So now I tell my family that although my face may be towards the sunset and I may be on the downhill trail, I don't feel 55, and I'll act as old as I feel. Perhaps one day when I'm an old, old lady I'll give up races with my little dog. I might settle for a seat in a rockingchair by the fire, my slippered feet poking out from beneath a crocheted woollen blanket, and a quiet purring cat sitting on my lap. But not yet.

CHAPTER NINE

Living and Dying

I WAS really looking forward to the 1996 annual conference of the Royal New Zealand Coastguard Federation. It was being hosted in Picton by the Marlborough Volunteer Coastguard. In September 1995 the Sounds Emergency Services was wound up and its assets gifted to the Marlborough Volunteer Coastguard. Joe became a committee member.

In the months leading up to the conference I'd heard snippets of what was planned. I was especially looking forward to hearing Commander Larry Robbins, commanding officer of the *Monowai,* speaking about the rescue of the yachts in the Pacific during the storm at Queen's Birthday Weekend in 1994. I'd never been to a coastguard conference before and I hoped to meet other wives and partners, and listen to their feelings when their men are involved in rescues. Like fishermen's wives, they had to be anxious. Best of all, on the three nights we were staying in Picton we were dining out. I wouldn't have to peel one potato or wash one dish.

Three nights before the conference, Joe went into Picton for a coastguard meeting to run through the programme and check that everything was in place. As well as hosting the conference Marlborough was launching its new rescue craft, *Tranz Rail Rescue*, which had been donated by the rail company. She had been built by Naiad Inflatables (NZ) Ltd, Picton, and had been on loan to TVNZ during the America's Cup campaign in San Diego. It was from this craft that Peter Montgomery with his commentaries had made yachting come alive for New Zealanders. Peter was to be the guest speaker at the wind-up dinner on the Saturday evening.

I was pleased when Joe rang me before leaving Picton and said he'd be home by 10.30pm, and 40 minutes later when I heard the speedboat coming into the bay and slowing down I could relax. I knew the minute Joe walked into the bedroom there was something wrong. He had a sheepish look on his face, and he stretched out on the bed, obviously prepared to talk.

"What's wrong?" I asked.

"Nothing. Well, nothing really wrong." His words, "I've got to tell you something," had me sitting up in bed.

His next words pushed all my enjoyment of the conference out the window. "They want you to be a guest speaker." I sat up and turned on my bedside light to see if Joe was joking or not and when I saw his face I knew that this was for real.

"Who does? Why me?"

"All the members there tonight agreed your book's been so popular and you've written about lots of search and rescues. Everyone thought you'd be a good choice." His, "You'll be fine, love," made me remember a conversation we'd had when the conference was in its infancy and I'd spoken those same words to Joe. "Hang on a minute. I thought *you* were going to be speaking. You've damn well passed the buck, haven't you?"

I didn't know what to believe in spite of his loud protestations and assurances and I spent the night thinking what I could talk about that would hold the interest of 200 or more delegates from throughout New Zealand. At least, I thought, he didn't want a divorce. This had actually gone through my mind because of the funny way he'd said he had to tell me something.

The next morning I spoke to my publisher on the phone and when I told her I was to speak and that I'd been told I was to sign plenty of books she said Cape Catley would donate the proceeds from those book sales to the Marlborough Coastguard.

Doug Kidd opened the conference. It was the 20th anniversary of the Coastguard and he read out a letter from Sir Michael Hardie Boys on behalf of HRH the Prince of Wales who is the patron of the New Zealand Volunteer Coastguard, and another from Prime Minister Jim Bolger.

Business followed and then it was time for Commander Larry Robbins to speak about that 1994 Pacific storm and the rescue. When I saw the man dressed in his naval uniform and heard his very correct English voice I was back in Pearce House in 1981, studying for my skipper's ticket. I shuddered as I remembered those hateful days and the way I'd been treated by a retired English sea captain who had tutored some of our classes.

Loud laughter in the room caught my attention. I looked up at Larry Robbins. He was standing with his two hands lifted in the air, elbows level with his shoulders, forearms bent at right angles, palms facing the audience and bending from the waist and swaying from side to side. "This," I heard him say, "was us rolling." He said the rolling instruments measured the rolls regularly at 35 degrees but one was read at 48 degrees. "*Monowai* was only making four knots in the conditions," Larry said, and when he told us how she'd rolled regularly I could understand him when he said it was sometimes better not to have the modern instruments telling them how big the roll was. "We still had room to roll," and he performed his rolling again. "Our angle of maximum stability is 58 degrees and we could in theory go to 88 degrees."

I tried to imagine him doing his roll to 88 degrees and decided he'd be nearly touching the ground if his ship rolled that far. This short man grew in stature as he related his experiences that day. "If we'd gone to our theoretical limit of 88 degrees everything on the high side would've joined everything on the low side and the equation would've changed. Even at our angles of roll some equipment which had been in place since the ship was commissioned 17 years earlier pulled away from its mountings on the bulkhead." One of those casualties was the senior ratings' beer cooler. It had them all up and securing it during the early hours of the morning.

"The wind was a steady 65 knots, gusting to 85 to 90 knots. The deck edges are six and a half metres above the waterline, and," he told us, "they were rolling under all the time."

We heard that when the ship was in a trough, the water was above the level of the bridge, and water was washing in through portholes and watertight doors. The fear of losing one of his crew overboard was paramount. "We'd never have got him back. We kept going off course. We'd roll off a wave or be hit by a gust of wind. In all this," Larry told us, "I endeavoured to remain calm, cool and collected."

He, along with his crew, also saved many of the yachties who were caught out in the storm. For this, Commander Robbins was awarded the OBE. During the rest of the conference Larry's rolling motion was referred to as the *Monowai* Shuffle.

Then it was my turn to speak. I could feel everyone's eyes on me, no doubt wondering what on earth I could have to say. What an act to have to follow. I asked Larry Robbins if he was thinking of becoming a tutor at the Nautical School in Wellington when he retired. "If so, I'll be along to do my coastal ticket," I told him.

As usual I had small notes to help me with my speech but as my eyes swept the room and I saw all the men I changed my mind and came in on a totally different angle from what I'd intended. "I'm speaking for the women," I told them. "Your wives, partners, mothers, and daughters. How many of you here today think about them when you are taking part in a rescue in foul weather?" I knew I had their attention.

I was able to impart my feelings to them as I related some of the extreme rescues that Joe, Young Joe and James have been involved in. The times I've sat at the Heads at the entrance to Tory Channel, thinking I'd never see them again in the rough seas. Rescues I've been out on myself, and of course the ones where the thought of the recovery of bodies had kept me at home.

But living right on the scene makes me aware of what is happening. Not so for the women in a town or away from the sea. "They," I reminded my audience, "have to sit at home, and wait and imagine."

At the close of my speech I knew it was the right thing to say. Many of the men came up to me later that afternoon and throughout the rest of the conference to thank me. The words were nearly always the same. "You know I've never thought about my wife's feelings. I'm out at sea and I know what's going on, but until today I hadn't thought about her."

On the Saturday afternoon there was a SAREX (search and rescue exercise) planned for Picton harbour. A cruise ship, in fact the Interisland freight ferry, *Arahunga*, was to catch fire, and 120 passengers - actually Coastguard members - had boarded the ferry at Picton's ferry terminal in time for her scheduled afternoon sailing. They were to be rescued. Six or more vessels plus two helicopters were available to rescue the passengers.

The control centre was set up at the Waikawa Bay Boating Club with six units each with five people. Each unit appointed a radio operator and one person to be in charge. I found myself being responsible to the press, and answering any questions an appointed newspaper reporter asked about the incident. Starting with number one, each unit ran the SAREX for 20 minutes before handing over to the next unit. Although it was only a SAREX I found myself caught up in the drama. Our unit was number six and by the time it was our turn we were left with the mopping up. The drama was over. All we had to do was stand down all the rescue craft and make sure everyone was accounted for. It was discovered that the passenger ship had hit a submarine, from the country of Chaos, in Picton harbour. When it surfaced its crew were taken aboard one of the rescue boats. The passengers were rescued off the ship which was on fire, the rescue boats returned to base, and the *Arahunga* became herself again and sailed for Wellington.

All the crews off the rescue boats, the passengers and those involved in the control room came to the debrief which followed. From the exercise one thing became clear - there had been a communications break-down and this would have to be fixed.

At the dinner that evening Peter Montgomery entertained us with his stories of sailing in the Southern Ocean with Sir Peter Blake, and many anecdotes from his years of broadcasting for TVNZ. Commander Larry Robbins sat at the same table as Joe and me so we were entertained with more of his stories as well - a great evening to wind up the conference. As we were leaving, the president of Marlborough's Volunteer Coastguard, Bill Gibb, came up to Joe and told him that Peter Montgomery would like a trip out in the *Tranz Rail Rescue*, and would Joe take him out in the morning as Bill had to stay at the conference.

It was a perfect morning to introduce someone to the Marlborough Sounds. This was my first ride in the new boat. Speeding up the Sounds, travelling at a speed of 30 knots, was a great way to take in fresh air after having sat inside for the last two days.

When Picton lost its float plane company in 1995, a large hole was left in emergency services, but this 12.6m Naiad will help fill the gap. With the newly built cabin she offers comfort for the sick and injured and the crew. *Tranz Rail Rescue* has all the modern navigational aids including GPS, radar and sounder as well as being equipped with all the necessary safety and rescue equipment.

Our trip was short as Peter had a plane to catch but being on the boat gave me time to think about the immense amount of work that so few men have done. The Marlborough Volunteer Coastguard is an organisation run within a small community, and these volunteers deserve all the support they can get.

The day I spoke at the conference was the ladies' day out. I was disappointed at not being able to meet some of the women and hear their thoughts about some of the rescues their men had been involved in, but I hope the men think more about the anxieties of those who wait at home for their men on the sea.

Joe and I had just arrived home at Okukari on the Sunday afternoon following the conference when our phone rang to alert Joe to the fact that a small yacht was missing out of Cloudy Bay. When last seen it was drifting south. We were put on standby. Two fishing boats in the area were asked to keep a watch out for the missing boat, as was the *Joseph Day*, the Sumner Volunteer Coastguard vessel, as it steamed south after the conference.

Our ears were glued to the VHF for the rest of the day - praying it would be found and we wouldn't be called out. At dusk we heard the message that made us breathe out in relief. The boat had been found pulled up on Marfells Beach. It seemed the owner had drifted ashore and left his boat. We were told the police would be speaking to that yachtsman.

The next few days were one non-stop whirl. In between mustering the merinos in for shearing, and baking for the morning and afternoon teas, I went to Picton mid-week, on the *Felix*, to keep a speaking engagement. Although still nervous I was finding myself relaxing more, especially when speaking to Picton folk. This time I spoke about writing and putting a book together, as I was aware that some of my audience would have heard me speak already at other functions.

Then it was back to Okukari Bay with one day's respite before shearing began. The second day of the shearing I had to leave my daughters-in-law to class the wool. I knew they were capable of doing it and I'd shown them what I wanted done with the wool. Having only 1000 merino wethers, I class to a fine, medium and a strong line. Short wool, and off fleeces - fleeces that are cotted (matted), yellow or very seedy - are kept apart from the three main lines. I told Joy and Lisa to keep aside any of the in-between fleeces they weren't sure of, until I arrived home.

I'd received an invitation to be the guest speaker at the opening of the third Picton Sounds Spring School. I was staggered. Why me? I was thanked for the recognition I'd given the school in my many interviews when all I'd done was tell the story of how I came to write my first book after attending the first Spring School. The invitation had come 14 weeks early, which made it easy to accept. A quick calculation had me thinking shearing would be over by then - it wouldn't be a problem. I'd forgotten the big part the weather plays in shearing schedules. Continuous rain had put our shearing back.

"I can't leave the shed," I cried, "but how can I ring up and say I won't be at the opening?" At the end of our shearing my stencil would be on each bale so I felt I had to be in the woolshed to make sure the clip was classed correctly. As usual it was my placid Joe who sorted me out with his question, "How many years have the girls worked alongside you? If they can't do it now, they never will. Just go. Any fleeces we're not sure of, we'll put aside."

How often words of my father come back to me. As I steamed down the channel in the speedboat, to the Spring School, one of his ditties came back to me.

> Some time when you're feeling important
> Some time when your ego's in bloom
> Some time when you take it for granted
> You're the best qualified in the room,
> Put your hand in a bucket of water
> Put it in right up to your wrist
> Take it out and the hole that's remaining
> Is the manner in which you'll be missed.

I was back working in the woolshed by 11am, my town clothes discarded in a heap on the bedroom floor and the orchid corsage they had given me now on the table, the only visible signs that I had been anywhere apart from the woolshed. And my father was right. My girls had managed without me.

By the end of September 1996 I was exhausted. In one week I'd had four speaking engagements and for each one I'd taken myself into Picton and back in the speedboat. When I turned over the calendar for the start of October I had only two crosses. One was for the first weekend when I was travelling to Auckland for the Women's Book Weekend which had been organised by Carole Beu of the Women's Bookshop. I had been invited to speak with two other women about our books, Pauline Grogan and her *Beyond the Veil*, and Neva Clarke McKenna with her *Angel in God's Office - My Wartime Diaries*. Our three-women session had been given the title, Ordinary Women, Extraordinary Lives.

I was driving up the country with my publisher. We had to be at the ferry terminal at 4.30am and as I pulled the door of Pauline's and Dene's house closed I realised I wasn't the only living thing awake when I heard a rooster crowing somewhere in the darkness. Once I was on the ferry it should have been easy to return to sleep but as usual I stayed wide awake until it was time to stand at the rail and watch Okukari slip past. When we'd cleared the entrance I couldn't close my eyes on the sun rising above black hills, and lighting up Cook Strait with shades of colours not seen on a painter's colour chart.

I had a great weekend. Meeting other women writers and finding that their worries were similar to mine, listening to them speak about their books, read from them and hear other women read out their poetry was like the best vintage wine - I savoured the taste.

Chris was staying on in Auckland to work with another writer. I'd decided to catch the overnight train to Wellington, then the Picton ferry the next morning. I curled up in my seat and the rhythmic clackety-clack of the wheels soon had me drifting off to sleep. I thought about the weekend. I'd noticed there were quite a few lesbians in the audience and I understood how much I'd grown as a person since I'd written my book. I thought back to 1994, to the first writers' workshop I did. I was staying with our older daughter, Helen, in Picton. When I'd arrived home that first day Helen had asked me how it had gone, and I remember my feelings of shock as I told her there was a lesbian, Hannah, in our class and a young man who had been on drugs and was certainly rather strange. My island world had been so small. Today I count Hannah as one of my special friends, and I'd felt at home among all those many different women in Auckland.

I had one day to spend at Okukari before I was off to Picton again to speak to a group. I'd picked up a red pen to write the time and date and now I found myself thinking this was a red letter day. The last time I had to go to town for ages. No more speaking. I could be just me. My next appointment was four weeks away - the dentist. And for now all I wanted to do was get back into the swing of life in Okukari Bay again, the place where life is always busy, and things always seem to be happening, but at the same time its peace seeps into my very soul and renews me.

For eight days I enjoyed the quiet. I ran on the beach in the early morning, the sea's special smell filling my lungs. Words flowed and grew into chapters, and the last two hours of every day spent in my garden soon had fewer weeds growing and the next day's writing planned.

This comfortable routine was shattered with a phone call telling us that Bill Gibb, Marlborough's Coast Guard president, and Picton's senior constable, was very ill. We knew he was having an operation and that it was cancer but I don't think anyone knew just how serious it was. After Bill had got over the initial shock, he decided he didn't have

Cancer, the big C, the one that no one spoke of. He had a complaint with a little c, and he was going to fight it.

Joe and I found ourselves asking each other questions. All the "hows" and "ifs" and "whens", and mostly the "whys". "All the rotten people Bill has had to deal with over the years. Why not them instead?"

I questioned my faith. "How can a loving God do this?"

We wanted to visit Bill but thought we'd wait until he came home. Instead, three days after Bill's surgery, Tricia, Bill's wife, rang and told Joe that Bill would love to see us.

My Joe, rugged outdoor man of the sea, wanted to visit Bill but his track record of hospital visits isn't good. He had vivid memories of ending up in the next bed when he was visiting me after one of my operations. I'm told it is the hospital smell and the heat, but, whatever the cause, Joe tells me that on that particular occasion he thought he'd died and gone to heaven because when he came to on the ward floor all he could see were lovely legs and lacy petticoats and knickers as nurses hovered over him.

Joe's memories put him off making a hospital visit for one day, but the following morning he woke up and said he was going to see Bill Gibb.

As we steamed down Tory Channel and past Maraetai Bay I couldn't believe that it was only three weeks ago that Bill, with Tony Groome, John Evans, John Dixon and Willy Abel as crewmen, and local doctor Nick Binns, had used the new Coastguard vessel, *Tranz Rail Rescue*, to pick up a person with a suspected heart condition from Maraetai Bay. That night there were northerly winds of more than 60 knots and heavy rain and we'd heard later of the mountainous seas but the boat had handled the conditions well, doing what she was designed to do - bringing help and comfort to the sick and injured. There was no other way the patient could have received help that night. It was right that Bill had skippered the boat on its very first rescue. Since he'd come back to live in Picton in 1983, it had been his dream that the Sounds should have a rescue craft, and the smaller *Interisland Rescue*, a 6.8metre rigid-hulled inflatable craft, powered by two 115hp outboard motors, was the beginning that led on to the new *Tranz Rail Rescue*.

As Joe and I climbed the stairs to the ward where Bill was, Joe suggested that we stay for only 15 minutes or so. "I hate these sorts of hospital visits."

I will never forget our last hour we spent with Bill. The room was filled with warmth and love. Laughter came easily as Bill related some of his life's stories. Tears came close when Tricia made me sit next to Bill. "Hold his hands," I was told. I felt a trespasser. Tricia had so little time left and yet she gave Bill to me for an hour while she sat at the foot of his bed.

"Bloody lousy fish in here, Joe. It's made me crook," and at these words Joe promised Bill fresh groper when he came home. "That'll be Thursday," Bill told us. Bill was coming home to write his special life stories, and when I offered, with tongue in cheek, to come and help set up his computer, we were all in laughter as Joe informed Bill about my computing skills.

I never for a moment dreamt as I hugged Bill and said our goodbyes that his time was so short. As the door of his room closed behind us and we stepped into the empty hospital corridor, I shivered. The love in that room was so powerful, life so certain, that I knew Joe and I had been witness to something very special.

The news of Bill's death four days later, on 25 October 1996, stunned us. He was 49.

Bill had always been there, co-ordinating so many of the search and rescues that my family have been involved in. We had worked together in life and death situations. He'd been my hitting-post when I needed one during searches when I believed I'd never see my husband and sons again. The times when they'd had to go out in horrendous seas to rescue fools or search a wild but empty sea for a missing boat, I could always ring Bill. He believed in Joe, and he made me realise I must believe too.

Since Bill's funeral I have asked myself many times, "How can a funeral be wonderful?" Bill's was. As Christine Cole Catley wrote in Bill's obituary for our local paper - 'Everyone truly mourned at Bill Gibb's funeral last week, mourned but laughed too, as Bill would have wanted us to.' It was the largest funeral I have ever attended. Picton was in shock.

This honest, brave, sensible, wise and fair man was carried through the police honour guard into the church by friends, to the sound of two pipers outside. I watched as his friends in the Coastguard, Police and yachting slowly made their way up the aisle with eyes closed as they tried to stop the flow of tears.

I played the organ. Bill had chosen two hymns, Amazing Grace, and, because it was the seafarers' hymn, written for those in peril on the sea, Eternal Father. Tricia had asked me if I would play something as a tribute to Bill. I thought of his last trip he'd had in the Sounds in those shocking conditions so short a time ago. In the blackness the lights would have lit up Bill's journey, so I chose the following:

> Lead kindly light amid the encircling gloom,
> Lead Thou me on;
> The night is dark and I am far from home,
> Lead Thou me on.
> Keep Thou my feet; I do not ask to see
> The distant scene - one step enough for me.

Tricia, and daughters Jacqueline and Elizabeth, chose special verses. I found myself wondering at Tricia's strength as she read the wellknown lines of W H Auden: 'Stop all the clocks, cut off the telephone, prevent the dog barking with a juicy bone.' As she read on I remembered the day my mother was killed. When everything had stopped for me, too. The ferry had passed us in the channel and jolted me back to the present as I realised that life just keeps on going.

Bill's family and friends carried him out of the church to the strains of the bagpipes playing The Scottish Soldier. Rosemary Powell, who conducted the funeral service, ended with words which gave us all much to think about. "Make the most of every minute of every hour we have to live. It was so rewarding to have known him, this kind, strong, brave man of the sea, who didn't suffer fools, who cared deeply for people."

One month after Bill's death, a crewman off the fishing boat *Lady Anna* had good reason to give thanks to this "man of the sea" who had had the vision to order a pair of night-vision binoculars for the *Tranz Rail Rescue*.

In the budget for setting up the new rescue boat, $1400 had been allocated for buying two sets of binoculars - one set for day use, the other for night. Before Bill became ill he'd ordered one of the sets, and it wasn't until after his death that Dave Baker, a committee member who had been given the job of ordering the equipment for the cabin, received a phone call saying that the binoculars had arrived. Dave said he was horrified when he saw what they cost, but he believed that "Willie knew what he was doing."

A Mayday signal had been picked up by Wellington Radio on 29 November 1996, at 1am. A crewman had been lost overboard from the *Lady Anna* as they were steaming out of Picton Harbour, and he was missing for 10 minutes before the crew realised what had happened. Picton Police were notified and a crew for the rescue boat was called out.

At 1.15am *Tranz Rail Rescue* skippered by Dave Baker pulled out of the Picton marina with Ken MacKenzie and Dave's son, Jason, as crew. "It felt strange not having Bill with us," Dave said to me later.

Dave is a commercial fisherman, and both he and Jason had been diving for paua the day before. "The phone had woken me from a deep sleep. I'd been diving all day and as we steamed out of the marina I was trying to work my brain. Thinking, planning - all the information I'd been given was bubbling in my head and I was trying to form a picture of events."

In the rescue craft's cabin amidships a brass plaque is set at eye level. It reads: 'In memory of William John Gibb. 14-5-1947 - 25-10-1996. Whose spirit sails with us on this vessel.'

"My hand brushed over the plaque. Bill seemed very close," Dave said.

The Interisland ferry, on its way into Picton, had been called in to help search, as was the smaller rescue boat, *Interisland Rescue*.

It was presumed the man had fallen overboard half a mile north-east of Mabel Island, near Picton Point, so a search was begun on the line the boat had been steaming. "It was a cloudy night, very little light and we had about 10 to 15 knots of northerly," Dave said later. "Ken was up the bow of the boat following the beam of the spotlight that Jason was working from the wheelhouse." I felt for Dave when he described his feelings and said how he knew he must make the right decisions. "A man's life was in my hands."

The sea remained black and empty, and Dave said he was positive they'd be looking for a body in the morning. "Suddenly Jason remembered Bill's night-vision binoculars and grabbed them out of the locker. As we steamed closer to Picton Point I had a hunch and came close to the shore to begin a search between Picton and Picton Point. With the binoculars Jason was able to see beyond the beam of light. As he swung the binoculars across a bay - right on the edge of the light he picked up what looked to be a body on the shore. It was 1.35am.

"We really thought he was dead. He was in a foetal position with his feet in the water. All the clothes he was wearing were dark. There is no doubt in my mind that we'd never had seen him without Bill's binoculars."

Dave nudged the boat ashore and Jason leapt over the side. His father had warned him that the man was probably dead but when Jason shook him he grunted. Dave called up Wellington Radio as well as the *Interisland Rescue* to tell them they'd located the man, as it was easier to lift him aboard the smaller boat. He was wrapped in a silver hypothermia blanket, as well as woollen ones, and Constable Marty Parker cuddled him to share his body warmth as the boat raced into Picton to the waiting ambulance.

One night search, one person saved. All because one man, Bill Gibb, had the determination to equip the boat with the very best, and the strength not to give in when his wisdom in buying such expensive glasses was questioned. The rescue vessel is truly Bill's legacy to seafarers in our area.

Since having the *Tranz Rail Rescue*, we seem not to have had call-outs at the same rate. There have certainly been boats reported as missing in the Marlborough Sounds when they failed to return at the time they gave. The Coastguard has swung into action only to be told later the errant boatie has returned, extending his day out in the Sounds without notifying anyone of his change of plans. And as long as the sea flows in and out of Tory Channel we'll receive calls from boaties who cannot enter the channel because of the fast-moving tide, and I'm in no doubt that Maydays and calls for assistance will still punctuate our lives.

On 29 January 1996 we had received a different type of call for assistance. I always think later that the rings of these calls have sounded more strident. A voice identifying itself as from Civil Aviation told us that a small plane, a Caravan, with six people aboard, was overdue on a flight between Wellington and Koromiko, the small airfield situated halfway between Blenheim and Picton. A signal from an EPIRB had been picked up, believed to be that from the missing plane, and we were requested to go out in the boat and search the coastline as far south as Rununder Point at the entrance of Port Underwood.

The message made me cold. Chris, my publisher, was in Wellington. I knew she was coming home that afternoon and she often flew with that airline. As I ran down to the boat every step pounded out "Not Chris. Not Chris. Not Chris." Joe soon had the boat up to full revs and we left Okukari behind in a mist of spray picked up from our foaming wake by the northerly wind.

"We've got to look on the shoreline and out to sea," Joe told us. "We've only been given the general area and there's a possibility that it might have gone down in the sea."

But once we were out of the channel and heading south down the coast, it seemed obvious where the plane would have crashed. I found it hard to swallow with the lump that was building in my throat as I visualised Chris, probably still busy editing, as the plane slammed into the shrouded hillside. The craggy skyline had been smoothed by the blanket of fog that was no more than 1000 feet above us. I kept staring into the clouds, imagining.

"Out to sea as well!" Joe yelled at me several times as I kept wanting to sweep the hills with the binoculars.

Off Rununder the Westpac helicopter flew over us and a short time later we received the news that wreckage had been sighted on Mount Robertson. All I could do was wait until I heard who was aboard the plane.

Later I heard. Because Chris's business in Wellington had been closer to the ferry terminal this time, and because there had been so many broadcast reports of a likely sub-tropical cyclone, she had changed her mind about flying in a small plane and opted to catch the fast ferry, *Lynx*, instead. She was on the ferry coming home when what would have been her plane crashed into the mountain. Chris was to tell me later how, when she woke the following morning, the day had never been brighter or the birds sung louder. She was alive but the five passengers on board the plane were dead. Only the pilot, badly injured, survived.

CHAPTER TEN

Lesson Time

ALL SORTS of things happen when you've written a book and live in a small place. You really do become "the speaker". I thought I'd beaten my nerves until I received an unusual invitation - to speak at Picton Primary School during Library Week. Three separate classes, I was told, and for about half an hour each. I knew these children would be my most attentive listeners yet. I decided that as it was Library Week I'd tell them how a book was written and put together, similar to a talk I'd given to a women's group recently. Knowing how children like to be 'hands on', I brought along my props.

I was taken first to the oldest children's class, and told some were working on and publishing their own stories. They were using computers and I wondered what they'd think if I told them what happened when I was learning to use my word processor. Instead I began, as I did in every class, by asking them who had been across to Wellington on the ferry. Most hands shot up, and I then described where we live. I had brought my map of the Sounds with me to show them where I'd come in from that morning. In every class I was asked how far it was and how long did it take.

I've kept everything I wrote while I worked on *Weather Permitting* and so the first thing I told the children was how I'd attended the Picton Sounds Spring School in 1994 and worked with Christine Cole Catley in her writers' workshop. I passed around the very first chapter, handwritten and unedited. I'd stapled the pages together so it could go around the room, and eager hands reached out for it when I passed it to a child in the front row. Next I told them how I'd bought a word processor, and gave them the same chapter, now printed and edited, to look at.

An important thing, I told them, is the author's contract, and my contract was soon being looked at as it went around the room. When I picked up the complete typewritten manuscript and told the children this was how it went to my publisher, there were gasps of amazement. Immediately a forest of hands shot in to the air. "How long did all that take to write?" "How many pages?" "How many chapters?" Children asked these three questions in each of the classes I spoke to.

I showed them the ISBN, and explained how my book was the only one in the world with that particular International Standard Book Number, and that if they were in China or Timbuktu they should be able to track down my book if they quoted my ISBN. I spoke about the acknowledgements and the jacket blurb from the back cover, and the naming of the chapters.

When I talked about the cover of the book I asked who knew Ian and Fi Garrod from the Happy Snappa photography shop in Picton. More hands shot up, and I told them how Ian and I had gone down to the beach one cold southerly day in Picton, and he'd taken that photo. "But Miss," one little boy said, "it doesn't look like you." I had to explain that I was dressed up in my town clothes to visit the school. On the day of the cover photo I'd been wearing a Swanndri for unloading fish off the boat.

Originally I was going to have a painting on the front cover of my book, showing my piano arriving on the beach at Okukari. We liked it but thought it was more suited for a children's book. The artist, Gary Hebley, had sent me the original, which I passed around the class. The children enjoyed touching and holding the things I had with me. This brought back so many memories of my own teaching years, with our four children on Correspondence School lessons. I could see my children's gentle hands gathering worms to make a worm colony, and younger hands feeling textures, to find rough and smooth.

The next question brought me back to the present. "How old are you?" My answer brought so many "Wows" and "Gollies" that I wondered what they'd been expecting.

Blenheim Bookworld had given me a copy of the booksellers' list which came out on 7 June 1996, when my book had reached number one in the list of New Zealand books, and I'd brought this in with me. I wondered what the children were imagining when I said that one of the most exciting things to happen to authors was seeing their names on this list, and it too was handed around. I watched them, and wondered whether any of them dreamed of becoming writers. Would I have, if I had met a real-life author when I was their age?

The teachers had brought a copy of my book to their classes that day, and, as I'd brought one in too, the children were taking turns with the books while I spoke. I noticed how they all turned to the photos, so I told them the story of how I'd taken a big suitcase filled with photos and albums to my publisher's house and we'd spent an evening going through hundreds of photos, sorting out the ones which best told a story. Then we had to decide on the captions for each photo.

I had brought the colour proofs with me and passed these around the room. One child was indignant when the little boy next to him had looked at one page for more than 60 seconds and he wanted a turn - I was glad I'd had only four children in my classroom in my teaching days. These children were fascinated when I unfolded the 12ft fax that had come to the publisher from Hong Kong before the book was printed, so we could check that all the right captions were under the photos. I could see they were most impressed that it had taken 15 minutes to come through the fax machine. The teacher in this class then asked me if I could read something from my book, so I ended the talk with the story of Lucky, the pet lamb.

The next two classes I spoke to similarly, remembering they were younger. They asked many of the same questions. Then came some different ones.

"Are you Pauline's mother? She operated on our dog."

"How old is Pauline?"

And, from one little girl, came the contribution of the day: "Pauline killed our cat."

I stopped short. More than 30 pairs of eyes were fixed on mine. What could I say to that?

I thought of our children's pain when any of their pets died. "Your cat must have been very sick or Pauline wouldn't have had to put it down."

A slow nod. Then, "It had cancer."

In the last class the subject of the cruise ship *Mikhail Lermontov* was raised - interestingly, because adult audiences have always asked about the sinking of this ship, too. I was asked if I'd been there, and had I seen her sink. I explained that my husband and two sons had helped in the rescue and had seen her sink. I was asked if Joe had been honoured for his bravery that night, so I told them it was really for his willingness to go out and help search for, or rescue, many boats over the years. In this class I ended by reading out the part in my book about the sinking of the *Mikhail Lermontov*.

I know the New Zealand Book Council arranges for authors of children's books to visit schools and talk, but I'd never imagined being asked to do this myself.

I learned a lot, too. In fact it was a morning I won't forget. The journey home seemed shorter than usual as I thought about those bright-faced children.

When I told my editor-publisher about it, and we'd delighted in the children's questions, she said I should have given them a short lesson on how to use a dictionary, based on the mistake she said she'd made when editing my book, when (among other things) she'd checked my spelling. She'd looked twice at a word I'd used, 'hyperthermia', to describe a near-frozen condition. It didn't look right to her. So, in a rush, she'd looked it up in the dictionary, seen that it was spelled correctly, and gone straight on to the next matter.

"What I didn't do," Chris told me, "was read the definition. If I had, I'd have seen that 'hyperthermia' means excessive temperature and the word we wanted was 'hypothermia'. Next time you talk to children, feel free to tell them how silly I was - then maybe they'll remember to use a dictionary properly, and read definitions."

It made a good lesson for my grandchildren on correspondence lessons here in the bay. The year 1996 was when the Okukari roll grew to three. Haydn, Lisa's and James's son, began his schooling in June. Then six months later, Rachael, Joy's and Joe's older girl, finished form two and left the Correspondence School to begin her secondary schooling at Marlborough Girls' College.

I remembered from my teaching days the difference it made when there was one fewer to teach. Each time one of my children left home for college, the heavy load I seemed to carry all the time became lighter. But I still believe the hardest time was when number one first began his lessons. I'd do exactly what was set out for each day and decide it was easy, but then at night doubts would assail me and I couldn't see how I could take this child through his daily lessons to the stage where he'd be independent of me. Especially with three other children waiting in the wings.

The day the first of Haydn's lessons arrived I wasn't home and I felt saddened when I heard he'd received them. I'd wanted to see his face when he opened up the boxes with all the art, maths, extra reading books, and the workbook for Lisa as well as his own. Then there'd be the all-important letter from his teacher.

Joe and I had arrived home late that night and the following morning the phone rang at 7.45am. It was Haydn. He'd kept his boxes to open when I was there. Joe, who'd never shown an interest in his own children's school, beat me down to Haydn's and we watched in delight as this child's new adventure was scattered over the lounge floor. I saw the pleasure on Joe's face and at last I understood. Just as James couldn't be there to watch his son with his school work, neither could Joe in those early years. He was always away fishing or working on the farm - as James was that day. With our sons running the boats now, Joe goes fishing only when he wants to and he is enjoying seeing his own children through his grandchildren.

With having to teach school, Lisa found her days changed. The times when she'd decide to go in to Picton on the spur of the moment if the boys were unloading fish now didn't happen. She told me that extra school lessons would then have to be done the next day or caught up with over the weekend. She is finding she has to plan ahead more - and I couldn't help grinning to myself when Lisa told me how on days when she wants to go out and knows that the day's work is easy, it is always just those days that nothing goes right and the school takes much longer. I'd been through it all before her.

Haydn had nearly completed his first term of school when I caught up with him during a music lesson. I walked in the back door, not to the usual sound of the stereo playing pop music but Haydn and Lisa singing, 'This is the way we wash our clothes'. No one heard me come in and I stood at the door of the school room feeling as if I were in a time warp. To me it was James singing along with the tape and doing the actions of the song, and then I noticed the empty stool while Danielle cuddled up on her mother's lap. It brought back to me the days I'd had to teach while at the same time having to pacify a sick child. Then the voice on the tape told Haydn to repeat after her a little poem about the wind blowing through the treetops. The effort he put into it as he said after his teacher, "Blow wind blow wind, blowing through the treetops," made me clap my hands and I was back in the present again. I joined in the last of his lesson for that day and heard a recorder being played, a harmonica and a saxophone. All wind instruments. This was followed by a guessing game and we heard other wind sounds. The first was easy - someone blowing over the top of a bottle. I couldn't guess the next one - blowing through cupped hands - but the last one Haydn recognised, a sheet of paper rustling in the wind. Danielle perked up and helped Haydn make his 'whooing' noise around a house, especially when he had to make a strong wind, then a wind dying out.

That morning Haydn had learnt the letter 'n'. "It's the last letter in my name, you know, Grandma." He showed me the other letters he knew and I was surprised how much he'd learned in one term. Besides recognising half the alphabet he read me one of his readers. His fingers automatically slipped across each page from left to right, pointing to each word. This was a story about a boy called Tim. "Where's Tim?" Haydn read, and I was told what a question mark was, a full stop and a capital letter. Lisa checked her booklet to make sure she had covered the morning's work and I noticed that the person who taught the lessons was no longer a supervisor. She is now a home tutor.

In Haydn's most recently marked set he'd had returned there was a 'warm fuzzy award' for extra neat printing. It was pinned on his wall and I had to admire it. Warm and fuzzy is how I always felt when my children's work had a special mention and I always felt it wasn't only an award for the children but for their mothers as well.

This one was beautifully coloured in orange and green. The warm fuzzy was green with a yellow and orange curly nose, orange eyes, and outlined in yellow. There was a buzzy bee with purple wings glued on to a yellow and apricot round sticker. "See how my teacher's kept inside the lines, Grandma," showed me that this too was another type of lesson for Haydn.

By December 1996 Joy was counting the days until the end of the school year when she'd have taught Rachael's correspondence lessons for the last time. But this was a different December for correspondence mothers. For the first time since 1949, mothers of children with pupils over the age of 11 wouldn't be welcoming home exhausted but satisfied children after they'd spent a month in Palmerston North at the residential school at Massey University. The previous year the month had been reduced to three weeks because of government cutbacks in funding. Now the whole scheme had been wiped. It meant that about 70 pupils from isolated areas in New Zealand, 15 from Marlborough alone in 1995, would miss out on one of the highlights of their Correspondence School years.

In the past I'd stood at the airport with Joy, waving our goodbyes along with the other mothers from Marlborough. I was sad for Angela, Rachael's younger sister, when I thought of the things she'd miss: the experiences of visiting work places, the entertainment, the fun of mixing with a lot of other children, and the learning of social skills - in my mind the most important thing for a Correspondence School child. These children living away from home for a month had to learn to think for themselves and respect others' needs, all so valuable, especially when most of them would soon be heading off to a boardingschool for their secondary education.

In place of the residential school there was to be a five-day trip to the Temple Basin skifield in Arthur's Pass. This was arranged and 10 students from Marlborough/Nelson, West Coast, Canterbury and Southland, the four South Island regions, could attend. Altogether 31 children took the opportunity, with Marlborough being able to send 14 because students from places where skiing was commonplace had opted out.

Three mini-buses left Picton at 7.20am, picking up students en route. Although mothers met the same sort of exhausted children as when they'd arrived home from Massey, I still wondered if there was the same sense of achievement for every child at the camp. I felt for the child who couldn't ski as well as his or her peers. At the residential school there was room for so many achievements, and a child could always find something to excel in.

Joy and I discussed her feelings now that Rachael was finishing correspondence schooling, and half of Joy's workload was gone. Her feelings ran parallel to mine when I'd taught our children. "It's the constant pressure. School is always in my head." I nodded with her as I remembered the days of finishing one set to get it away in the mail and then starting the next one. Dates to be met, finding things left out, and the checking.

Joy continued, "You know what I mean. I ask myself, am I doing it right? Is it good enough? And, do you know what I'm realising now? It's Rachael's last year and I'm wishing I had a little bit more time to teach her something else. Suddenly this is it. I haven't got any more chances."

Just as I had, Joy too worried for their future. "All the years I've anchored Rachael's school and now I'm scared that when she goes to boarding school everything I've taught her might go out the window."

Angela burst into our conversation, needing help from her mother. "And that's another thing," Joy went on. "Some days I find it so hard to be patient. I'll sit over Angela, wanting her to come up with a suggestion or an answer to something. I nearly always end up telling her or I'd be waiting all day." How vividly I remembered days like that, when I felt as if I had to think for four children as well as supervise their lessons, and when Joy told me how on bad days she'd love to take the day off - "but you can't because school has to be done regardless" - I could sympathise.

If only all children could be the same, quick to learn, life would be easy for a mother teaching school. Just as I had recognised James had a speech problem, Joy had recognised that Angela had a reading one. As she began each new set she struggled more and more. The language section became harder because the child couldn't read. "Somewhere along the way she must have missed a vital point," Joy told her teacher.

Joy basically started Angela's new reading programme from the beginning, while keeping on with the other set work. Easier books came in with Angela's school work and gradually she gained the ability, and more importantly the confidence, to read. Today she has caught up with her age group and, I tell Joy, all credit must go to her.

There have been advances in other areas of school since I taught our children. Under-fives have the opportunity of doing pre-school. I've seen my young grandchildren's excitement when they've received their sets in our mailbag, filled with books for their mother to read to them and many puzzles, jigsaws and ideas for art work. For a mother with older children on the roll it is a wonderful system for keeping the under-fives busy and feeling important when their 'school' arrives in the same way as their siblings' does.

During my teaching years we had other events as well as the residential school and a week up at Lake Rotoiti in the Nelson Lakes district in early December. We had the summer picnic, and a school week when the children were integrated into a local school, and the winter party which was held in Blenheim in July. Today the Marlborough Parents' Association runs a two-day camp at Mistletoe Bay in Queen Charlotte Sound in February. Here the activities are centred mainly on the water with swimming and canoeing, and the mothers have time to talk and compare. Later in the year an activity week is held in Blenheim. The main focus is on learning to swim, and half the time is spent at the heated pool. The rest of the time is spent working in groups with art and games. On the last night there is a social and the pupils are divided into two groups, one for the very young and one for the older children. The week up at Lake Rotoiti in December is still held for children over eight.

Okukari Bay in the 1890s. Painted by Captain E F Temple.

I chase cattle. The same rugged hills as in the above painting are in the background. (Paul Palmer photography)

Two weeks after launching, my book reached number two on the New Zealand bestseller list. Haydn liked this colour photo (accompanying an interview) better than the usual black and white pictures. "It's not a dirty picture like the other ones, Grandma," I was told. (Photo, Timaru Herald)

Going to church at Aotea. From the top of the picture are: Katherine, Peter and Ethan McPherson, Joy, Lisa and Haydn, and Joe and Danielle.

Young Joe and I baiting groper lines to set at first light.

Joe and I preparing floats and lines for the cray season.

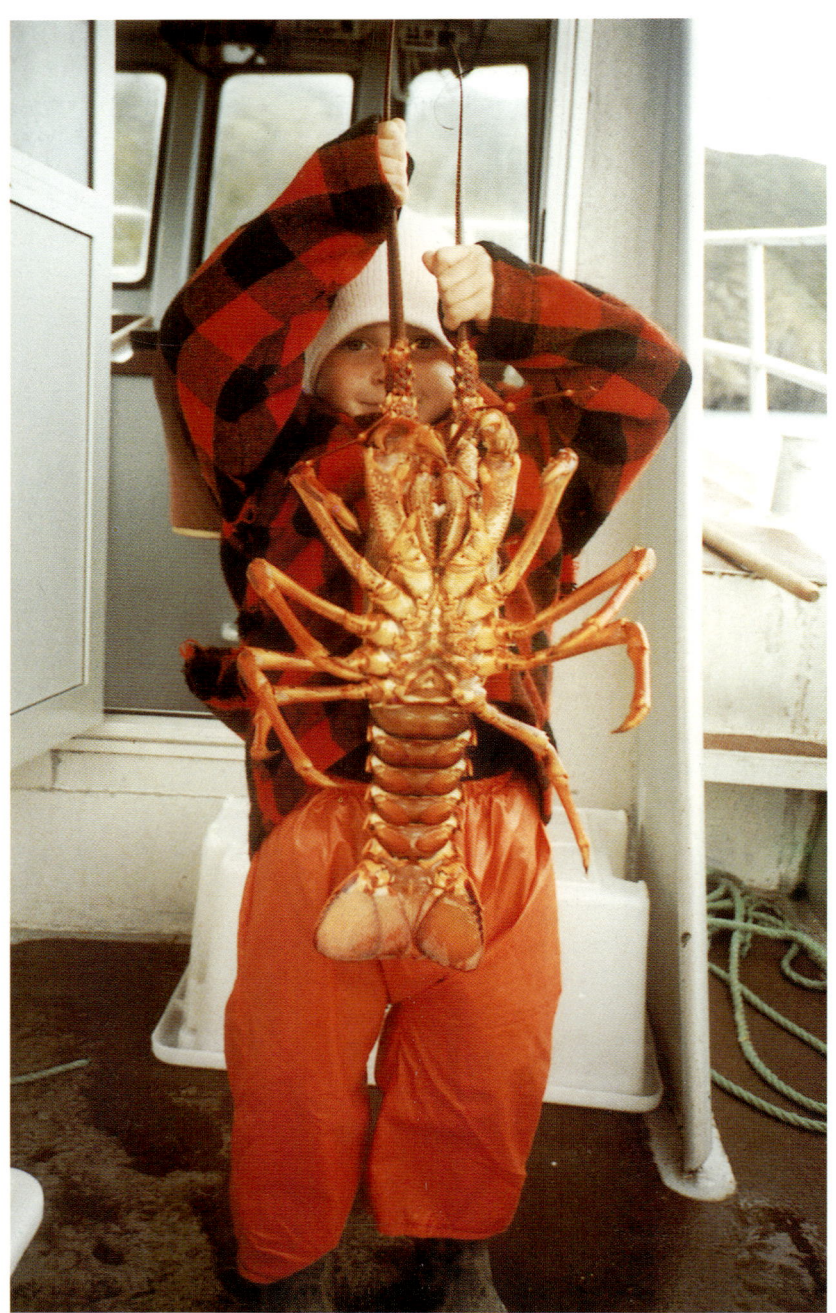

Haydn with a big buck cray.

During 1996 I had the chance to visit the Correspondence School once more. I had been in Wellington with Joy, Rachael and Angela to see the ballet, Swan Lake. Joy is an insulin-dependent diabetic and the next morning she had an appointment at Wellington Hospital for her twice-yearly check with a diabetes specialist, and I was taking my two granddaughters to meet their teachers at the school. I wandered through passages that opened up on brightly lit rooms. Teachers sat in their cubicles, surrounded by some of the art work sent in by their pupils. I noticed a list of children's names with their birth dates written next to them. Rachael's and Angela's birthdays were never forgotten. Now I knew why.

The school had grown since the days I brought my children to visit their teachers in the old school in Clifton Terrace with its poky little rooms that always appeared to be bursting with high stacks of sets to be posted, sets to be marked, paper, books and everything else that made a school.

Computers in the room seemed to take away a great deal of the clutter that I remembered. I was shown how, when a set comes in, it goes through a scan and its arrival is automatically noted on a computer. The same thing happens as each set is marked and sent out to the pupil. Computers on the teachers' desks made me realise how teaching had changed. But there was still that glorious smell of books and paper, and as I walked around the huge room and spoke to many of the teachers it was like a drug that kept pushing me back over 20 years to my teaching years. Years that I can enjoy now, but ones that I certainly didn't enjoy at the time.

When Joy arrived from the hospital and after she had caught up with the girls' teachers we took a taxi down to the Interisland terminal to catch the Picton ferry. The trip gave me time to reflect on the years that have passed, especially the years when I was totally swallowed up in teaching our four children. I never dreamt that one day I'd be sitting on the ferry with a daughter-in-law and two grandchildren, listening to their excited chatter about their visit to their teacher. I dozed, and thoughts drifted with my body, bobbing in and out of wakefulness. Tchaikovsky's music from the ballet throbbed in my mind: my feet tapped out the catchy beat of the dance of the little swans. "What are you smiling at, Grandma?" woke me up. I'd remembered the first time I took Helen to a ballet, while in Auckland visiting my parents. The lights dimmed in His Majesty's Theatre, the orchestra played the overture, and beside me Helen perched on the edge of her seat. The music built up to its crescendo. Then silence. The curtain rose and I heard Helen's gasp as she took in the dancers, all poised waiting for the music to bring them alive. A gruff little voice echoed round the theatre, "Mummy, those men haven't got any pants on." I was glad of the darkness as I tried to slide down in my seat.

I thought that my life is like a pebble thrown in the water. All the circles of ripples that come from that one little pebble are like my life, growing bigger as each new ripple is formed. But it wasn't until we came into Tory Channel and I went out on deck to watch Okukari pass by, then the remains of Peranos' whaling station, followed by Te Awaiti, that I realised I wasn't the pebble that had been thrown into the water. That pebble would have been James (Worser) Heberley who arrived at Te Awaiti in 1830 with Captain Jacky Guard to start up a shore-based whaling station. I was only one of the ripples.

CHAPTER ELEVEN

Worser Heberley Began It All

I WAS born in the year 1809, on the 22nd Jany, my Father was a German belonging to Witenberg, my Mother was an English woman, my native place is in Weymouth in Dorsetshire, my Father was taken Prisoner by my Grandfather in a Privateer, in the year 1790 brought into Weymouth, I was the first Son born, and my Mother set great store by me, and gave me to much of my own way, and I was a spoilt child, when I was about 5 years old I was sent to School, till I was 8 years old.

This is the first entry in James (Worser) Heberley's diary which he wrote in a school exercisebook. It was his dream to publish it, and at the time of his death preliminary arrangements had been made to prepare the story for the printer. His dream died with him. The manuscript is now in the Alexander Turnbull Library in Wellington.

Jacob Heberley married Elizabeth Curtis in Weymouth on 2 January 1809 and although James wrote that he was born on 22 January 1809 it seems probable that he was a year out. The Wyke Registry in Weymouth that records his parents' marriage also records that James was christened on 28 February 1810. His brother, John Jacob, was born in 1811, followed by John Lovelace Smith in 1816 and Frederick Mathew in 1817. The parish records show that the four boys were christened. There is no evidence of any girls yet James refers to sisters in his diary, and in the parish records of Abbotsbury in Dorset it is recorded that, on 27 May 1839, a Mary Gibbons Heberley, daughter of Jacob Heberley, mariner, married a William Guy.

Jacob Heberley died in 1817. James wrote in his diary. *My Father died on board the Nancy Brig belonging to Weymouth, my Mother then had to go out washing to maintain me and my Brothers and sisters. I myself was taken from school.*

The eight-year-old child was sent to the Isle of Wight to live with an uncle who owned property in East Cowes, and was also the manager of Lord Henry Seymour's estate. James used to visit the castle with his uncle, and became a favourite of Lord Henry's. *He took me out a shooting one day for the first time in my life I shot two*

Geese which pleased Lord Henry very much, My Uncle was very severe with me, My Aunt sent me to gather rent, it was late in the evening, and I had to pass through a garden, I saw some fruit I gathered some I did not taste it, I gave my Aunt the Fruit, and said Mrs Richman gave me some nice apples I gave them to my Aunt and she tasted them and said they were Greengages.

Later this Mrs Richman told James's aunt that she hadn't given the boy any fruit so as punishment his uncle sent him back to his mother in Weymouth. There his mother found him work in a rope-walk, a long piece of ground used for twisting rope. He earned three shillings a week and stayed 12 months.

The sea was in his blood and at the age of 11 he sailed as an apprentice on board a fishing boat for two years, before breaking his indentures. James arrived at the London docks where he shipped on board the *Sarah Margaret* and stayed on her for two years as cabin boy. Then the master to whom he'd been apprenticed found him and ordered him back to the fishing boat, where he beat the youngster with a dogfish tail. When his mother became sick and James asked to go and visit her, he was refused. She died, and when he asked if he could go to her funeral he was given another thrashing, this time with a piece of rope, and held on the vessel for two weeks.

In his diary James calls this man a tyrant, and after he managed to escape from him for the second time he made trips to the West Indies, America and Hamburg. These voyages were no easy ride for a lad of 14 or 15. He was sent aloft to 'square the yard'. He found everything frozen so came down, whereupon the mate thrashed him. So he left that ship and signed on a man-of-war. The doctor's assistant or *loblolly boy* was always threatening to pull James's ears:

> *On Christmas Day he struck me, so I returned the compliment, so we had it out I striped to the waist, and at it we went, the Master came and told the Boatswain to take us on deck, the Master cut two ratlins* (small lines fastened across a ship's shrouds like ladder rungs) *out of the rigging he gave one to me and the other to the Doctors boy, and gave orders to thrash each other, the rope was frozen, and the Master said that the one that gave in first he would flog.*

When I came to this part in the diary my eyes scanned ahead and I felt relief when I read that James won and his messmates gave him a glass of alcohol. I couldn't begin to imagine what his life must have been like, and I kept comparing his life with that of his namesake, our second son James at the same age - our son who had a life where three meals appeared on the table daily, whose clothes were washed, mended and ironed, who had an education and a family and a mother to look after him when he was sick. I studied the one photograph we have of this first James Heberley, taken when he was most probably in his 60s, and I tried to see beyond the rugged face as I grew closer to the young James.

In 1826 James arrived in Sydney, and from there he drifted into the whaling business. It was whaling which brought him first to New Zealand in 1827 aboard the *Caroline*, a sperm whaler.

Of his arrival in the bay of Islands, James writes:

> *The Natives were at war with one another. We were obliged to lift our Anchor and shift farther out, to get clear of the shot, the war lasted for three days. Then they came on board and traded we got a good supply of Potatoes and Pigs we laid there about a fortnight, the Women came on board and every Man took a Wife to himself, we gave them Shirts and Tobacco which pleased them. There was a Slave Girl on board, she had a child on her back by accident she dropped the child overboard, belonging to a Chief, the child was not drowned, but the Chief took the Slave girl on shore, and hung her up by the heels and stabed her in the back of the neck and sucked her blood until he was tired, then the Chief Wife took a turn at sucking the Girls blood till she was tired, and so on, till the girl was dead. Then they cut her up and cooked her in a copper.*

James stayed with the *Caroline*, sailing as far as Japan, until April 1830. When he was paid off in Sydney, he shipped aboard the *Waterloo*, a schooner belonging to Captain John Guard, my mother-in-law's great-grandfather. John Guard had enticed his crew with stories of plenty of houses in Te Awaiti, and plenty of native women. And, they were told, all they'd have to do was go out in their boats and catch the fish for the women to clean and cook.

The ship sailed from Sydney on 1 April 1830 and arrived at Te Awaiti on 14 April. James wrote:

> *I found he had made a fool of me, there was no houses there, only places built of high posts which the Natives used to keep their Provisions in.*

Armed with a tomahawk, James went into the bush to cut timber to build himself a house.

> *I saw a great many dead bodies. I suppose there was about 50 or 60 on the ground besides Heads Arms and joints, some of the joints were cooked, there was like a young child stuck upon a stick before a Fire that had been lighted the Natives had their full and left the rest. The Natives had gone to Kaipoa* (Kaiapoi) *to fight, they left a few Natives behind to look after there land.*

I couldn't imagine all these experiences happening to one person in a lifetime. But James Heberley had seen all this, and he was only 20 years old.

The Maori living at Te Awaiti helped James build his house and he paid them with tobacco but while his house was being built he slept in a Whata (Maori food-house). One morning he was woken by a chief's daughter calling, "Ai tangata whata haeremai mou te kai." Translated it meant, "Oh, man of the food-house, come and get your breakfast."

The natives called him Tangata whata from that day although the whalers called him Worser, thought to be a European corruption of the word, Whata. I still prefer the more colourful version of his name which originated in his piloting days on Wellington Harbour. When he was asked to forecast the weather, his frequent reply was, "It's getting worser and worser."

Worser Bay in Wellington was named after him but whether it came from the corrupted version of Whata or his gloomy predictions of the weather is unknown. In James's diary he admitted to being better known by the name of Worser.

Whaling began two weeks after Worser arrived in New Zealand.

> *We pulled to the Heads of Queen Charlottes Sound, some go on shore and some stop in the Boats fishing, till sundown. Sometimes we go to Rununder Point in search of whales, but more often to the Heads.*

Worser was at Te Awaiti when the Maori returned from Kaiapoi on 10 May 1830. A truly dreadful time then ensued, just around the channel from us.

> *There was about 2000 Natives including females and children, among them were 500 prisoners, they had from 60 to 70 Canoes, the Canoes were decorated with dead Mens*

Hands and Heads they landed at Te Awaite. They had a feast, the Chief Te Rauparaha send some of the Prisoners Slaves in the bush to get Firewood to make a Copper. That is a hole made in the earth and a Fire made in it, as soon as the oven was ready then the Chief took his Tomahawk and kill the Slave Prisoners that fetched the wood to cook themselves, then some of the other slaves cook his friends, and dish them up in baskets and set the human flesh before the Chief got up and made a speech, after that they all sat down and feasted. They stopped about nine days on the beach with us.

Worser went to Port Underwood and it was here he met Maata Te Naihi, more commonly known as Te Wai, of the Ngati Awa tribe. Her whakapapa taken from the records of the Maori Land Court in the Nelson Minute Book 1/149150, shows she was a direct descendant of Te Kurakaewhao and Tuta.

I took a Wife I bought her for a blanket, she was not a slave. I took her to Te Awaiti and she reared a large family.

Worser and Te Wai spent time in both Te Awaiti and Port Underwood. He writes of living in the Port during the summer and while there built houses and readied the fishery in that place before going back to their old station at the fall of the year, or the autumn - the whaling seasons, I remembered, always began during April.

Houses must have been rebuilt regularly.

The Southern Natives came back and set fire to our houses and destroyed our crops, we took to our boats and crossed the Straits to the North Island. We stopped at Kapiti Island until the war was over which lasted five weeks. The Natives came back to the Sound we all came back with them in our own Boats. The Southern Natives had gone back to Otago, and we went to Port Underwood and got ready for the season.

It was a man's world. To survive they had to be tough, but as for the women - their strength and resilience must have been superb.

My wife was confined on 27 December 1832 of a Girl, the following month we left Cloudy Bay, the same day we arrived in Queen Charlottes Sound we put up a bit of a Shanty to live in, and then we went in for gardening and sowing crops, and built fresh houses.

Once again Maori came up from the south. In the diary I read that there were about 60 natives living at Te Awaiti and they had what Worser described as a 'running fight' with the southern tribe before everyone from Te Awaiti took to their boats and canoes to escape the marauders who chased them part way across the Strait. Worser landed at Waikanae where he left Te Wai and her baby, Margaret, among her own tribe before coming back to Kapiti.

It was at Kapiti that Te Rauparaha saved Worser's life. I think about the might-have-beens of history. If Te Rauparaha hadn't intervened, I wouldn't have been one of those ripples on the ever-widening circle from that one pebble, and my books of course would never have been written.

> *One of the Waikato Natives jumped in the Boat with a toma-hawk in his hand, he was lifting the Tomahawk to strike me in the head, the Chief sang out in Maori language, do not kill him, the Chief threw a mat over me to save me.*

Worser paid his attackers off with all the tobacco he had. He stayed at Kapiti for two months and in June came back to Te Awaiti to find their houses and crops destroyed again. They lived on fern roots and fish until August 1934 when the *Shamrock* sailed into the bay under the command of Captain Williams. He agreed to purchase the bone of the whales that the men caught, and said he would sail to Wellington and bring back potatoes and pigs.

They made the return journey in a strong sou'easterly. A sudden squall capsized the ship in the bay. There were about 30 natives on board and four Pakeha. Only two Pakeha survived. The Maori placed a tapu on the area because their relatives had drowned there, and for the next six weeks, until another ship arrived from Kapiti and bought the whale-bone, the inhabitants of Te Awaiti lived off the lip of a right whale.

Worser left Queen Charlotte Sound and travelled down to Cloudy Bay where he joined up with the American whalers under the management of a Mr Furby. Once the whaling season finished he returned to the Sounds until the following autumn. In his diary Worser says that there were now many natives in the bay.

> *There was three Tribes of Natives, the Southern Natives paid us another visit, but they got a cold reception for we were ready for them, we met them at Cloudy Bay. We fought them and we lost about 40 men which they cut up and put*

> *in Baskets to eat and we killed 203. The fight lasted about three weeks. The last day of the fight, the Ngatiawa tribe wanted to charge them, but the chief Te Rauparaha sang out to stop till tomorrow, so the tribe retreated and several of the Southern Natives that night made their escape.*

Worser and some of the Ngati Awa tribe rushed the pa for plunder.

> *It was very dark, and the first thing I fell over was a man's Leg and thigh, after that I fell on my Face, into a basket of Shoulders and wrists. I and three more men captured a Woman and gave her to the chief. The Chiefs wife got jealous of her Husband, so the Chief killed the Woman and told the Slaves to clean her, and cook her, they made a fire and singed her like a Pig, they scraped her, and then cut her up and baked her. They did not eat much of her, they said she was to salt, so they threw the remainder of her to the Dogs. That was all the slaughter that year.*

Worser was 26 years old.

During the 1836 whaling season Worser fell into a pot containing 200 gallons of hot whale oil. He was rolled in calico and linseed oil, and was on crutches for four weeks before he returned to Te Awaiti, the place he called his summer seat, as he couldn't work for the remainder of the season.

A trader, Mr Ferreby, who was an agent for a firm in Sydney, settled in Te Awaiti, trading in flax, staves, spars and whalebone. He employed many men but they weren't paid for their work. Instead they had to take sugar, soap, tobacco, spirits or clothing. Worser sometimes earned £220 per year but it was money not seen when the Sydney merchants charged five shillings for one bar of soap and one shilling for a pound of sugar, and moleskin trousers cost £1 per pair. If anyone wanted to return to Sydney, the fare was £60 - when this is converted to dollars, there isn't much difference between it and a special low cost fare across the Tasman today.

When the *Hannah*, a Sydney-based schooner, arrived in Queen Charlotte loaded with general stores, her crew ran away, so the Captain asked Worser, Mr Barrett and Mr Love if they'd sail to Sydney with him as crew. They left New Zealand on 18 December 1836. The voyage took 13 days, and when they were paid off the three men received about £400 between them. They heard rumours that English settlers were coming out to New Zealand and they would arrive in the lower half of the North Island so they spent their profits on tobacco and blankets to use for trade.

Back at Te Awaiti, Worser found more hostilities and put Te Wai aboard the vessel, *James of Capetown*, for protection. In this year, 1837, their second child, John, was born. I tried to visualise Te Wai's fear, with the responsibility of a five-year-old daughter, pregnant and then with a newborn baby, and the natives fighting all around her. It is actually such a short time ago, yet it is almost impossible to comprehend - to compare her life with my own.

Worser's diary records that, when the fighting stopped, the tobacco and blankets were traded for land and pigs.

> *We had as much right to the land as the New Zealand Company for there trade was no better than ours the Natives will sell the land over and over again.*

The *Tory*, with Colonel Wakefield aboard, arrived in Ship Cove, Queen Charlotte Sound, in September 1839. A crewman walked over the hill to the settlement at Te Awaiti where he found the men trying out a whale, so the following day Worser and Dicky Barrett, with a crew, rowed a whaleboat around Arapawa Island to visit Colonel Wakefield anchored in Ship Cove. The whalers were invited aboard and were introduced to the Colonel. He wanted to know the best place for a settlement. When they suggested Port Nicholson, Wakefield asked Worser to sail with him and pilot the ship, and Barrett to be his interpreter. The following day they sailed back around the Sounds in the *Tory* to Te Awaiti, where they anchored for two weeks until the whaling season was over.

Wakefield described Te Awaiti in his journal, dated 1 September 1839:

> *There were about 20 houses presented to our view; the walls generally constructed of wattle supple-jack, called kareao, filled with clay; the roof thatched with reeds; and a large unsightly chimney at one of the ends, constructed of either the same materials as the walls, or of stones heaped together by rude masonry. A nice stream runs through the middle of the settlement. Some of the whalers were dressed in their Sunday clothes, but a large gang were busy at the try-works, boiling out the oil from the blubber of a whale lately caught. It appears that this is a process in*

which any delay is injurious. The try-works are large iron boilers, with furnaces beneath. Into these the blubber is put, being cut into lumps of about two feet square, and the oil is boiled out. The residue is called scrag, and serves to feed the fire. The oil is then run into coolers, and finally into casks for shipping. The men are unshaven and uncombed, and their clothes covered with dirt and oil. Most of them are strong and muscular men; and they reminded me, as they stoked the furnaces and stirred the boiling oil, of Retzsch's grim imagination of the forge in the forest, in his outline illustrations of Schiller's ballad of Fridolin. On asking one whether they always worked on Sundays, he answered contemptuously, 'Oh! Sunday never comes into this bay.'

Wakefield went on to describe the beach and ground in the area as being saturated in oil, and the stench of the carcasses and scraps of whale flesh lying about in the bay as intolerable. In later years the station housed as many as 700 people.

When Worser left aboard the *Tory* to pilot the New Zealand Company's first ship on its land-buying excursion, he left behind Te Wai and their two older children and their three-month daughter, Sarah.

We brought up at petone and traded for land the trade was muskets and fowling pieces powder lead red blankets pipes Beads jews Harps umbrellas tomahawks calico print tobacco and such like things. There was no writing to show the boundarys or any quantity of land but a certain hill or point.

Worser piloted the *Tory* on to Wanganui and New Plymouth. While becalmed, Worser amused himself by catching barracouta using a nail which was driven through a piece of red wood, then bent in the shape of a hook. Arriving in New Plymouth, Worser and Barrett were put ashore and asked to wait while the *Tory* sailed north to Kaipara.

Dr Ernst Dieffenbach, the German scientist, had come to New Zealand aboard the *Tory* and he too left the ship in New Plymouth, and, with two Maori porters, he attempted to reach the summit of Mt Egmont. Barrett lent the cook as he himself, although in his 30s, was too fat to take part in the expedition. It failed, and on their return to

Wanganui Dieffenbach asked Worser if he would accompany him on his next attempt.

> *We started on the 13 of December 1839, the party consisted of Dr Dieffenbach and Black Lee myself and three Natives belonging to Wanganui we were 12 days going to the top we did not travel fast as the Dr was looking for specimens, I carried my gun and blankets, the natives carried our provisions.*

On Christmas Eve they camped on a ledge covered with English grass and buttercups, and the next day set off on the last stage. When they reached the snow the natives sat down, took out their books and began to pray, but Dieffenbach, Black Lee and Worser kept on until they came to a steep ridge of burnt clay and small pumice stone: *It was loose we had great difficulty to ascend we would go eight or nine steps up and slip back three or four.* Black Lee slipped and Dieffenbach went to his assistance. Worser didn't stop.

> *I got on top of the mountain about 20 minutes before the Dr. I wanted to call it mount Victoria, there was not room for two men to stand on top there are three rocks they stand in a triangle we found a skeleton of a rat on top, we lit a fire with sum small wood we fetched up in a handkerchief we put snow in the panikan and boil the snow water to measure the height of the mountain we found it to be 8883 feet above the level of the sea.*[1]

Worser is credited with being the first Pakeha to reach the summit of Mt Egmont, the official height of which is now recorded at 8260 feet or 2518 metres.

It is generally accepted that he was also Wellington's first pilot.

An article in the May 1982 edition of the Wellington Harbour Board's magazine, *Beacon*, read: 'The first harbour pilot, James Heberley, was appointed in 1842 but it was not until the early 1860s that the first official pilot station was established at Tarakena Bay.'

As more immigrant ships arrived, it seems apparent that Wakefield commissioned Worser to act as the pilot.

---

[1] At a lower pressure, water boils faster because it boils at a lower temperature. Dieffenbach would have had a table which gave the temperature of the water and the pressure at which it boiled, and another with the pressure and the conversion of the height he boiled the water. It was a measurement close to the official one of 8260 feet, when all the men used was a thermometer and a pan of boiling water.

*Colonel Wakefield sent me to the heads as pilot I remained
there two years there was no salary given no pay but what
I got from the shipping, there were two natives which was
grandfather and uncle to my wife they gave me the bay
known as Worsers bay to live they pulled down the old hut
and lent me a hand to build a new house the piloting was
not sufficient to pay me a crew and I left it and came to
town and started fishing and in the whaling season I went
to the sound whaling.*

Tarakena Bay lost its name years ago. The propeller of the *Wahine* sits on one of its headlands as a memorial to one of New Zealand's worst maritime tragedies when the *Wahine* went aground on nearby Barretts Reef, with the loss of 51 lives, on 10 April 1968. No doubt when Worser told people where he worked he'd have described Tarakena Bay as being "outside the Heads and facing Cook Strait. The first bay, west of the western ledge reef between Chaffers Passage and Lyall Bay." Although sheltered from the nor'west and giving a clear view of Cook Strait, it is exposed to the southerlies. Whether or not Worser did much piloting after the first two years is speculation but he did commute across the Strait regularly in his rowing boat.

In 1841 the Wesleyan missionary, the Reverend Samuel Ironside, came to Te Awaiti and baptised about 200 children and married about 40 couples. His Register of Marriages shows Worser and Te Wai were married on 13 December, and his Register of Baptisms shows their three children were baptised the same day.

Over the years I have accumulated pages and pages of family history. Now as I pored over them for this book I was caught in Worser's time-frame. At night my sleep was filled with dreams that I could always link to what I'd read and written that day. They were graphic dreams that left me breathless with the remembered pain of birth, or sick despair when I recalled my own loneliness in the first months I lived at Okukari. On other nights I'd wake with pounding heart as I relived the times when I've had to deal with a sick child or cope with death. Now it was no longer Worser's face I studied. It was Te Wai's face which fascinated me as I tried to merge into the life she led.

Between 1841 and 1856, Te Wai had five more sons to Worser - James, Thomas, Jacob, Joseph and Henry. By now Te Wai and Worser were living a further three miles down the channel from Te Awaiti, at

Yellaton, so with Worser either piloting or visiting Wellington, away whaling between May and September, or else fishing, Te Wai must have spent most hours with only her children for company.

Ropoamo Te One and his wife Haneta Torea, (Toea), Te Wai's uncle and aunt, gave Worser and Te Wai the block of land known as the Yellaton Run, of 1156 acres. There are varying dates as to the year he was given this land but I found a clue in a diary kept by the South Island explorer, Thomas Brunner. He was in the Marlborough Sounds in 1854, surveying various reserves claimed by the Maori in accordance with the terms of the purchase of their lands by Sir George Grey. On Christmas Day he wrote that he had dined with the Heberleys, and that James Heberley had been living there about 20 years and had a good house and garden. Worser also claimed a small piece of land at Te Awaiti - about 120 yards by 40 yards. I wondered if this was where he built his original house when he first arrived in New Zealand.

I discovered Worser must have been a great letter-writer. I carefully read his many letters as he tried to establish his legal right to land in Queen Charlotte Sound and even in Wellington at the site of Pipitea Pa, an area bounded by Moore Street, Pipitea Street, Thorndon Quay and the pa. He was successful in his land claim in Tory Channel and mention was made of the fact that, as he'd assisted with the colonisation of New Zealand with his piloting skills, his claim should be favourably considered. His land grant for Yellaton stated it was Worser's and Te Wai's for their natural life and then it would pass into the hands of their children.

Gaps opened up in the record of his life, and I can only presume that as he grew older he began to fish more. Brunner wrote in his diary that he gave a message to a settler informing him that he (Worser) had received the money for the fish but no accompanying letter.

When he was in his 60s Worser still rowed across Cook Strait to Wellington. He became one of the best-loved characters of the new town. During the 1870s the skipper of the coastal trader, *Falcon*, spotted him sailing his 14-foot dinghy across the strait. A stiff nor'wester was blowing and in reply to an offer of a tow Worser replied, "Tow? Why should I want a tow? I'm all right." They left him sitting there, "cosy and smoking an old black pipe with only a dog for company".

I like to think that in the latter part of her life Te Wai saw more of her husband and that her life might have been easier, especially after

John and Charlotte were married and Worser and Te Wai lived with them in Oyster Bay. She died in June 1877. Before her death she had buried three children, Margaret, aged 30, Sarah, aged 23, and a son, Thomas, aged 23. Her son Jacob was only beginning his career in Maori carving, with his first carving being documented in 1869. Jacob carved a walking stick for his father which he used till the day he died.

Joseph, Te Wai's seventh child, acted as Picton's harbourmaster at times. He died at the age of 35 and his sons, Herbert and Thomas, came to live with Jacob and his family in Petone. Under Jacob's teaching, Thomas became a skilled carver. In 1926 he was appointed Government carver and for the last 10 years of his life he was employed by the Dominion Museum in Wellington, refurbishing and restoring many items and preparing collections for display.

Picton became Worser's home, and a house built in Surrey Street for him remained in the Heberley family until 1967. He lived here with his new wife, Charlotte Emily Joyce, a widow whom he married in 1879. I was intrigued when I read that one of Charlotte's granddaughters from her first marriage, Lottie Godfrey of the wellknown Marlborough family, was the mother of Janet Frame, the leading New Zealand writer. Janet Frame refers to Worser Heberley in her autobiography, *To the Is-land*.

Worser became wellknown in the town and it was only in the last few months of his life that his health deteriorated and he became weak and cantankerous. The night before he died he appeared downhearted and admitted to being not comfortable in his mind. This comes from Henry Joyce, his stepson, who had known him for 20 years and who had spoken with him that night.

Worser died on 26 September 1899 at the age of 90. It seems that he had wandered, for he drowned in the shallow water of Picton harbour, caught in the mud, still clutching the head of the carved walking stick Jacob had made. He was buried with the end of the stick in his hand. A new head was carved for it, and Charlie, my father-in-law, uses this stick today.

It seems ironic that a man who had served such a long apprentice-ship to the sea should die by it. In his lifetime he had seen New Zealand grow from heathenism to Christianity, and move towards European civilisation. He'd witnessed the purchase of Wellington for a cargo which included slates and slate pencils, and Jew's harps and beads. But through his children he left behind the chance that one day his story would be recorded.

Charlotte, his widow, died shortly after Worser.

John, Worser's and Te Wai's second child and first-born son, took over Yellaton Run. He married English-born Charlotte Hockey and they had 10 children in the years between 1859 and 1887. A son, John, drowned under the Picton wharf when he was seven. Another son, born in 1875, was given the name John Thomas. Arthur, born 25 November 1880, was my Joe's grandfather while Charles, the youngest son, was killed in France during the First World War.

In 1888 a Lease in Perpetuity was granted to John Heberley for 1048 acres in Oyster Bay. This adjoined Yellaton, and the rent of 20 pounds 19 shillings and 2 pence was to be paid twice yearly in advance. It was in Oyster Bay that John and Charlotte built their home and raised their family.

Joe and I took my in-laws to Oyster Bay in 1996. Charlie pointed out where John's and Charlotte's home had been. Only a small area of cleared ground with a poplar tree growing to one side remains. "The poplar tree grew from the branch that had been Grandma's clothesline," Charlie told us. The house had been built on the water's edge and he recalled stories his uncles used to tell him of how they'd lie in bed with a fishing line tied to their big toes with the lines out the window. They'd catch groper that swum into the bay, feeding off bloater or sardines.

Today the water in the bay is shallow from the mud that has swept down the hill from the bulldozing which has been carried out over the years as the land usage has changed from farming to forestry. Where sheep grazed on cleared hillsides, straight lines of pine trees grow. Charlie told me how his grandfather, John Heberley, and his uncles had cleared the steep gullies in Oyster Bay. "It was called a drive," Charlie recalled. First of all, the undergrowth was cut, then four or five bush-fellers climbed the steep faces, scarfing the trees as they went. At the top each man took a tree and yelled, 'Right!'

The top trees fell on the trees below, and all the scarfed trees created a domino effect. The noise could be heard as far as Okukari. Now covered in pine trees, the land has completed a full circle.

John Heberley was not only a farmer. He had his Master's Certificate of Service, granted on 21 May 1885. It stated that he was employed in the capacities of Master in the British Merchant Service in the Home Trade. He whaled alongside the Jacksons, Nortons and Thoms, from the rowing boats based at Te Awaiti until the early 1900s

A controlled burnoff.

And one of its casualties. Joy, on the right and Rachael try to bring relief to the merino caught in the fire.

The Endeavour

*Bud, one of the pet lambs,
refuses to be caught.*

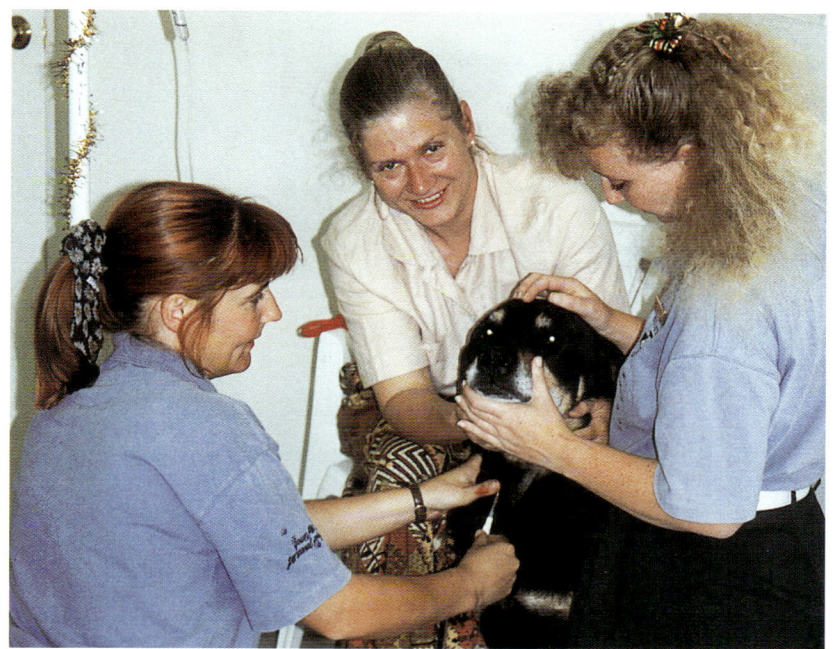

Pauline inserts the catheter into Toby for his chemotherapy treatment. He is held by his owner, Sue Edwards, and vet nurse, Kerry Kinder.

The seventh generation at Christmas 1996. The four girls from left are Amanda, Rachael, Angela and Danielle. The boys from left are Carl, Haydn and Glen.

With His Excellency the Governor-General, Sir Michael Hardie Boys, after Joe had received his Queen's Service Medal at Government House, Wellington, on 15 May 1997.

From left: Dene, Joy, Young Joe, me, Joe, Sir Michael, Ruby, Charlie, Lisa, James and Pauline.

Helen and Peter, unable to be present, sent flowers to Joe at Government House. (Photography by Woolf) when he set up a whaling factory at the head of Yellaton. They had a Cornish boiler and digesters which were about five feet high and four feet in diameter. The blubber was pushed into these while the men set the fire going in the boiler to raise the steam which was then piped into the digesters. The only way they could replenish the water was by drawing the fire out, then letting the manhole go to let off the pressure. Water was bucketed back in, the fire relit and the process started again. Whale numbers were dropping, and problems with the boiler, as well as the five miles to the entrance of Cook Strait, made the 70-year-old give up the idea of his own station.

Shore whaling wasn't as profitable as it had been at the turn of the century. When a Gisborne man, Captain W H Tucker, who leased Campbell Island, approached the men at Te Awaiti asking if they'd like to work on his station and shear his 7000 sheep and lambs in summer and hunt whales in winter, a group of the young men decided to go. Among them were Charles, Harry and John Thomas Heberley. John Thomas led the expedition. They sailed from Bluff aboard the *Hinemoa* early in 1909 and among their equipment were building materials, a launch and a whale boat. They built huts in Northwest Bay where they lived during the winter months when they were whaling.

Charlotte had died in 1908, and while John was in Bluff waiting for his sons' return from Campbell Island, he too died on 2 September 1909. They brought his body back to Picton where he was buried on 12 September.

The Heberleys stayed with the group on Campbell Island for two years, and many of those days were too rough to whale or shear. Notes from a diary belonging to one of the men give an insight into some of those days: 'Nothing doing all making trinkets out of Sperm whale bone.' Another entry: 'Went out on harbour, got sea lion, others trinket making, August making a model.'

Arthur Heberley took over the farm in 1909. He married Ada Louise Rolinson and they had four sons: Joe who was born in 1909, Herbert 1911, Jim 1913, and Charles 1918, and when the wife of one of Arthur's cousins died in childbirth in 1911 they adopted the child, Mona Agnes. They built their home at the head of Oyster Bay where it stood until it was bulldozed to the ground around 1968 after Herbert Heberley, Ada and Arthur's second son, sold the property.

The boys grew up with a 3000-acre backyard to play in. Work was always turned into games, and they were inventive. When their old draughthorse died their father was away and they had to bury it. They faced up to things that few of today's children could or would handle. Charlie told me they dug the hole beside the head horse. When the hole was deep enough they tied ropes on its legs and pulled the horse into the grave. It fell in with its legs in the air, and the four small boys couldn't lift it out so they took their father's saw and sawed off its legs. They laid them beside the horse and then gave it a decent burial.

Another job was gathering wood to boil water for their mother's washing copper. This had to be in short lengths, so Charlie said they used to go up to the top of the wood wire where his father would send bundles of firewood down on a wire which was about 300 metres long, and coming from a height of 60 metres. A favourite pastime was to hang on to the wire and slide down it the first few feet until their feet left the ground, when they'd let go. A visiting cousin, Noel Rolinson, was persuaded to try it - but he forgot to let go. With tears in his eyes from remembered shock Charlie finished the story. "In the middle of the wire's run there was a huge drop and Noel sailed over this. I closed my eyes. I couldn't watch. Then I opened them a crack to see him hit the ground at an angle and roll along the ground. If he'd hit the woodstack he'd have splattered."

The same cousin came back for more. Arthur wanted electricity in Oyster Bay. He had a waterwheel 12 feet in diameter made up in Wellington and had it shipped to Picton. It was sent over in sections and Arthur brought it up to Oyster Bay in his own boat. He built a dam across the creek which came from a large catchment area and flowed down the flats to the sea. A steel pipe, fifteen inches in diameter, which had been acquired from the site of the old Mahakipawa goldmine near Picton, was set into the dam, and, because there was no governor to control the power being generated, the water that flowed through the steel pipe on to the wheel had to be controlled. To do this Arthur had made a wooden slide that could be let up and down over the end of the pipe to adjust the flow, and at one end of the dam there was a spillway that could be opened in a flood.

The four boys often wriggled their way through the pipe when there wasn't any water flowing through. When it was Noel's turn his cousins lifted the slide up and let some water run down. A wide-eyed, skinned-face lad shot out into the creekbed to the loud laughter of his cousins as they ran to the end of the pipe to greet him.

A massive flood ate the end of the dam away, causing it to collapse.

It was then that Arthur brought one of the first diesels into the Sounds. It was a semi-diesel which had a little round bulb that had to be heated with a blow lamp to start it.

Arthur was another Heberley who fished, farmed and whaled. In 1911, two years after John Heberley's death, the first Perano whaler, Joseph August Perano, took over John Heberley's station in Yellaton. With the first of the motor launches he killed a total of six whales for the season. Yellaton also failed for the Perano family because of the distance the dead whales had to be towed. The following year whaling began out of Tipi Bay, a site immediately across Tory Channel from Te Awaiti. Joe and Charlie Perano with Arthur Heberley, Billy Gillice and Sid and Billy Thoms all had shares in the Tipi Bay station. Joe Perano later pulled out and set up the opposition station in Fishing Bay, the bay next to Te Awaiti and closer to the channel entrance.

Whaling was in Arthur's blood. He worked at Tipi Bay as well as being a driver or gunner on one of the chasers. When he wasn't whaling he fished for crayfish, cod and groper in Cook Strait, and also developed the farm into one of the best runs in the Marlborough Sounds, running 3000 romney sheep.

My father-in-law Charlie grew into whaling. He remembers as a child going with his mother to the whaling station in Tipi Bay and watching his older brothers, the oldest no more than 16, working alongside their father, cutting up whales. Their legs were laced with sacking up to their knees for protection, and on their feet they wore short boots. He remembers the day that Joe, his oldest brother, was scalded when a steam pipe burst. It was only his dash to the sea and diving straight into the water that saved him. He remembers the fear when that same brother and Tommy Norton Senior went missing. They'd shot and got fast to a humpback whale off Tokori, a rock near the Brothers Islands in Cook Strait. A southerly ripped through the Strait and Arthur Heberley ordered the men to cut the whale loose and get in out of it. They'd refused, and set off around the top end of Arapawa Island with the dead whale tied alongside the chaser. They steamed all night until they reached Wharehunga, a bay on the opposite side of Arapawa Island from Okukari, where they sheltered. Next morning they arrived in Tipi Bay with their whale. They'd steamed right around Arapawa Island.

The Tipi Bay station began its decline in 1924 when Joe Perano started his whaling from Fishing Bay. Fierce rivalry developed between the Perano brothers and their supporters. Faster boats were built until it reached the stage where seven boats were chasing one whale. A collision at sea resulted in a court hearing.

By 1927 Tipi Bay station was in serious financial trouble. Shareholders were asked to put more money into it. Arthur Heberley chose to pull out and put his money into the family farm. In 1929 the station closed down. The equipment at Tipi Bay was shipped across the channel to Fishing Bay with two of the whale chasers. Arthur Heberley took over the remaining two, the *Oria* and the *Crescent II.*

Back in Oyster Bay the verandah around three sides of the homestead was collapsing so Arthur built a concrete wall around it with windows and partitioned the area off into rooms. With all this space, and with declining wool prices in the years leading up to the Depression of the 1930s, Arthur and Ada decided to take in guests, a business which flourished for the next 25 years. The *Oria* was altered and used, in conjunction with the guesthouse, to take holidaymakers out on fishing trips and picnics.

I never met this man, my husband's grandfather, but from the many letters I received from people who had read *Weather Permitting* and who had also stayed at the guesthouse I grew to know him. One letter read:

> *I remember a reserved, perhaps taciturn man, quietly spoken, but who left one in no doubt that he was the 'Captain'. With never any fuss, with a wonderful economy of movement as in speech, the job was done. Looking after a boatload of totally inept fishermen from the city must have stretched his patience at times but I cannot remember any such occasion - lines were untangled, the regular visitations of blind eels quickly dealt with, and when we landed for lunch at a beautiful bay on the southern end of Arapawa Island, fires sprang to light immediately, one with billies boiling, the other ready for fish wrapped in leaves to cook to perfection.*

> *At the same time, he appeared to take great interest in children, taking time at the picnic to instruct us in the finer points of catching fresh water bullies with the spider webs common on rushes. Another day he stopped to scoop out a quantity of the tiny red swarm of shrimp, wrapped them in*

cloth then placed the bundle round the base of the exhaust stack to steam, then nibble.

The particular feeling of Oyster Bay was the return late afternoon, the only sound the beat of the diesel exhaust stack and the gentle break of water under the bow. A gentle following breeze allowed a slowly dispersing line of perfect smoke rings to mark our passage.

The *Crescent II* was converted to a fishing boat, with their son, Joe, fishing on it out of Wellington. On 30 September 1930 Joe with his crew of three left Island Bay at 6am. Later that day a southerly gale came in and around 2pm the engine stopped because of its dry batteries running down - not like the wet-cell batteries of today. Despite their putting out a sea anchor the boat was carried towards the coast near Owhiro Bay. They sent up rockets and when these were gone Joe soaked his jersey in petrol, lit it and used it as a distress signal.

An earlier *Arahura*, not the Interislander, had left Wellington at 7.30pm and people in Island Bay who were witnessing the tragedy signalled her to see if she could help. She came within 30 or 40 yards of the stricken boat but the horrendous seas prevented her from getting any closer. Attempts by fishermen to send a rescue party from the shore also failed. Cars parked on the shore shone their headlights over the sea. Many of the Italian fishermen jumped into the seas in vain attempts to reach the boat.

The *Crescent II* was swept broadside on to the waves and about 11pm she capsized, throwing the four fishermen into the sea. One man was never seen again. The sole survivor, Arthur Hodgman, later told his story. "We were all thrown into the sea. Heberley was trying to keep Hunter up. He could not swim. We had buoys off the lines. The last time I saw Heberley and Hunter they were struggling together in the water. I saw no sign of Perano."

An article in the *Auckland Weekly News* on 8 October 1930 tells of "a story of heroism which cannot leave one unmoved. Had Joseph Heberley, the skipper of the launch, which was wrecked in a heavy sea, endeavoured to swim straight in when the boat capsized, he would have probably reached the rocks and been rescued. Instead, he stayed in a vain attempt to help one of his comrades, Magnus Hunter, who could not swim, and so sacrificed his own life."

The sea kept Joe Heberley's body for 11 days until an Island Bay fisherman, Tommy Isbistor, found him floating. He was buried in Picton.

So, 31 years after the death of Worser, the sea had claimed yet another Heberley who had been involved with the sea all his life. Joe's leisure had been spent on the sea. Joe rowed for the Picton Rowing club and represented Marlborough. After his death his parents commissioned Tom Heberley, the Government carver, to carve a shield which they donated to the Marlborough Amateur Rowing Association in 1932, for inter-club welter-weight "eight" competitions between Picton, Blenheim, Wairau and Nelson. The centre of the shield is carved in a full Maori design with the sides left plain for the silver shields with the winning club name engraved. At the base there is a silver scroll with the inscription, 'The Heberley Memorial Shield'.

Arthur and Ada Heberley lived for 46 years at Oyster Bay. When they moved to Picton to live in Surrey Street, their second son, Herbert, took over the farm. Arthur died, five days short of his 80th birthday, on 22 November 1960, and Ada seven years later on 10 May 1967.

Nanny Ada was at Okukari and staying with Charlie and Ruby four years after Joe and I were married. I don't know why it happened to me, but a few days before Ada died I woke up one night with someone standing in our bedroom. It remains as vivid in my mind today as it did 30 years ago. I saw a man, dripping wet, with an old-style oilskin coat and sou'wester hat on his head. My screams woke Joe and he tried to pacify me, telling me it was only a dream. Then it became a joke and he'd tell friends that "old Godfrey, the lighthousekeeper, paid Heather a visit". That is until I read on his death certificate that Charles Godfrey had died of 'pyelites exhaustion' and most probably he would have died in his bed. Over the years I've had experiences when people I've loved have died and they've come back to me. I don't know if it's a figment of my imagination and I'm seeing those I long to see once more, or if love is strong enough to reach across the chasm that separates life from death. Whatever, although I never knew him, today I believe my visitor was the Joe who drowned at sea, looking for his mother as she approached death.

Charlie and Ruby, my parents-in-law, married in 1939 and lived at Oyster Bay for four years. In that time they had three children, Donna, Jocelyn and my husband Joe, who was born on 3 January 1943. Ruby has told me stories of experiences not unlike mine. At shearing times

166

while her mother-in-law worked in the woolshed, her own battles with the coal range. Cooking for four shearers and musterers. The smell of the shed. Baking bread. Making jellies for morning and afternoon tea, and trying to get them set in a house that sweltered in the summer heat and with a temperamental kerosene fridge already overloaded. Having to make fruit cakes when she'd never made one in her life. All this was juggled around cooking hot meals for lunch and dinner. "I often had to go over to the shed and get Charlie," Ruby said, "but worst of all was my very capable and efficient mother-in-law. She took everything in her stride. Worked in the shed like a man. Killed her own mutton, ran the guesthouse. All the linen was starched and ironed, and it was nothing to have up to 40 guests. It was always hustle and bustle." I knew what Ruby meant when she said how it made her feel so inadequate.

Memories of whaling stayed with Charlie. In 1941 he began working for the Peranos when he spent two years in the factory at Fishing Bay until 25 June 1943 when a gun exploded aboard a chaser, killing the gunner, Johnny Huntley.

The very next day Charlie was behind the gun. He remembers that day well. "It was a howling sou'easterly gale in Cook Strait. The wind was gusting 40-50 knots in the channel. Two whales came into the channel. I'd never been on a chaser in a hunt or used the gun before but I had a fair idea. I was worried about how I'd perform but I guess because it was in my blood I slipped into it. We managed to kill them fairly quickly. I learnt by experience."

In 1945 Charlie's brother, Jim, left Okukari Bay to live in the city and Charlie and Ruby bought the property that was to become my home. Charlie whaled and farmed until 1957 when he decided to finish with whaling and concentrate on farming.

The Hauraki Whaling Company built a factory in 1956 in Whangaparapara on the Great Barrier Island, 52 miles north-east of Auckland. When it foundered, the Barrier Whaling Company, which was a subsidiary of the Norfolk Island and Byron Bay Whaling Company, was formed. This company didn't know the technique of small boat whaling as they used the larger Norwegian-type chasers, and as Charlie was so familiar with them he was asked if he would manage the station - a position he accepted on his own terms.

Okukari was left in the charge of a farm manager, Joe finished off his fourth form year at college, and early in 1959 Charlie, Ruby and Joe moved to Great Barrier Island.

Charlie's ambition was to produce the best quality oil, to produce a product that was equal or better than anywhere else in the world. To do this, all whales caught were processed within 12 hours. Rather than have a poor quality oil, whales were left unharmed. My father-in-law showed me a photo of a 'blasted' whale and explained.

"If you've got 40 to 50 tons of meat and blubber from a warm-blooded animal in the heat, they deteriorate very quickly. They start to ferment inside and blow up - what we call 'blast'."

Charlie did all the testing in a laboratory at the station and kept the oil to a very low acidity content because of its use in margarine and pharmaceutical products. My father-in-law achieved his ambition and he has a letter from the oil-buyers in Amsterdam commending him on the fine oil that was produced from his station.

From the time I met my Joe in 1961, I found it difficult in some ways to distinguish him from his father. They were so much a part of each other. They lived together and worked together. Charlie drove the chaser and Joe was the gunner. I often heard Charlie say, "I've got a lot of pride in Joe. We're a good team. One of the best."

Ruby was a part of this team, running the base radio set and probably being the only woman in the world to have taken the helm of a chaser while a whale was shot.

In his childhood Joe had longed for his whaling career to begin. On days when he'd be doing his Correspondence School lessons, if the flag went up over on the lookout he'd be up the hill or down on the beach watching. In the evenings, for three months of the year nothing but whaling was discussed at the table. And there were the near-accidents - chasers were holed in the bottom or topsides regularly. "We listened to the stories. There was drama and danger, and as kids we lived by it too."

A fifth-generation whaler, Joe remembers his first day behind the gun. "I was scared as hell." He maintains it wasn't a job, it was more like a traditional sport, and even though it was dangerous the wet and cold were forgotten the moment a whale was spotted. His blood automatically raced when a whale was spotted. He'd grab his lunch tin and tear down to the beach and row out to the whale chaser moored in the bay. "All hyped up - probably like the All Blacks going out on to a rugby field for a test match."

168

At that time Joe and Charlie believed whaling was going to go on for ever with 104 whales caught at the Barrier in 1959, and 135 in 1960, a year in which a total of 361 whales were caught in New Zealand. That same year it was reported that the Russian and Japanese whaling factory ships had taken 42,000 whales. Before Charlie began whaling at Great Barrier, a Russian factory ship passing through Cook Strait had sent one of the 22 chasers it carried inside Tory Channel on a courtesy call. It came into Okukari where Charlie spoke with the skipper of the chaser, and was told that the factory ship could process up to 72 whales in 24 hours. Charlie likened these chasers among the whales to a pack of wild dogs in a mob of sheep in a small paddock.

Whales migrated up from the Antarctic in three streams, and the New Zealand whalers took whales from only one stream.

In 1961 only 26 whales were caught. The Barrier Whaling Company went into receivership in July. Although they knew whale numbers had decreased due to the whaling operations going on in the Antarctic, it was generally believed whaling could still continue from the Barrier, working the station on a profit-sharing basis. A group of men headed by Charlie negotiated for the operating rights, and in 1962 Joe was once again gunning with his father at the helm.

Day followed day when the men would leave Whangaparapara in the early morning darkness and steam down to their lookout on Cape Barrier, only to make the return journey in the dark without making one sighting. Only eight whales were caught in June, and on 7 July 1962 whaling ceased in the Hauraki Gulf. Joe says the devastation of the men was profound. The abandoned station became a ghost town. Grass grew up around the windows of the empty buildings, and the oil tanks rusted in the salt air while the waves and drifting sand removed any sign of an industry that dated back 132 years within New Zealand.

Charlie and Ruby came back to the family farm at Okukari until 1979 when they went to live in Nelson. I hope I'll remember Charlie's parting words when our time comes. "When young ones grow up, you've got to step aside and let them take over."

Our sons will never whale but they are like their forbears, men of the sea. In researching and writing this history I've learnt a great deal. At last I've come to terms with having a husband who enjoys working from daylight till dark, and the guts to get out and do something for others when conditions are bordering on the extreme, but who has the sense to pull out of a situation if it becomes too dangerous. I see something of all Joe's ancestors in him just as I can in all our four children. And as I watch our seven grandchildren growing up I feel I have been given something very precious when I see some of the same characteristics in them.

CHAPTER TWELVE

Fires - and the *Fugitive*

THE SEA is still our highway and source of food, just as it was for primitive man, and we make a living from it, but fire does more than provide warmth for us. Fire is also a way of clearing our land. I've watched it rage over the hills in a controlled burn-off, feeling the heat of the flames across two or three gullies, and watched the speed with which it engulfs everything in its path. I've shut my eyes against the heat and listened to the roar of the flames and crackling of the gorse as it burns and tried to imagine how I'd feel if it was our house that was burning. There'd be no fire brigade to call out here. Joe is the fire officer for our area, and, even with our two sons, one fire pump wouldn't do much.

Weather patterns have changed. My first sight of Okukari in 1962 was through a pall of smoke. From Dieffenbach Point where Tory Channel meets Queen Charlotte Sound, to Okukari at the Cook Strait end, the farmland on Arapawa Island was ablaze. "We burn every year," Charlie told me then. "It's the only way to keep the gorse and scrub down on this land," and by the look of the blackened land even I, the townie, could see what he meant. "One good shower and the hills will be green again," he added.

Over the years our summers seem to have become shorter. The hot dry nor'wester doesn't last as long, and there aren't the long periods without rain. Two or three years with little or no burning, and the scrub grows bigger and doesn't dry out in the summer.

Then forestry began on the island. I can still hear my father-in-law on how forestry would ruin the farms with all the restrictions that would be placed on the farmers. "There'll be no more burning, mark my words," he used to say. And many farmers, unable to burn to the extent they used to, gave up the struggle against the encroaching bush. Some returned their steep land to the Crown and in return were given permission to subdivide their flat land with beach frontages, making smaller blocks. More money was being made from holidaymakers looking for small parcels of land than from farming sheep and cattle. Other farmers sold their land for forestry while some grew pine trees themselves. One or two, like the Heberleys, diversified into fishing.

The remaining farms struggled against bureaucracy. When the land was ripe for burning, a total fire ban was put in place. Fire breaks had to be made - no mean feat when a bulldozer had to be barged in from Picton. Permits had to be obtained. No burning on Saturdays, Sundays or public holidays. If a fire did get away, even though it was burning scrub, a helicopter with a monsoon bucket would be called in to put it out, and the farmer had to pay. Today only three farms remain on Arapawa Island and the land that hasn't been taken up with pines is reverting to native bush.

My introduction to burning off, soon after I'd come from Auckland to Okukari, was supposed to be a day mustering on Sweetlips, a block overlooking Cook Strait. Charlie took Joe and me out in the farm boat and then rowed us ashore where, I was told, we'd climb a bank before starting to muster the seaward side of the block. After dropping us off Charlie would steam back to Okukari Bay where he'd meet up with another musterer, climb the hills behind the house and bring down the sheep on the opposite side from Joe and me.

My eyes didn't take in the climb above me. I was focused on the seas that were crashing on the ledge where Joe and I, and Joe's two dogs, were to be put ashore.

The swells rose and covered the ledge then fell back, sucking tentacles of seaweed and loose stones with them. A seething cauldron of white water formed at the base before crashing up on to the ledge again. As we rowed ashore in the dinghy I simply couldn't believe this was happening to me, and I tried to blot it from my sight. The roar of the sea became louder as we drew closer to the land. I felt the dinghy fall and I knew we'd be in the white water, then we were lifted up and I felt a thud as we landed on the ledge. "Get cracking!" Charlie yelled. "I'll wait for a lull in the swells before I head back to the boat."

With both my feet on the ground, relief surged through me until I looked up to where we had to climb. The bank was a cliff 15 feet high. "Some bank!" I protested when Joe showed me the narrow goat tracks we'd use. I was learning very fast that these Heberley men didn't stand around and wait while a mind was made up because I found myself being cajoled then pushed up the first eight or ten feet. Fear made my hands clammy. I ran my tongue over my top lip and felt a coating of dust caught on beads of sweat. Then I was stuck. Fear froze my body and I couldn't move up or down. My screams telling Joe I wanted to go back fell on deaf ears but Charlie must have heard them because he yelled that I'd have to keep climbing because he'd lit the scrub below me. Smoke filled my nostrils. White hot anger that this was happening to me kept me climbing and made me claw at the rocks. The crackling of the flames blocked out the sound of the falling stones and when I at last scrambled over the top I lay panting and abusing Joe at the same time. "You don't just clear land with your damned fires! You try and kill people!" If I'd had any idea what the future held regarding fires I'd have shrugged that experience off with a laugh. It was minor.

Later I became a fire-bug, vowing death to gorse. I'd set off up the paddock with a milk powder tin with the lid cut out, a wire handle twisted over the top and filled with diesel or kerosene. The end of a green manuka branch or thick gorse stem soaked in the diesel or kerosene burnt for quite a while and I'd enjoy running from bush to bush, poking my burning stick in the middle and hearing the whoosh as the flames leapt into the air. An occasional dip in the bucket kept it alight.

I've had a few close calls with fires but the worst one was when I was burning a large patch of tall gorse. Not concentrating, I was pushing my burning stick into the middle of the gorse bushes where it is always dry, gleefully watching the flames leaping 12 to 14 feet. Suddenly the daylight vanished beneath black smoke and I was surrounded by burning bushes. Aware that my bucket might feed more flames, I heaved it as far away as I could, sank to my knees, and buried my head in my arms. The heat was intense. This was the end, I thought.

But I was so lucky there was no wind that day, and as soon as the flames had roared through the gorse bushes around me it went out. A very smoky and subdued young woman arrived home to be met by a concerned husband. There was a strong smell of wool burning, and I guessed my jersey was singed. I was wrong. As Joe wrapped his arms around me he burst out laughing. Sitting on the top of my head was a thick branch of gorse, still smouldering, and when he plucked it off a chunk of hair came too.

New rules were laid down, rules I still follow. Now when I go burning I leave the bucket of fuel behind and instead I use a burner. This is made from one-inch copper pipe, about the same height and shape as a hockey stick with a cork in the top end and a tap fitted just above the curve. Strips of sacking are rolled into tight rolls then screwed into the pipe below the tap. Diesel or kerosene is poured into the top end, and the cork is pushed in. The flow of burner fluid can be regulated by the tap, and the wick kept burning or turned off as required. This has made me safer but it didn't stop me creating one of the more potentially serious fires in our bay.

It was only a little fire. I was burning rubbish in the back yard before we moved into our new house. Behind the little house there was a shelter of old pine trees. Years of pine needles lay beneath them, and fallen trees were overgrown with a wild creeper, much of which was smothered with rambling roses. A narrow ditch which had been dug for the footings when we added on the two bedrooms was the only clear space.

This was the most junk I'd ever got rid of on one bonfire, and just as I was going through the last box and deciding whether there were one or two things in it which I should be keeping, a gust of wind caught some burning paper and carried it into the creeper. The flames sizzled through the undergrowth towards the trees. Joe and Charlie were up the hill making fires for a burn-off, while Ruby, who'd run over to our house when she saw my flames, and I were trying to put one out.

I grabbed the hose and ran with it as close as I could get to the heat of the flames. "Wetting the bush'll help!" yelled Ruby. The water trickled out the hose. My finger over the end stopped it altogether. "You'll have to run up to the dam. Quick! The pipe might be out."

My heart pounded as I tore up the hill only to find there was no water. The dam was dry and we'd have to wait for the water to build up. By this time Joe and his father had arrived - they'd seen our fire. Water baled from the goldfish pond did little to halt the flames and in desperation the men brought the fire extinguishers up from the boats, but they proved useless in these circumstances.

Joe Perano, Gilbert's brother, was involved that day in catching porpoises for Napier's Marineland. He had a crew of five or six aboard his boat and they'd been netting the porpoises and holding them in a Para pool which had circulating water pumping through. They kept this on the breastworks of the closed-down whaling station, and from there they were taken to Picton and transported to Napier. Joe Perano had seen our fire as he steamed past the bay with his catch of dolphins, and as soon as they were in the pool they all arrived to help.

We had to let the fire in the undergrowth burn. There was no way we could stop that. But they dug a fire break around the pine trees. Just on dark we got it under control, but not before two pine trees went up in flames. The sight remains with me still. If I close my eyes and imagine the roar, I can see the whole tree lit up from the bottom to top and engulfed with flames, the branches black within the orange flames and the thick smell of the burning pine mixed with the smoke.

The box of rubbish that I'd been wondering whether or not to burn moved up to the new house with us. My fire-lighting days were over for a while.

The aftermath of this fire came more than a week later. Something woke me. My eyes shot open and I could see a red glow reflecting from the paint on our bedroom door. Yelling at Joe I jumped out of bed and ran into the kitchen. Through the windows over the laundry tubs I saw flames. All I could think of was that our children were asleep in the two rooms against that back wall. Joe woke the girls and I ran to the boys. They were asleep in their bunks and I brushed against the wall as I pulled their blankets off. It was red hot.

That night we had water, and although we could get the fire out I was past sleep when we got back to bed. The thought of what could have happened took a long time to go away. The fire must have smouldered deep down in the pine needles, and the strong nor'westerly wind we had that night had fanned it so it burnt back through the creeper. And it had all started with such a little fire.

Joe didn't let me live my fire down for a long time. Part of me didn't want to forget it, either, as it made me realise just how terrible a fire can be. For months after my fire I'd wake up bathed in perspiration. Always the same nightmare had me seeing our four children burning in their beds.

Joe's was the next fire to cause trouble but it also gave us the name for the new boat we were having built.

True to Charlie's words, we now needed a fire-permit to burn. Many farmers took it lightly and didn't bother to obtain a permit or ask permission to burn. Joe had watched fires going up from nearby farms until he couldn't stand it any longer. "They can't have one," he argued, when I told him he'd better get a permit. "It's a Saturday."

Before long smoke was drifting out of our bay and mixing with all the other smoke. When Joe arrived home he was met on the wharf by a local policeman, who happened to be a friend. He'd come down on the boat with the Rural Fire Service and he greeted Joe with, "What the hell do you think you're doing, mate? These guys mean business."

Not long after this, Joe was served with a summons to appear in court, charged with lighting fires without a permit. A very nervous man left home that morning and it was just as well we were connected to the telephone by then because he rang me four or five times before his court appearance, needing to talk. By the time he was due in court he'd made me as nervous as he seemed to be, wondering what the outcome might be. He was fined, but he always maintained that the land he'd cleared was worth it.

Sitting at the table that night Joe told me how he'd felt like a hardened criminal while waiting to go into court, and in the middle of relating his story he hesitated before blurting out, "We'll call our new boat *Fugitive*."

Joe didn't say much to anyone else about his day in court and on the day of the launching there were many who wondered about the name of the newly-launched fishing vessel.

Being greeted by men from the Rural Fire Service and a local policeman were nothing compared with the advice which was offered to Joe another time when he'd just arrived off the hills after burning-off all afternoon.

It was a stinking-hot day and from all the smoke that had been pouring out of the bay I knew he'd had some great fires. Joe told me later that when he got closer to home his tongue started to hang our for a nice cold beer. As he was walking across the bottom paddock he noticed an aluminium boat coming in to the beach. Two men climbed out and met Joe at the top of the track that leads from the beach. He'd stopped to talk to them, hoping they weren't going to hold him up. "I was hot and buggered. Thinking of that beer in the fridge. One said to me, 'Nice farm you've got here, Joe, but you're wasting your time, you know.' "

Joe didn't know who he was talking to but he sailed into him and asked him what he was talking about.

" ' The world's going to end in a few years,' he said."

These two Jehovah's Witnesses hold the record for having the shortest visit to Okukari.

Losing the smell of burning wood collected from the beach and being able to sit in the darkness looking for patterns in the flames in the open fireplace was nothing compared with the joy of opening the door to a room now warmed with our new slow-combustion wood-burner. Gone were the days of raking out dead ashes every morning before I could light the fire and start to get warm. No more down-draughts that sent choking smoke down the chimney, a film of ash over the room and the fear at night that a log might roll out of the fire. Our new fire had left primitive man far behind.

On this occasion Joe was in Picton with the *Fugitive* on the slip and at home I was making the most of my time alone, sewing some of the 8000 beads on to lace motifs for Pauline's wedding dress. I'd sat in front of the fire sewing until my eyes made me give up, and as I was on my own I left everything lying on the floor.

A southerly gale lowered the temperature and I shut the lounge door so I would get up to a nice warm room in the morning. The wind whistling round the house and the noise of the sea crashing on the beach woke me about 5am. I'd stoke the fire up, I thought to myself, and bring my bead work back to bed and sew while my eyes were fresh. The house was freezing except for the lounge so after I'd stoked the fire up I closed the dampers and gathered up my sewing. On the way out I slammed the door.

For an hour I sat up in bed sewing and when I'd completed a motif I decided to snuggle down into the warmth and perhaps drop off to sleep again for an hour or so.

Days when Joe is away and not going to be home are long, especially when the weather keeps me inside, so I was delighted to find it was after 8am when I woke up for the second time. I felt great. I'd slept well, I already had some bead work done, and when I drew open the bedroom curtains I could see the rain had stopped.

My great feeling evaporated when I opened the lounge door. All I could see was smoke. It appeared to be coming from the wall where our log fire was, rising to the ceiling, curling over and down the opposite wall before pouring over the floor. The sight of the rolling smoke mesmerised me for an instant but the sound of my own indrawn breath snapped me out of the trance and I remembered the golden rule I'd learnt when I studied for my skipper's ticket - keep the hatches shut on an engineroom fire. My lounge wasn't an engineroom but the thought made me shut the door in a hurry. I don't know how long I stood on the other side of that door. I was swallowing hard, trying to still my pounding heart. Big breaths pulled me together and I phoned Young Joe for help. I still had no idea what was burning, or why.

He ran into the room and opened the windows and ranch-sliders, and we could see what had happened. The glass in the firebox had blown out. Glass lay over the floor except for one shard that still hung in the hole. The force of the explosion in the fire-box had thrown out most of the wood which lay burning over the floor. What was left in the fire-box kept on burning but with the dampers closed there was no place for the smoke to go. It stayed in the room. My carpet was covered in smouldering wood and embers. Some had burnt through the carpet and rubber underlay to the particle board.

As the smoke cleared my heart sank deeper when I saw the mess. Cobwebs of soot hung from the curtains that I'd made less than a month ago. They clung to the walls and the ceiling. I brushed some off a wall, and black greasy splodges remained. But in all the mess I could only look in wonder at the spot where I'd left my sewing overnight. Thank God I'd come out early and taken it back to bed with me. It would have been totally destroyed. I thought of the hours I'd spent on it and wondered if I'd have been able to start all over again. The relief carried me through the day as I scrubbed the ceiling and vinyl wall paper and took the curtains down so they could be taken to the dry cleaners when a boat was next going to Picton.

A call to the log fire agents to order a new door horrified us when we were told that it was the third such accident they'd heard of. The problem could have been closing the damper before the fire was properly burning, so gases built up. In those days, too, the glass doors weren't always as strong as they are now.

An insurance assessor came down as I don't think our insurance company believed our story. He just gaped when he saw the path of destruction in front of the fire and across the floor. We were all thankful our carpet was wool and not synthetic or the place would have gone up in flames.

Wet summers had prevented successful burn-offs for some years and gorse and scrub had taken hold on some of the blocks. The big ridge that rises from the head of the flats to meet the road which winds down from Puriri Bay boundary gate had become difficult to muster. Sheep would stand in the thick gorse, and as this is my mustering beat I'd arrive down at the bottom with a lot fewer sheep that I should have had. Each season I'd threaten that this was my last muster.

Every year Joe spends more than $20,000 on aerial spraying. We don't seem to be winning the battle against gorse but it's reached the stage where we can't afford not to do it or the previous year's spraying will have been a waste. We decided 1996 was to be our year for land clearing. The highest block on the farm was to be sprayed, then burnt, and grass seed flown on. The other block Joe hoped to spray and burn was the big ridge.

The boys were away fishing when Colin Bint, who flies for Marlborough Helicopters, phoned and said he'd be in the bay at first light, weather permitting. I spent a night scared to go to sleep as I knew I had to start early to have the spray over in the paddock in the early morning. Colin would want to spray before the wind came up. Daylight was just breaking and as I waited with the spray I watched two Picton fishing boats, their tuna poles reaching to the sky, steam up the channel and head out into Cook Strait bound for the tuna grounds. Gold in the sky must have assured them that settled weather could be expected for the next few days. The thump of rotor blades drowned out the boats' engines as Colin flew into the bay, circled where he was going to spray, then landed beside me. His son, Innes, climbed out and soon had the pump in the creek. The operation began. Spray was measured in the tank first, mixed with a penetrant and then the water.

As Colin took off I squatted behind the bike to keep out of the way of the stones, sticks and water whipped up in the air. Quita, my brave guard dog who'd growled and barked at Innes when he jumped out of the helicopter, now cowered behind him, her coat ruffled in the wind. Before I left for home I watched a couple of loads of spray being dumped and it seemed as if I would be able to keep mustering the big ridge after all.

The gorse slowly died. At first it went dull and then the tips all bent over. Gradually we could see that a good job had been done. Windy days, some very hot, dried out the sprayed gorse. Home from fishing Joe kept an eye on the weather, wanting the gorse to get as dry as possible. Hearing a midday weather forecast with heavy rain predicted made up his mind. He would burn the big ridge that afternoon. And he had a permit this time.

From the house I could see flames roaring up the gullies and high in the sky where they were mixing with thick grey smoke before being carried over the hills into Queen Charlotte Sound. I'm always relieved to see the bike cruising back down the hill so I know Joe is safe - memories of fires are vivid in my mind.

This day when Joe arrived home he was elated with the success of his burn but when I heard his story about how he'd had to take cover in a waterfall when the fire jumped the creek I shuddered. "But it roared up the other side. Come outside and have a look with the binoculars."

From out on the bank I could see the whole of the big ridge. It was black. A log was the only thing still smoking. "Give me a look?" and the binoculars were ripped out of my hands. "Shit! It's the power pole." No "Are you coming?" or "Goodbye." Joe took off on the bike. The sound of the phone ringing made me run inside.

It was Marlborough Electric. "Colin Graeve here, Heather. You got power?" I glanced around and realised nothing was on. When I told him he said he'd make some enquiries and get back to me.

Every time our power goes off I have this urge for a cup of tea while I wait for the power to come back on, so I fill the electric jug. Then I remember - no power. This time it hit me. Joe's power pole. Maybe that's why the power is off? Just as I finished telling Colin that Joe might have burnt a power pole, he rode up to the house on his bike. "Tell Colin it's on the ground," Joe called out when I told him who I was talking to.

It was a pole on the line that feeds electricity out to Perano Head for the radio beacon owned and operated by the Airways Corporation of New Zealand. It provides electronic guidance to aircraft within the Cook Strait, Marlborough and Nelson areas in two ways. It provides pilots with their bearings from the ground station and also their distance from the sight. It means that pilots can fly using instruments rather than visual references and the 30-metre diameter dish sends out its signals to about 250 kilometres. Colin told us he'd send a helicopter out to the island with some men to pull the pole fuse where the line splits sending power out to Perano Head and down into Okukari Bay. "It'll give you power tonight. We'll send a crew down in the morning to replace the burnt pole."

I sailed into Joe. Planes might crash and it would be our fault. And the cost. "It's user pays now," I reminded him. My placid Joe reminded me that planes hadn't crashed before it was built so why should they now. "Anyway," he informed me, "it's all duplicated to provide a reliable service. The standby batteries will have swung into action now. They can run for at least 10 hours or so."

When I rang our insurance company to check that a burnt power pole was covered I was assured it was. The bright efficient voice dropped when I told her the helicopter was just landing in the bay to pull the pole fuse. Our $15 we'd paid for the cover was a wise investment, we decided, when we received an account, for the total job, of nearly $4000 from the Power Board.

Joe wasn't allowed to forget the trouble he'd caused with his last fire, and, when it came time to burn the second block, quite a few pointed comments came his way. But he assured everyone this fire would be safe because there weren't any power poles to burn. We'd left this block longer as we'd used two chemicals. Before Christmas we'd sprayed the gorse with one chemical, and the scrub was sprayed later with another. For this burn Joe wanted a westerly wind and a hot sunny day.

I knew it was no place for a woman or children but I had to see the block burn. Rachael and Angela came up the paddock with me and we climbed a hill and sat on the next ridge over from the block. It was a long wait as Joe, Young Joe and James worked out where each of them would begin the burning. I lay back in the grass, shutting my eyes against the sun's brightness and listening to Rachael's and Angela's conversation. The smell of the warm earth mixed with the sweet smell of drying grass made me sleepy; their voices faded. I entered a magical world with dinosaurs, seals and faces with big ears until little girls giggling woke me up and had me staring in vain for the things their youth could see in the clouds.

I could see the three men were ready. Young Joe was going to burn down the fenceline, James was disappearing out of sight down a ridge and Joe was coming further down on the motorbike. It was easy to follow Joe and Young Joe but the only way I could keep track of James was noting new spurts of smoke as he progressed down the ridge and into the gully. I watched in disappointment at the fires. They weren't going to clear much land, I thought.

But suddenly fire took hold. It looked as if all the hundred acres were burning at the same time. The flames roared and joined into one and we couldn't speak above the crackling and roaring. The heat drove us further away. Rachael and Angela panicked when they couldn't see their father and while I was reassuring them I was anxiously scanning the burning land for signs of Joe and James. This was a time when I had to put my trust in their commonsense but I found myself praying. Now and then I'd catch a glimpse of my two Joes but again the only way I knew James was OK was seeing new fires springing up further down the gully. I felt the same fear as I've felt so often when they've been out in the rough seas either fishing or on a rescue, knowing I couldn't do a thing and longing to catch sight of them.

At last three blackened forms appeared and I relaxed. James told me his story.

"I couldn't believe it," he kept repeating. "You've no idea - the noise and roaring of the wind!" He told us how the fire had generated winds of up to 40 knots, and how sticks and pebbles picked up in the wind had stung his face. "I don't mind admitting I was scared. The wind whipped the water in the creek into willywaws. It was feather-white." The story was told with many "awesomes".

As Joe came down the fenceline he saw two merino sheep against the fence on the far side of the block so when they all met up at the bottom they decided to go home and have lunch, then come up, chase out the two sheep and light the other side of the block. In the middle of our lunch billowing smoke blotted out the sun. "Bloody hell. It's jumped the creek." The chair was knocked over in his hurry to get out and, as he took off on his bike I saw James doubling Young Joe up the paddocks. They too had seen the smoke.

But there was nothing they could do to halt the fire's path. Joy and Rachael were already up there and by the time I arrived the face was black.

One merino lay dead against the fence and the other was struggling to walk down the hill. We brought it down and while Rachael and Joy held it in the creek I brought the bike up to it so we could bring it home. The burns were too much for the sheep and it died two days later but I liked to think we at least gave it some relief in the cold water. The elation of such a clean burn was gone when I thought of the two sheep we'd lost but it brought home to me once again the elemental power of fire.

CHAPTER THIRTEEN

An A-Z of Workers

WITH a farm to run as well as a fishing business we employ a wide range of people during a year. Of course with the farm we have shearers as well as the casual workers who are mainly for scrubcutting, spraying and fencing. But with our fishing base at Okukari we also employ one or two extra crewmen to work on our two boats. Fishing is the bigger side of our business.

The wet fish such as shark, groper, butterfish and so on can be stored in the shore-based fish freezer or in our boats' fish freezers. When we are crayfishing we keep our fish until our holding tank is full. Consequently people see us with quantities of fish and think fishing must be a great way to make money. All these fish, especially the crayfish, make the dollar signs come up in many of our employees' eyes. "Fishing is for me," they assure us.

They don't realise the hard work that has gone into catching the fish they see. The men are out in most weathers, eyes reddened and stinging from the constant wind and spray, with a workplace that's never still, and the 3am or 4am starts usually carry on to a 12 or 14-hour day. There are days with great catches but there are also the times when they catch very few fish.

After 34 years my wages record book reads like a *Who's Who*. When I read through it my mind wants to make it into lists: the non-workers, the players, the workers and the no-hopers. It is my *Employees' A-Z*.

The first person Joe employed I'd place in the worker column. Alfred (I shall change most of the names) came to live with us in 1966 after we'd had the *Heather* built. He was a young Maori boy, brought up on Correspondence School lessons. He couldn't tell the time or barely sign his name and I never saw him pick up a newspaper except to look at and comment on the photos. At that time Young Joe was two and Helen was nearly one. "If this is what Correspondence School produces, count me out with your kids," I told Joe.

Joe had known the lad's family and it was, Joe said, the result of a mother not prepared to put effort into teaching. When Alfred asked me if I'd teach him to tell the time I felt I had been given a quite precious opportunity, and I loved seeing his pleasure in learning. While he was with us he learnt his letters and when he left he was able to read simple books.

Alfred had one fault - he couldn't keep a secret. Before the days of the GPS, fishing grounds were well-guarded secrets. Some 'spots' had been handed down through families for generations, and they regarded them as theirs. Now of course with the GPS anyone can pinpoint the area where another boat is fishing if they want to move in on that particular ground.

Joe and Alfred came home with a good load of groper. As they stacked them away and readied the boat for another day out in the same spot I heard Joe tell his crew, "Keep it under your hat. We don't want all the other buggers coming out there."

Next day they did even better, and set off to Picton to unload. Joe told me later how, on the way to town, he'd reminded Alfred not to "mouth off". Joe said he couldn't believe his ears when this stranger strolled down the wharf and commented on the nice load of fish they had.

"Off the Brothers drift, bro, off the Brothers drift. Couldn't go wrong."

But it was a good lesson for him. Next day they left home in time to set their fishing gear at daybreak. As the light lit up the water in Cook Strait it showed three other boats already setting their gear. Alfred couldn't believe his eyes until Joe reminded him about the previous day.

I'd have to slot Bob in the no-hopers column. We'd acquired him from a boarding establishment. All he wanted to do was be a fisherman, he told Joe, and yes, he could row a dinghy.

During the 1970s we targeted mackerel to use as bait for groper and shark, and we had a market for the fish we didn't need for bait. They are a pelagic fish, but schools of mackerel come into Tory Channel in June and July, and we'd catch them using a drag-net. The net was run evenly into the stern of two dinghies and when the tell-tale shiny patch of water was spotted the oarsmen would row quietly, close to the outside edge of the bubbling water. The person in the stern of each dingy threw out the net, as the rowers pulled hard in opposite directions around the shoal of mackerel, and then headed for the beach. A rope was tied at either end of the net and this was used to haul the net ashore. If we landed them on our beach, the whole family joined in. Today we obtain all the mackerel we need for bait from the fishing company and we no longer catch them to sell. For the work involved and the poor return, it isn't worth it.

Bob arrived in mid-June. We needed him to be able to row. The first sighting of mackerel swimming around our bay had everyone excited, and the net was quickly run into the stern of the two dinghies. Joe yelled at Bob to row the one he was in while Charlie and his crew would take the other.

His words, "But I can't row properly," had Joe roaring at me to take over the oars and "Leave the bastard behind." I felt embarrassed. But this was Okukari and neither Joe nor his father was a patient man - especially when there was a huge shoal of mackerel in the middle of the bay. We soon had the net around the fish and Bob was able to help then.

A few days later Joe and Bob, with Charlie, were working on the *Heather*, tied alongside the wharf. They needed a particular tool and Joe didn't have one. "Quick," Charlie said to Bob. "I've got one. Row out to my boat and bring it in. Get some rowing practice."

It took him ages to reach the boat and longer to work out how to come alongside but it was when he arrived back at the wharf that we knew, as did Bob, that fishing most definitely wasn't for him.

It was a spring tide and dead low water. He let the boat go but grabbed a wharf pile as the dinghy floated past. Holding the painter in one hand he tried to clamber up the pile. The dinghy drifted away.

"Help! Help!"

Joe and Charlie crouched down on the stern deck and peered between the piles. "For Christ's sake, man!" Charlie yelled. "Just slide down the pile and you'll be able to walk ashore."

Con and David I'd slot into the non-workers. They could do the work but didn't like the long hours. One man lasted three days, the other slightly longer, but he finally gave up after a three-day trip down the Kaikoura Coast. Con told Joe that all he wanted to do was be a fisherman and make lots of money. "I'm not afraid of hard work," he boasted. Joe told me that after two poor days he was thrilled when they finally got on to the groper and they were "slaying them". By 11am they had more than 150 on board and as each line came up they were rebaiting then setting straight away. To make up for the two bad days, Joe intended to keep fishing until it was time to leave for home. Joe was disgusted when Con wanted to stop for a cup of tea and a rest.

When Joe told him he'd never have it any better than this and reminded him that he wanted to make money, Con gave in his notice.

Elle and Fred were players. They never came to work but arrived at our place on the recommendation of a friend who'd had them to stay for a couple of days as they passed through the country on the New Zealand leg of their overseas holiday. Once they arrived at our place they didn't want to leave. "We'll work for our keep," they told us, but this fizzled out after the first three days. As the days grew into weeks I knew they had no intention of leaving until they were due to fly out of the country. Two extras not only put a strain on our grocery bill but a strain on Joe and me. Joe would be out on the farm or away fishing, and some days I'd see Elle and Fred only at mealtimes. They'd stay in their room until I called them. I'd visit Lisa or Joy just to get away but of course I always had to come back and find things were just the same.

They boasted that they'd smuggled things out of Australia in their car. When I told them there were some things they shouldn't have brought into our country, they just laughed. They had detonators in their bag - "a New Zealand farmer gave them to us", they said. More likely stolen, I thought. James was horrified when they offered them to him.

One day they'd gone for a walk around to the old whaling station and when I came into the kitchen I saw a navy-blue wallet lying on the kitchen table. I knew Joy had one like it and as I picked it up I wondered when she'd left it. There was a flash with a loud bang. The wallet flew out of my hands. I tore outside to find Joe. He ran in, picked up the wallet and found the remains of two contacts.

I was waiting for them when they arrived back to the house. Fred vowed he didn't leave his wallet out on purpose, and he certainly didn't booby-trap it, and he made the excuse that perhaps one of his friends might have done it to catch him.

My reasoning was that he must have left it out to catch someone. After all, why else would he have his wallet out here? There aren't any shops on Arapawa Island.

I was in shock with tears waiting to spill down my face any second as explanations flew around the room. It got too much and I left the house, telling Joe I'd come back home when they'd gone. From Lisa's I watched Joe launch the speedboat and Elle and Fred walk down to the wharf with their bags. As I watched the boat speed down the channel I felt six weeks' tension drain away.

Lisa and I discussed the things they'd told us they were taking back to the States. "I'm glad I'm not on the same plane," I remarked to Lisa. I wondered if the detonators could explode. We knew the date they were leaving the country and where they were leaving from. New Zealand Customs were very interested.

Graham was one of our best workers. We have had many like him. He came to us with a solid fishing background and left to further his career in fishing. I remember Graham for his brief appearance on television when the team of the TV3 show, Nissan Gone Fishin', had stayed at our home and gone groper fishing in Cook Strait with Joe aboard the *Te Wai*, a programme aimed at the recreational fisherman. As they were filming Graham cutting up the small mackerel for bait, he held up half a fish and in a solemn voice mimicked the TV commercial: "This is what happens to your goldfish if you don't pay your TV licence." Judging by the comments we received after the programme went to air, viewers loved it.

My finger ran down the names and I felt a smile crease my face when I came to Harold. I'd definitely slot him into the workers' column. He was an asthmatic, very slight, but the years he had spent building up his body to help fight his asthma had made him sinewy, and he'd try his hand at anything.

It was in the days of my coal range and Joe had brought a load of coal home on our fishing boat and dumped it on the wharf. As they walked past the bags, Joe suggested they each carry one up to the house. "Bend down and I'll put it on your back," he told Harold. Joe slung his own one over his shoulder and strode ahead. I was following and saw Harold struggling to take the weight. He couldn't straighten his legs and he staggered from side to side of the wharf. Each stagger grew wider until he veered right to the edge and fell in, the coal still on his back. I peered into the water. He burst through the surface, laughing, and was still laughing as he swam ashore and walked up the beach. At low tide Joe and Harold rowed out in the dingy and fished up the bag of coal with a grapple.

Harold could always laugh at himself. He worked hard to overcome the limitations brought on by his asthma but his slight body probably saved his life on one occasion. We had been working with cattle in the yards. One of the bulls escaped and as the men tried to bring it back it suddenly broke and started pawing at the ground and tossing its head around. I heard it give a loud snort and watched in horror from my safe place in the yards as the enraged bull turned towards Harold, who didn't need the loud yells of everyone telling him to run. He spun in a couple of circles before heading over the wide open space towards the yards. I watched aghast. Harold's legs were going like pistons but the bull was catching him. The giant disks, left lying in the paddock since Joe had last used them, were his only refuge. I saw him drop down and squeeze himself between the disks while the frustrated bull could only tear up the dirt as he tried to reach his quarry. He gave up after a while, and then a very dusty and dishevelled boy eased himself out and stretched his stiff body.

Harold was a caring person and whenever we went to Picton he always liked to catch up with his mother. He knew they were shifting house but wasn't sure when. I'll never forget taking him out to his parents' house in our car and as I was driving away he asked me to wait while he made sure they hadn't already left. He came running out to the car. "They've gone."

"Are you sure?" I thought they may have been at the local shops.

"Yes. The kitchen sink is gone."

There was nothing I could say after that.

Ian was a no-hoper. He could work, but drugs got the better of him. A trip to Picton gave Joe the information he needed to fire him on the spot. The needles we use to inject our sick sheep with penicillin are 18-gauge or 1.25mm in diameter. They kept disappearing from their container in the woolshed and I blamed Joe for losing them. He assured me he hadn't used any - it must be me losing them. I knew it wasn't.

We reeled in horror when we were told Ian was supplying the local addicts with "as many pricks as you need". He never came back and his gear followed him on the next mailboat out of Okukari.

Jim was another worker who began his fishing career with Joe and went on to own his own boat. He brought his wife and young children down to the bay and they lived in a bus that Jim had shipped from Picton on a barge.

Ken was a likeable player. As my finger slid down the column past his name I wondered what things he and Joe had got up to that I never discovered. When I found out about one escapade I held it over Joe for weeks.

Joe and Ken had taken the boat to Wellington to have some work done on the electronic equipment. It took longer than they expected and they ended up staying in Wellington overnight, on the boat. Next morning on the VHF radio in the kitchen I heard snippets of a conversation between Joe and a local fisherman. It sounded as if they'd had quite a night in Wellington. When Joe came home I asked him what he'd done in the big smoke. "Nothing much. Went up the street, had a feed and saw the sights." He shrugged off any further questions.

I didn't think anything else about it until two weeks later when Joe and I were in Picton. While Joe and Ken fuelled the boat up I talked to Ken's wife.

"What do you think about the boys going to the Purple Onion?"

I couldn't believe what I was hearing. The notorious massage parlour! And more! That broken conversation I'd heard on the radio came flooding back. I was going to find out about this.

"Yes. What a scream. What did Ken say about it?"

Before long I knew all about it, and Ken's wife had no idea I hadn't been told. When Joe called out to say we were leaving I noticed he had a strained look on his face as I ran down the wharf and jumped on to the boat. All the way home I stewed about his visit to the strip-club. If he'd told me I wouldn't have cared, but the secrecy made me seethe and it was with an effort I kept my voice bright and a smile on my face. I noticed I was being called love and darling more than usual, too.

It was still the days of the generating plant and once we were ready for bed Joe would run out to the shed to turn it off while I lit a candle in our bedroom. Earlier in the evening I'd found two lacy hankies and a pair of iridescent, purple-pink clip-on earrings which I laid out on the dressing table. The minute Joe left the house I lit the candle and stripped off. I tied the hankies together at two corners. If I'd worn my bikini instead of the hankies it would have looked very modest in comparison. I clipped an earring on to each nipple and posed, like a ballerina waiting for the overture to end and to commence the dance.

I was still furious with Joe but the sight of myself in the bedroom mirror against the backdrop of the shadowed room built up such laughter that I pressed my fingers against my lips to try to suppress it. The backdoor slammed and Joe burst into the room.

"La la-la," I sang, and gyrated.

He fell back against the door and slowly slid down the enamel paintwork. I warmed to the situation and danced over to him. The earrings caught the light.

"I knew it. I knew it. She told you, didn't she?"

When we were both able to speak I asked Joe why he hadn't told me that he'd been to the strip-club. I told him how hurt I was, finding out the way I did.

"If I'd known you'd take it like this, I would've told you."

He had the last laugh. As I lay on the bed, feeling the righteous wife, he plucked the purple-pink clip-on earrings slowly off my nipples. It hurt.

A number of names come under L. These were young men who were attending Lincoln College and for some years Joe and I employed two to cut scrub during the Christmas holidays. They were all workers. Some returned two or three times and we enjoyed their company.

Matt and Pete were having a break from working and were going to Wellington for the weekend. They had arrived at the ferry terminal early and they watched as the ferry began to turn in the harbour before it backed in to the link-span. But they fell asleep, and woke up to an empty ferry terminal. Their first night was spent in Picton.

The Marlborough Sounds is one of the areas in New Zealand where a great deal of marijuana is grown, and the dope helicopter was a common sight over the Sounds. Matt and Pete told us how they'd been using the two scrubcutters and the first thing they saw was a shadow passing over them. The helicopter swooped over them a second time and they said it gave them such a fright they threw their machines down and ran for cover in the steep gully. We could imagine them parting the scrub and peering up in the sky and not coming out of hiding until the helicopter left. Joe was concerned the police might be back to investigate our property but when no one came to check us out it must have been decided we didn't have two growers minding their patch on Okukari.

Some have wanted to work with us not only for the fishing but because there are a lot of pigs on Arapawa Island. I remembered Maurice as he had a pig-dog. He fitted into all the columns except the non-worker.

His dog was uncared for and frequently I'd find it on the chain without water. It wasn't fed regularly, either. One evening it got too much for me and when it was time for dinner I dished up one meal fewer. "When you've fed your dog," I told Maurice, "I'll feed you."

He did stay on and work with us for some time and the dog was better looked after.

Nick was a worker with a capital W and we were sorry when he left to travel overseas. He is the only one in my A-Z book who has exercised on the for'ard deck during the slack times of the day when we were out tuna fishing.

When I came to the next name a vision of wild pork crawling with maggots came into my mind. Owen was retired and lived a short distance down the channel from us. He wanted a season fishing so he came to work for Joe. I loved the arrangement. For one year I didn't have a crewman living with us as Joe picked him up each morning and dropped him off at the end of the day. He was a worker and when he wasn't fishing he had a wonderful garden and kept us supplied with all our vegetables.

But I shuddered when I thought of the time Joe had hunted and killed a wild pig that had been seen close to one of our lambing blocks, as he wanted it killed before it added lamb to its diet. It was a full-grown boar, "too strong to eat", I was told, when I asked him why he didn't bring it home.

Two days later Joe mentioned his hunt to Owen, who couldn't believe that Joe had wasted all that good meat. When they arrived in from fishing he walked out and cut off the back legs and brought them back to Okukari. The pig hadn't been gutted and we'd had two typical spring days. As he threw the meat on his boat I noticed some maggots crawling away and it made me rub my scalp. The following week he presented us with a leg of pickled pork that he'd done himself. Swallowing the bile that rose in my mouth I tried to show my delight. Not even the dogs ate that meat.

As I read further down my list I found myself chewing the end of my pencil as I debated which column to put some of these people in. Many could be slotted into all of them. Paul had to be another no-hoper but he was working on being a healthy one. He arrived in the bay with his clothes, a sack of organically-grown wheat and a mincer. His breakfast was freshly ground wheat and he was always suggesting I try it. He assured me I'd love it but I declined when I opened his sack of wheat and discovered that mice also loved it.

Over 34 years there have been a few that I'd have to slot in the Qs as questionables. Some left and the next time we heard of them they were in prison. Others we heard of through Accident Compensation -

they were trying to obtain money from the ACC by saying they'd hurt themselves while working with us. My diaries have been useful when it has come to reported dates of injuries, and we've discovered they've still been fishing with us. Some have managed to go hunting after their 'serious injury'. We have noticed this happens mostly in the cray season when a great deal of money is made in three or four months. These Qs come in, work for the crays, leave, and if they can swindle ACC for the rest of the year they can make a good wage. We have got to know quite a few of the staff in the ACC office.

My finger stopped at Roy and his name reminded me to order a new tyre for Joe's motorbike. Roy lives in Aotea and Joe employs him to spray the gorse, scrub-cut, and fence. I have to group him with all the other workers but next to his name I scribbled in the word, innovative. To reach our place Roy needs his two-wheeled motorbike to ride the 10-kilometre farm track which is very steep in places. He seems prone to breakdowns but, like the mail, 'he always gets through'.

Roy's inner tube was beyond repair and until a new one could be brought out to the island his bike was immobile. Roy found some black polythene hose and wound it inside the tyre three or four times. He fitted the tyre back on to the wheel and lashed it with rope, between the nobbles on the tyre, over the rim and through the spokes. It hung together until his new inner tube arrived.

For a long time I wanted new vinyl laid in our kitchen, bathroom and laundry. Having to organise someone to come out from Picton or Blenheim seemed to be such a hassle as well as expensive. Roy was at our place when Joe and I were discussing it. "We know a guy, Jimmy, who'd do it. Comes and stays with us," and Roy thought he'd jump at doing it for some spare cash. On his next visit to Aotea he rode over the hill and measured the floor, with a promise to come back when I had the vinyl.

Now it happens that occasionally wild cattle stray on to our land. They come from the bush, descendants of farmed cattle that strayed from farms many years ago. A ginger-coloured bull, that looked as if he'd been crossed with many breeds, came in with our cows. Joe thought he'd weigh at least 1000kg. His head appeared to be growing out of his broad shoulders and his mean eyes focused on anything that moved - and then he charged.

Joe invited me to ride on the back of the motorbike to see him, and as we drove along the opposite side of the creek he raised his head, watched us for a few seconds then started to charge in our direction. I wasn't happy until we had at least two fences between us.

"Get rid of it! Eat it! Feed it to the dogs!" I yelled at Joe as we rode away. "Imagine if it took to one of the kids."

"It'll come in with the cows in the next day or so," and Joe promised me he'd get rid of it then.

I was so peeved when I heard from Young Joe and James what happened. I'd have loved to have been there. Apparently the bull came into the yards without any bother at all but when it was time to separate him from the cows he turned mean. Young Joe could hardly talk for laughing, "You should have been there, Mum. Dad, James and I were fighting to get to the woolshed first. Dad won and slammed the door in our faces."

"I was safe." I glanced at Joe when I heard the laughter in his voice. These Heberley men were all hysterical, I thought.

James's words ran over the top of his father's. "Shit! I've never scaled a fence so fast."

"But we had the last laugh," spluttered Young Joe as he wiped tears from his eyes.

They'd all decided the only way to get the bull out of the yards was to drive him out with the tractor. Joe drove it at him, trying to make him move. With a toss of his head he charged at Joe. "I knew the bastard would get me there," so Joe told me he'd climbed over the top of the engine and up into the bucket. Young Joe and James were in hysterics by now, and they had to let their father tell me how they'd crept up and let the bucket drop to the ground. Then it was Joe's turn to make a mad dash to a shut door. When the bull finally left the yards he made straight for the gate out on to the hills and soon disappeared over the skyline.

Just then, over this same skyline, Roy's friend Jimmy rode his bike on his way to lay my vinyl.

When he could speak he told us that he'd passed a mob of cattle standing on the track, and driven through them. He heard a sound and turned around, and "this big red bull was thundering after me". He wound up the throttle but as he approached the next corner the bull charged the back of the bike, "and I spun out". He landed in thick gorse and managed to sneak down the gully. "I left the bull attacking the bike."

We took a shaken young man to Picton to have his knee stitched up. My vinyl-laying was delayed until he could kneel again, the bull was shot, and Jimmy became known as Streak.

My nephew, Tom, fished with us for two years. He was another worker with a capital W. He too has made a career in the fishing industry.

Unique - having no like or equal or parallel. This definition from the *Oxford Dictionary* describes Jummy - a worker and a player. Numerous stories have unfolded after his weekends spent in Picton with his mates. On one occasion, for a dare, Jummy scaled one of the light towers at the railyard only to find on reaching the top that his mates had scarpered and in their place was the local constable, shining his torch on Jummy, and demanding that he descend immediately. I'm not sure if he ever received his winnings of a dozen DB.

His next weekend off had him fast talking to the same constable once more. This time Jummy and his mates had raided a local farmer's corn paddock and filled up the back seat of the car. As they drove back to Picton they shucked corn and threw the leaves out the car window. After a complaint from an irate farmer, it took little detective work on the part of the same constable to follow the trail of corn leaves and eaten cobs to Jummy's parents' house. The next time Joe and Jummy were in Picton unloading fish, Joe had a visit from this constable who was also a friend of ours. He suggested that Joe keep Jummy safely out in the Sounds.

Joe always said Jummy was a skipper's delight, and he enjoyed working alongside him for more than two years. He was a crewman Joe trusted.

The no-hopers still turn up, and Vince was certainly one. He came to us through a work scheme. He is the only one who ever threw a saleable crayfish back to the sea. "Tangaroa needed that one," he answered an infuriated Joe who believed the Maori sea god already had all the crayfish he wanted or needed on the seabed. We learned that Vince's erratic mood swings were chemically induced so he was told to leave.

Willy. The one who fell overboard in Cook Strait. It wasn't long after he'd finished working for us as he'd wanted to go back into town to live, and was now working on another fishing boat out of Picton. A Mayday was issued for assistance to lift Willy back on board. Willy was a big man with a weight problem, and before he worked with Joe he had been in hospital to lose weight. All the time he was with us he watched his diet carefully and we could see his weight going down.

Joe and Willy were friends from the whaling days and after he left us we were saddened when we saw how his weight ballooned again. His heart couldn't cope with the strain, and he died.

In January 1996 Joe hurt his knee while tuna fishing. The constant movement of the boat aggravated the injury and he came ashore for 10 months, working around the farm and going fishing only when Young Joe or James needed a crew. With Joe off the boat, a new crewman had to be found. My finger passed over quite a few names that took up only one line in my book. It was easy to put them in the non-worker column. Xavier spent his spare time in his room drinking rum so he was replaced by another who had seen us unloading a week's catch from two boats and was positive he wanted to be a fisherman. He didn't take winter weather into consideration and after spending a week at home waiting for a southerly to die down he decided fishing wasn't for him after all.

Zak. He fitted every column. He was here for a year and when he started he was a worker. He grew from a juvenile to a young man while he was with us and he often came to Joe to ask for advice, especially when he started to earn big money during the cray season.

When he had money in his pocket a gradual metamorphosis took place. He became a player. It seemed as if sex and alcohol were ruling his life. A trustworthy young man changed to a no-hoper and we were disappointed. I didn't want to dwell on Zak so I closed the book and walked out of the office but my mind kept returning to him.

Joe and James had been away fishing in *Te Wai*, while Young Joe and Zak were doing day trips from Okukari Bay in the *Fugitive*. Zak wanted to visit some friends over the hill and asked Lisa if he could borrow her four-wheeler. I tried to push away the burning anger I always feel whenever I think of what he put my daughter-in-law through that night.

Lisa told me she must have been sleeping lightly, waiting for Zak to arrive home with her bike. "It was some ungodly hour in the morning that I heard him drive up to his hut and park the bike."

A short time later she heard a noise. "It sounded like someone coming up the stairs on to the decking. I jumped out of bed, ran to the top of the inside stairs and flicked on the light." When Lisa came to this part she burst into tears. "He was naked and inside my house. He closed the door."

What worried Lisa most was the thought of what would have happened to her, or Haydn and Danielle, if she hadn't woken up. She gulped back her tears, then laughed when she said he opened the door and shot out, straight over the edge of the balcony. "It's a shame he didn't injure himself when he landed on the wheelbarrow."

Joy and Joe live next door, and Lisa quickly rang Joe up. He ran out to see where Zak was and told us when he saw his shape in the bed he closed the door on him. He knew he would have been charged with assault if he'd confronted Zak that night. Joy and Joe spent the remainder of the night with Lisa, talking her through her ordeal.

At first light Joe told Zak he had 20 minutes to pack his gear and get down to the wharf, where he'd be waiting with the speedboat to take him in to Picton.

Lisa just wanted him gone but when we talked about it I made her see that he shouldn't be allowed to get away with a thing like that. It upset me to think that this person we had helped in so many ways could do such a thing, and to one of my family. Lisa took the matter further and reported the offence. A police officer was waiting for Zak when he arrived in town. He was charged with, and found guilty of, being unlawfully on private premises.

Looking back we've certainly had an assortment. They've come and gone with the regularity of the tides. I have only touched the surface of my memories, and it has been like exploring our beach after a southerly storm, poking in the piles of kelp or lifting up pieces of driftwood, and kicking away the rubbish that always washes ashore on the flood tide. Amidst all of this there is usually something good to be found. And so it has been with our workers.

CHAPTER FOURTEEN

Yarns From Whaling Days

JUST as frustration leads my men to the playing of pranks when they are at sea, so did the long hours of boredom when the whalers sat in the lookout, keeping their vigil over the sea for a spout from a whale. Some of the stories I've heard Charlie relate have had us in non-stop laughter, and it seemed as if each man had to out-do the other with the tricks they played. As I've listened and watched memories light up his face, I've glanced around the room and seen everyone hanging on his every word.

Okukari has no need for a tractor with a horn, but when Charlie bought such a tractor in the early days of his farming, its horn came in very handy.

"There were no toilet facilities over at the lookout. I decided to build a long drop there. Every morning I'd take a couple of bits of timber or some old sheets of iron that were lying around the place. The hole was dug and the shed around the hole was built as we carted the materials." Memories made Charlie burst out laughing. We all waited for him to go on.

"We left the seat loose and drove a copper tack on the bottom and a copper tack on the top to make a contact. I screwed the horn in underneath the seat. There was a lead from this to a battery hidden in a flax bush outside."

When he asked us if we remembered the engineer, Gordon Cuddon, it was easy to think of the big man whose engineering kept Peranos' whaling station operating. "Well, he was our next visitor to the lookout. He had a stutter," Charlie added. "He goes in there and sits down and the horn goes 'urrrr'." Charlie doubled up with laughter and tears ran down his face. "Old Gordon shot out with his trousers down around his ankles, fell over, and all he could do was stutter. He couldn't speak for about five minutes."

It was probably just as well the second part of the plan didn't happen. Charlie told us they always intended to get a fly swat, coat it with treacle and set it up with a spring. When the horn went off it would release the fly swat up on to a bared bottom. "But we never got around to that part of the trick," he ended with a sigh.

"The spaghetti one was one of the best," and he launched into the next yarn.

"The National Film Unit came to the whaling station. The chap's name was Roger Mirams, wellknown in the film industry. He stayed aboard the mother-ship, the *Tuatea*. When he went back he sent over a parcel of food because of the kindness shown by the boys. In it were some tins of spaghetti."

Every morning the chasers would steam up to the *Tuatea* to take on fuel and explosives. "One morning I sneaked below and stole a tin of the spaghetti. Over on the lookout hill I soaked the tin in water and took off the label before cutting the tin around the middle."

The contents weren't wasted. "Joe Perano (senior) and I sat outside in the tussock and ate it cold. At that time the wireless operator on the lookout was a local farmer and he'd brought some sheep to graze around the lookout hill, so there was sheep dung lying around. Joe and I gathered some up, along with kelp bubbles off the rocks, filled up the tin, then soldered it back together. Once we'd glued the label back it looked and felt like a full tin of spaghetti. That night I slipped it back into the *Tuatea*'s stores."

The *Tuatea* was used for whale-spotting as well as towing back to the factory the whales that the smaller chasers had killed. "A few days after the spaghetti episode we'd caught a whale and while we were tying it up to the mother-ship I went aboard to replace some of our gear. The boys had been given a groper by an Italian fisherman." Charlie pinched it. When the cook realised it was gone he took the tins of spaghetti from the cupboard, put them in water and heated them up. Charlie couldn't go on for laughing, but Ruby finished off the story. She said she can still remember the looks on the crew's faces as they tried to describe the dinner they'd been dished up.

Arapawa Island has no rabbits or possums and it was easy to forget that West Head, where the lookout sat, was the mainland. "But there was a strange animal on the lookout," Charlie carried on. "Every day apple cores, scraps of bread, banana skins - scraps of the boys' lunches - were thrown outside. They always disappeared."

Everyone debated what sort of animal it could be. "Too big for a mouse or rat." So they set a trap.

Charlie had been in Australia when World War Two broke out and when he came home he had brought back some fox furs and had them made up into stoles. Ruby's stole was worn out so Charlie cut the tail off and took it over to the lookout. He tied a string on the end and put it beneath a flax bush, with only the tip showing. He told one of the gunners, Trevor Norton, the plan.

"Max Kenny, he owned Okukari before the Heberleys bought it, went outside. I bailed him up and told him to come and have a look at this. When he saw the strange tail he got everyone else to come and see. Trevor stayed inside and each time Max tried to grab it, Trevor yanked the string." I tried to imagine grown men grovelling around under flax bushes and in the dirt until it was finally caught.

"We set a trap and in fact it was a possum."

Sometimes the men remember old pranks when they're doing some present-day jobs. I'd helped Joe build that extra-strong chookhouse for our new chooks and while I was struggling to hold a sheet of iron in place while he nailed it to the frame he started grinning and then laughed. "What's so funny?" I demanded.

"Just thinking."

"What?"

"When Mum and Dad had chooks. I was only a kid. The chookhouse was over there on the bank," and Joe pointed to the steep bank above the beach immediately in front of our house. "It was winter and the men were whaling. The *Tuatea* used to anchor in our bay. This night all the dogs were barking and Dad took out his .303 to fire it into the air. All the dogs were gun-shy and it shut them up good. What Dad didn't know was that Charlie Perano, the skipper of the *Tuatea*, and Billy Gillice were sneaking up the bank through the gorse to raid our chookhouse. They thought Dad was shooting at them, and took off. Dad didn't know a thing about it until the next day when Gilly told him. Apparently they were digging out gorse prickles for weeks."

Early whalers were hard men. They had to be to survive the conditions they worked under. Whaling was not for the faint-hearted. But in their spare time at sea many men carved designs on the teeth of the sperm whale - scrimshaw. In the midst of the danger, blood and guts, even death, they could turn a whale's tooth into a thing of beauty. Modern whalers too could see beauty. I've heard poetical descriptions of sunrises in Cook Strait from some of the toughest men I've met, and a story my father-in-law told me made me realise that Charlie, too, sees beauty in the sea.

They had been to Oyster Bay to dredge for oysters, and were late coming home. A full moon lit up the channel. As they passed Te Awaiti, Charlie noticed lights on the *Cachalot*, one of the whale chasers. When he went over to the boat to turn off the lights, Gilly was on board waiting for him. Ted Huntley, who worked in the whaling station's bone department and lived in Fishing Bay, had seen two whales spout in the channel. "I jumped aboard. The other whale-chaser with Trevor Norton and Joe Perano was trying to follow the whales up the channel. We were off Okukari when one spouted. It was the most fantastic thing I've ever seen. The water was lit up with phosphorescence and when the whale lifted there was just this big golden ball coming up - you couldn't see the whale. I shot at the ball. It was a great sight to see this damned thing coming up with all the phosphorescence streaming back on it." He shook his head and repeated, "Fantastic, just fantastic."

The savage beauty of Cook Strait was exchanged for a different type of beauty in 1959, when Charlie was asked to manage the whaling station in Whangaparapara Harbour on Great Barrier Island. Here the lookout was at the southernmost tip of the Barrier. Joe has described the sunrises he'd seen as the sun had lifted over the edge of a purple, mirrorlike ocean, the black clouds sitting on the edge of the Pacific suddenly transformed as the sun edged them in gold.

I was lucky, and saw such a sunrise when I spent a weekend at Whangaparapara in 1962. It was over an hour since I'd said goodbye to Joe's mother at Whangaparapara, and after the ride in the dark in the whale chaser with Joe and Charlie, in the company of the other two chasers, and then the climb up the hill to the lookout hut, I welcomed the hot drink that was thrust into my hands.

Suddenly everyone was quiet. I heard myself swallow. Like them, I watched the light as it moved across the sea and lit up the jagged windswept coast to the north. The light coated the walls of the hut. When we'd watched our fill, chatter and laughter filled the room once more.

The Barrier whalers, too, dreamed up ways to play pranks on one another. But in Auckland they came up against a tough adversary in the wellknown Freddy Ladd with his amphibian plane. His business, Tourist Air Travel, which operated out of Auckland, meant that Great Barrier Island was only 30 minutes away. On his scheduled flights he'd drop a *New Zealand Herald*, wrapped in plastic, on to the deck of a chaser. Joe says he can recall many times at sea when Freddy swooped down on them, and then the roar of the plane's engine and the flapping of his wings as he flew away left them with hearts racing and threatening fists punching an already empty sky.

Then there were the days when Freddy dropped flour-bombs from his plane. "It got to the stage when we didn't know if we were having a newspaper or a bomb delivered," Joe said.

Before the whaling season began a chaser steamed in to Auckland to pick up the explosives that were used in the guns. Tom Norton, gunner, and Tom Gullery, driver, who worked on the same chaser, were steaming past Devonport's naval base on their way back to the Barrier when they spotted Freddy Ladd's plane taking off through a sparkle of white spray on the opposite side of the harbour, in Mechanics Bay. He must have seen the chaser because, as soon as he was airborne, he banked steeply and then swooped. This time, the two Toms were ready.

The harpoon-gun fitted to the gunpost at the bow of the chaser had been loaded with a paper wad rammed down the muzzle of the gun as far as the cartridge of explosive powder, but the harpoon head was not in place. As Freddy flew his plane a few feet above their boat, Tom Norton fired the gun. A roar - and pieces of burning paper and smoke "shot" the plane.

The whalers' glee was short-lived. Anywhere else but next to a naval base, and their prank might have gone unnoticed. They had a lot of explaining to do, and were severely reprimanded.

A well-dressed Canadian worked out at the Barrier for a season. He wore his thick-soled fancy suede shoes everywhere, much to the disgust of the rest of the workers who wore gumboots. One day when he'd taken his shoes off in the heat he found them nailed to the decking of the factory. When he tried to pull them free the soles peeled away from the uppers. He became like the rest of the men, and wore gumboots.

But there is another side of whaling. When I began to do this research I thought the light-hearted stories and pranks would go on for ever, but I soon realised that they were just diversions, fun to help cover up the realities of one of the most dangerous occupations in the world, performed in one of nature's harshest environments. Charlie describes it as a very dangerous game, and "damned hard work. But, it was an industry. It was a job. It was a necessity."

Whale oil was used in margarine, cosmetics, pharmaceutical products and chocolate, and during the war it was used in the hardening of gun metals. Frozen edible whale meat was also sent to Britain.

The sperm whale had a large bulbous-shaped head. At the back of this was a cavity filled with a massive sac of a waxy-feeling substance that looked like honeycomb. It melted when touched. This produced an oil of the highest quality and was used in fine machinery such as clocks, finest-grade candles and ointment.

Charlie said the whalers all agreed the spermaceti was there for a purpose and they all believed it may have had something to do with the depths the whales dived. He recalled a story of the remains of a sperm whale being found twisted around the Atlantic telephone cable. It was held firmly by its jaw, as if the whale had grabbed at something, taken the cable, rolled with it and become entangled - proof that these animals do indeed swim to great depths.

Many involved in the whaling industry had a dream, to get on a chaser as a driver or gunner. Charlie, one of New Zealand's top gunners, who shot more than a thousand whales, remembers what the dream was actually like.

"A man can expect to be soaking wet from the moment a chase starts until he arrives home at the end of a day. It doesn't matter how much clothing you have on, standing at the gun on the for'ard deck of a 36-foot chaser travelling at a speed of 25 to 30 knots in a two to three-metre swell, and you get drenched. I've been at the gun when we've hit a big sea, and it's washed me away from the gun and along the deck almost to the stern."

Charlie had lived in a time-frame of New Zealand's history, spanning the kind of whaling which his father did for two years, in open rowing boats, to the 36-foot planing hulls, some of which were capable of speeds up to 45 knots. He saw the lookout hut grow from a dug-out on top of the hill to a hut which was built after the end of the Second World War. The navy had built a lookout on Westhead for the gun emplacement across the channel in Whekenui Bay on Arapawa Island. It had a generating plant and water tank and various other things that were left after the end of the war. The whalers soon used them to build the hut, which is still in reasonable condition today.

He has lived through a time when there was no radio-telephone link between the man on the lookout and the chasers out in Cook

Strait. He has told me how they used the Indian style of smoke signals when a whale was spotted. I love watching his face as he recalls those times. It lights up with memories that have been fondled so often they have grown into a legend, a legend I am compelled to write for future generations.

"From the lookout we had a vision of 17 miles to the horizon and from where we sat it covered from Cape Campbell to the south and north to Paremata and Plimmerton. We estimated our vision covered 250,000 acres."

For this they used 7x50 binoculars which were fitted on the backs of home-made chairs so the men could sit, reverse style, watching. When a whale was spotted the binoculars would be locked on it and the whaler then gave directions to the others, using, as fixes, land in the North Island or a lighthouse. Once all glasses were locked on the whale they would determine which way it was travelling and when that was established they'd try to work out the distance it was swimming between each spout. Each man moved his binoculars one glass vision ahead of the other and this kept quite an area covered. When they'd determined the distance from the lookout they'd take off from the hut and charge down the track to the beach at the bottom of the hill.

"The first man down the hill always grabbed the oars because then you'd row to your own boat first and get a head start on the others. There was keen competition - especially between the gunners."

At sea-level the whale was hard to see so they'd head off in the general direction of the last sighting and when they were out far enough the man remaining at the lookout would light up some tussock that he had ready. This was the smoke signal for the boats to stop. If the boats were too far north he'd light another fire south of the first.

"Then we'd go south," Charlie explained. "When we got far enough south he'd put out that fire and we'd know we were in the vicinity of the whale.

"Once fast to a whale we worked our boats like a trout fisherman works his rod. The boat is the rod. When the whale dived we let the rope out."

The two-inch rope was fastened on to the harpoon which had a diamond-shaped explosive head with three toggles or arms, that lay back against the shank of the harpoon. When they went into the whale and the whale's weight came on the rope, then the toggles hooked and spread out like the barbs on a hook. This held the harpoon under the blubber.

His next words made me grateful that these hard men hadn't lost their compassion. "Once a whale was harpooned we wanted it killed soon as possible."

Charlie went on to explain how the explosive head often stopped the whale straight away and they were able to kill it by using a hand-made killing bomb. The bomb was placed in the back of the neck before being fired with an electric detonator. The bomb was three plugs of gelignite encased in a sharpened galvanised pipe which was attached to an electric wire that ran back to the boat.

"And as I said earlier, when we were travelling at speeds of 25 knots or more in a swell it was hard to stand up, but it was even worse on a rough day when the bomb had to be thrown by hand. We always used both arms and all we hung on to the deck with were our feet."

My father-in-law has seen a whale lift a chaser clean out of the water and almost toss it over by coming up underneath. I watched his craggy face light up and his eyes focus on something I couldn't see. He was oblivious to my presence as he reminisced.

"There were two whales running north off the Brothers, both swimming shallow. I could see the shadow of one and I had my eye locked on it. Take your eye off it and you'll lose it."

Charlie was guiding the driver with hand signals and not watching the other whale. "It came up sharply beneath us. His nose came through the bottom of the boat right next to the engine."

These boats were built with two water-tight bulkheads dividing them into three sections. This meant if one or possibly two sections were damaged they would still have enough flotation.

Two whales were lucky that day as the other two chasers came to assist the stricken chaser back into Tory Channel. And while that picture was still vivid in my mind he began another story.

This time a whale lashed out and made a big hole near the bow of the boat. "We always wore oilskins," he told me, "so I became like the Dutch lad who saved Holland by holding his finger in the dyke wall." I pictured my father-in-law sitting with his bottom in the hole as the driver brought the boat back.

As I listened I relived the day I was pitched over the side of the boat when I was out fishing with Joe in Cook Strait. I recalled the deep colour of the water above me as I struggled to the surface and the bubbles that tingled my face when the crayfish pot that Joe was winching aboard the boat passed me. This paled in comparison with Charlie's next words.

Whales nearly always died on their sides with one side of their fluke - the tail - out of the water, Charlie said. The gunner threw a lasso over the fluke so the dead whale could be drawn alongside the boat and held tightly while a hole was cut in it. A wire rope was passed through and around the fluke. A heavier rope was put on to the wire rope, then passed to the mother-ship before she began to winch the whale alongside.

"This day we thought the whale was dead and in our hurry to get it passed over to the mother-ship we pulled the tail in very quickly." Charlie stopped for a moment with his memory of pain and fright. When he went on he told me that they wanted to get rid of it fast and have another go at the second whale. Just as he leant on his stomach over the side of the boat to cut the hole, the whale lashed out and broke the rope holding it. Charlie fell overboard close to where the tail was, so when the whale came back for his return kick the blow wasn't so hard.

"But when it hit me across the back of my shoulders it drove me down deep. A peculiar feeling - all the bubbles of froth, and I couldn't see anything." His main thought was, am I going to try and get to the surface, and take another smack, or dive deeper?

This time my father-in-law was lucky. When a whale moves its tail it travels forward as this is its propulsion, and with the second kick it moved far enough away to allow Charlie to come to the surface. Bad bruises from his knocking around, and a damaged jawbone, were all Charlie had to show for his ordeal. "By God, it was frightening down there."

His stories had me trying to imagine what work must have been like for the generation of whalers before Charlie. They'd hunted whales in the same area, with similar weather conditions and using rowing boats. Stories I've read or heard told by my father-in-law have horrified me. Stories that for me, living in the 20th century, are incredible.

Geordie or Jordy Thoms, a whaler from Te Awaiti, was dragged overboard with a rope in a half-hitch around his left arm. Every time the whale came up to spout, Jordy took a breath. Then the whale would go down again, taking the man with him. When the accident happened the whale was nearly dead and instead of diving for the usual eight-ten minutes it would have been diving shallow and surfacing every minute or so. Jordy survived because the whale didn't.

And in the same recollections of Joe Timms and Gilbert Perano recorded for the Picton Museum in July 1977, when I'd learnt about Joe Timms being Charles Godfrey's eyes, (Charles, the keeper of the lights at Whekenui), I heard another story about Jim Norton getting swept out of the rowing boat with a rope as he stood in the bow ready to lance the whale. The rope was running through his legs when it came out of the chocks and knocked him overboard. Harry Norton grabbed an oar and jumped in with his father, then shoved an oar under his fathers arms to hold him up until they could be brought back to the boat.

The early whalers were hard men. The conditions they worked in wouldn't have passed today's standards. They didn't have factories as the later whalers did, and at one stage the whales were cut up in the water.

"I've watched my dad," Charlie began, "after they've pulled the blubber off the whale, and cut underneath its ribs. Dad would dive down in the water to get inside the chest cavity to fix a chain on to its heart. He'd come up for a breath before going back down again to pull the heart out."

All this because the fat around the heart produced a huge amount of oil. Even if it was a cold southerly day, he said, you'd see the men diving down in the water to get inside the cavity. "I can remember once, when I was only small, Mum and I went to visit Dad. I think she was taking him food. In those days," Charlie continued, "they used a thing called a whale spade for cutting the blubber. It was sharp like a paint-stripping knife but on a larger scale with a handle and a very sharp face. They'd chop with it to cut the blubber."

When Arthur came out of the water Charlie said they saw a big cut across the front of his gumboots but when they remarked about it Arthur told them he was all right. He couldn't feel anything. But when he pulled off his gumboot, two toes fell out.

Joe's own whaling career began at Whangaparapara, Great Barrier Island, and ended at Peranos in Tory Channel with modern boats, a streamlined factory, and up-to-date communication with radio-telephones. It was still a dangerous occupation but, Joe always added, exciting.

Joe's biggest fright in his whaling days was when he saw a whale charge the *Colville*, a Fairmile, 115 feet long with a triple-skinned hull. It had been built for the Navy during the Second World War, before being converted to a chaser and mother-ship for the whaling station. He said he watched as the whale did a great arc, came to the surface, lined the Fairmile up, and charged. The whale drove its head six to eight feet into the topsides, then backed off with its nose and one third of its body out of the water, draped with bits of wood and pieces of sheet from one of the bunks in the accommodation area.

"I knew this guy meant business."

And another time Joe said he wondered why the boat was rising out of the water so suddenly.

"It was a whale coming up underneath us."

The only damage that day was that a little bit of the chafing batten came off the bottom of the keel.

Incidents like that happened quite often and Joe has laughed when he's repeated them to people. Even the experienced men have been so excited they've given wrong directions and slipped off the back of a whale.

"Alf Nimmo was the gunner and Max Kenny was the driver. Alf was following one whale and hadn't seen the other. The second whale came right up underneath and the chaser fell off the side of it." Through laughter Joe finished the story. "I can still see Alf letting go of the gun and hanging on to the gunpost on his hands and knees, wondering what the hell had happened."

Joe maintained they had to see the funny side of these incidents, knowing all the time that the whale only had to give one swipe with its tail and it would have the side out of the boat. "But we'd laugh like hell if no damage was done."

Tom Gullery had been the seventh foreman at the Perano whaling station before he'd left whaling. He was working in Picton when he was invited to go up north with Charlie to work at the Whangaparapara station as his driver on one of the chasers. Tom told me he was surprised. "I felt very honoured, actually. Charlie's a good workmate. I'd trust my life with him."

Tom recalled his first day out with Charlie. "It's lucky it wasn't my last."

"We had just arrived in Whangaparapara with our boat, the *Oria*. We pulled up to the jetty and heard that a crew from one of the other boats had sighted a whale south of us, off Tryphena. We got directions from the RT and set off - flat out." Now Tom's face lit up. His mind was free of the body which has kept him imprisoned since he suffered a stroke. "This whale spouted in front of us. Bang!" I was enjoying the full description. "Charlie was fast to it."

Tom had never been fast to a whale before and as the rope started to run out Charlie had yelled at Tom to 'take a turn'.

Emotion, memories, the effects of his stroke, all three had him wiping his eyes as he carried on. "Silly bugger, me. I picked up the rope and put two half-hitches around the logger-head." In the silence I was imagining what Charlie had said. I think we both knew the boat could have been pulled under, the harpoon pulled out, or the rope could have snapped. Tom's voice broke in, "We got it off. We were OK but at the time all I could think was I'll hang on to this bugger."

Once again I heard Joe saying they'd laugh like hell if no damage was done, while at the same time I knew from Joe that when a whale was running hard it might take out 40-50 fathoms of rope in one dive. All that rope had to be played out by the driver around the hardwood logger-head at the stern. Certainly not tied with two half-hitches. Joe has said he has seen smoke coming off the logger-head and some of them have almost burnt through in a season.

Whalers became masters of innovation. Most new ideas were born and developed in response to the needs of the job. During the Second World War the whale meat that was sent to Britain had to be frozen. If the explosives were used on any mammal they went right through the meat, contaminating it. Carbon-dioxide was to be used and this drove the oxygen out of the blood. These professional innovators decided to try CO_2 in a bottle with a hose connected to it and they joined the air spear to the hose. In theory it sounded good. Once fastened to a whale with the harpoon, the air spear was poked into the whale and the CO_2 turned on. Joe's father and Gilbert Perano were to try it out.

"When I put the air spear in and Gilly released the gas, we never thought about putting on a regulator. The gas went out with a rush and froze the whole cylinder. We were left with a whole block of ice. The whale took off, and the air spear wouldn't pull out so we had to throw the cylinder and everything overboard. We killed the whale by the usual method."

Then the electric harpoon was invented. This, Charlie told me, had a specially wired 230V generator with a very high amperage. The idea this time was to fire the electric harpoon into the blubber. They taped the flex to their ordinary whale line. Once the line was fast to the whale, the electricity was applied and the whale killed.

To me, electricity and water sounded a lethal combination - the water was used as the return circuit which caused the boat to become part of that circuit. Gordon Cuddon had assured the men that it was safe as it had been tested in Picton harbour. Charlie still worried. Cook Strait was not Picton harbour. Out in the Strait they were never dry.

Charlie remembered once firing the harpoon into a whale. He said he was pulling back what he thought was the rope with the electric cable attached to it. He didn't know the cable had broken and when he got it near the boat he looked over the side.

"I could see this damned great blue flash of flame under the water as the electric flex swung round. As it came up and over the rail it hit it. There was a shower of sparks. After that we decided it wasn't safe."

During the trial of that harpoon they used the ordinary type of shanks that they used with the all-explosive harpoon. These were two half-inch shanks that went down the barrel of the gun with the head fitted on the front of it.

The guns didn't have any recoil system. The only thing that took the jar of the gun was the flexibility of the gunpost that the gun was mounted on. That was laminated - similar to a cricket bat handle.

With the electrical circuit, if the harpoon was sticking out through the blubber it was shorting and the whalers weren't getting the full power through so they decided to build a harpoon up using Australian hardwood for the shank. There was no give in that at all, and when the gun was fired it almost knocked the gunner over. Charlie grinned and looked down at his thumb.

"I had the habit of putting my thumb over the back of the gun when I pulled the trigger. I fired this hardwood shank out, the gun kicked out of my hands, came back and caught my thumb."

He had broken it at the first joint but he didn't knock off. "Gilly taped it with insulation tape and I continued whaling for the rest of the season."

That too, joined the 'unsafe' heap.

A big percentage of whales sank when killed in the early days. If the water wasn't too deep they were towed along the bottom. The boat that was fast to it was connected by the harpoon line and because that rope went over the bow the other two boats helped by towing the boat and whale backwards.

Later, they used an air compressor driven off a clutch at the front of the engine to stop the whales sinking. An ordinary garden hose was connected to the compressor with an air spear on the end of that. The spear was made out of half-inch galvanised pipe, sharpened at one end with holes in it to allow the air to come out. Just before they used the killing bomb, they'd push the air spear in the stomach or in the throat area because the whale has a massive tongue which would inflate. Not much air was needed to give them flotation.

All of this is now history. I find it hard to believe it all happened in my lifetime and so close to where I live today. Men like Tom Gullery, Joe and his father, some of the last whalers, all agree. "It was only a job. When we caught a whale we were happy as we'd achieved something - no more cruel than a pig hunter or a trout fisherman. It was a challenge."

They all agreed there was stress and this built a strong sense of community and friendships that are still firmly in place today. They were together for so many years. They were brought up together and their fathers were brought up together before that.

The women also played a big part running the office and answering phones, and whenever anyone was injured either on the boats or at the factory it was always the women who first came to their aid.

Joe still believes the whale had the last say. "Quite often the weather conditions made us steam away, keeping the whale safe. The whale had the capacity for going down for eight to ten minutes. In that time it could go a long way. Then it might come up and spout three or four times. We never knew what direction it was heading. Sometimes we got it right. Then when it would come up it could be a quarter to half a mile away."

The whalers needed that speed of the chasers to get to the whale because, Joe said, they would arrive as it was taking its third or fourth breath and down it'd go again. Joe believed the whale had a fifty-fifty chance or even more, and there weren't the electronic aids such as radars, sounders or GPSs.

I understood. For these men it was an art, and a skill - their skills against the skill of the whale. Today they all support its conservation.

Joe's last words summed it up. "It was dangerous, but that was part of the game. It got the adrenalin flowing. We enjoyed it or we wouldn't have been out there. I don't think there's any other job that you could pursue that was more exciting."

In my researches I came across an old ballad, *The Whekenui Whaling Song.*

It was composed by the whale chaser crews on the lookout hill at the entrance of Tory Channel.

The characters and places in the song are place names at Tory Channel entrance and nicknames of the men who worked on the lookout hill and on the tug boat and chasers.

Jordy Rocks are a set of rocks to the south of Tory Channel entrance.

Old Sid was Sid Thoms who had an impediment in his speech and was lookout man and wireless operator to direct the chasers on to the whale.

Old Joe was J. A. Perano Senior, founder of the station. When he retired as a chaser driver he used to go to the lookout and walk up and down and growl about the way the chase was conducted.

Shucks was Trevor Norton, a gunner.

Young Joe was Joe Perano Junior, a gunner, who was not a quick rope splicer so he would sooner tie a knot if short of time.

Nicky was Alf Perano, master and owner of the tugboat *Tuatea*. A very excitable man.

Steve is Alf Perano's son and was stoker on the *Tuatea*, which was a coal-fired steamship.

Puponga Point The point between Fishing Bay (whaling station site) and Te Awaiti. Puponga (sperm whale) was what the Maori people called William Henry Keenan. This point was owned by the Keenan family.[2] It was a good place to watch a whale chase should they come inside the channel entrance. Everyone living within the vicinity would rush up there to watch the kill.

Natives were the Maori and Pakeha locals.

---

[2] From *Keenan History* by Mr James K. Keenan, verified by Mrs Mildred Connor and Mrs Lily Reeves. In the Picton Museum.

The WHEKENUI WHALING SONG
To the tune of *She'll be Coming Round the Mountain*.

1 *They'll be coming 'round the Jordy's when they come, when they come*
They'll be coming 'round the Jordy's when they come, when they come
Now we'll all go out to meet them
And it's ten to one we'll beat them
For they're coming 'round the Jordy's when they come

2 *Now Old Shucks will splice an iron-on when they come, when they come*
Old Shucks will splice an iron-on when they come, when they come
But Young Joe will do a tie on
Yes Young Joe will do a tie on
For they're coming 'round the Jordy's when they come

3 *Now you will hear Old Sid a stuttering when they come, when they come*
You will hear Old Sid a stuttering when they come, when they come
And Old Joe will be a muttering
Yes Old Joe will be a muttering
For they're coming 'round the Jordy's when they come

4 *Now you will hear Old Nicky screaming when they come, when they come*
You will hear Old Nicky screaming when they come, when they come
You will hear Old Nicky screaming
"Come on Steve get her steaming"
For they're coming 'round the Jordy's when they come

5 *There'll be Natives on Puponga when they come, when they come*
There'll be Natives on Puponga when they come, when they come
There to see the lucky gunner
Just to see the lucky gunner
For they're coming 'round the Jordy's when they come

212

6   *Now the Boys will sharpen kni-ves when they come*
    Yes the Boys will sharpen kni-ves when they come
    Oh the boys will sharpen kni-ves
    Some will be in bed with wi-ves when they come
    For they're coming 'round the Jordy's when they come

    (Slowly to finish)
    Oh they're coming 'round the Jordy's when they come

Memorised from his experiences at J A Perano's Whaling Station, Tory Channel from 1933 to 1946, by T G B Gullery aged 76. February 1992.

CHAPTER FIFTEEN

Living in History

WE LIVE at the beginning of New Zealand's history, according to Maori myth. Stories handed down through Maori whakapapa tell how Kupe, the Hawaiki chief and navigator, discovered New Zealand in the 10th century.

Kupe was fishing off Tahiti but a giant octopus known as Te Wheke o Muturangi kept stealing the bait from his line. He chased it across the Pacific, eventually killing it at the entrance of Tory Channel. The blood coloured the water red, so Kupe called the entrance Kura-te-au (the red current).[1]

During the summer months, vast concentrations of red crustaceans come into Tory Channel, turning the sea red. Known as whale-feed or krill, they are the larvae of several species of crustaceans. Washed ashore by the flood tide they are left in thick patches on the sand for the seagulls to fight over. I wonder if this was what Kupe saw when he named the entrance to Tory Channel, Kura-te-au.

In my search for the history of Okukari I have discovered many differing stories, even the meaning of Okukari. I was always told that the name meant mad dog, but I discovered it also means place of a young bird. I have enjoyed searching through archives in the Picton Museum and Waikawa Marae - places I never imagined I'd visit. As I became more immersed in the history I spent time in the Blenheim Lands Title office and LINZ, (Land Information of New Zealand), in my hunt for previous owners of Okukari. And my awe when I saw a print-out of a plan, taken off a microfilm, showing the position of Charles Godfrey's house and boatshed in our bay in the late 1800s made me realise what a handful of people have done to preserve our history. It made my own research seem very insignificant. But from it all I have compiled a history of Okukari.

I was amazed at what I discovered. Hundreds of people, possibly thousands, have used our small bay during recorded history. The million or more ferry passengers who steam past our bay every year see only three houses tucked away, a wharf and a woolshed and an area of flat land backed by steep hills. There is nothing to suggest what

---

[1] *Kei Puta te Wairau*, W J Elvy p 12. Whitcombe and Tombs 1957.

Okukari has seen, or what has gone on in neighbouring bays in Tory Channel, for that matter. Yet, as Worser Heberley's diary shows, Okukari had long been a significant area for Maori.

All the history books I have read spoke of Maori tribes crossing Raukawa Moana (Cook Strait) about 1400 and settling in the Marlborough Sounds. A Taupo chief, Tumata Kokiri, and his tribe, the Waitara, migrated to Arapawa Island or Arapaoa Island as it was first named, meaning, 'to turn towards the smoke'. In the new-found safety their numbers grew and they spread westward. This was the tribe that met Abel Tasman and gave rise to the name of Murderers Bay.[2] Other tribes came south and I read of the Rangitane, Ngatikuri and Ngatira who were here when Captain Cook first came to New Zealand in 1769 and named Ship Cove in Queen Charlotte Sound.

My father-in-law believes the earlier Moriori people lived in Okukari as two skeletons have been discovered in the bank above the beach, both in a squatting position looking out to sea. Other skeletons, believed to be a race before the Maori, have been unearthed in the Kenepuru Sound, interred in the same manner.[3]

In the early 1940s Charlie was cutting firewood and throwing it over the bank to the beach when the soft sandy soil slipped away, exposing a skeleton. Before reburying it Charlie dug around to see if there were any artifacts that may have been buried with it but there was nothing. Thirty-five years later James and a friend were cutting a track down the steep bank in the front of our house to the beach when they unburied a skeleton. It too was buried in a squatting position facing the sea. There were screams of fear and excitement as they tore inside with the skull. It was shortlived as Charlie ordered them to put the skull back where they found it and rebury the skeleton. Today when I walk along the beach I can still see the first stage of the track. It was never completed for fear of finding more human remains.

There was a fortified pa at Okukari. Over the years ploughing has removed all signs of the pa but many Maori artifacts have been found. Charlie has told me he can remember, in 1945 when they bought the farm, still being able to see indentations in the paddock in the shape of a large rectangle. A 15-foot clay bank rises off the track that leads up from the beach to the flats and Charlie has pointed out to me where the palisade posts used to be. Years have rotted the posts in the ground, and

---

[2] *Old Marlborough*, T Lindsay Buick p 83. Hart and Keeling 1900.

[3] Ibid p 75.

constant erosion from the wind and rain brings down small slips exposing a strip of fine dark brown soil 18 centimetres, and approximately 70 centimetres deep. At the top of the bank that runs towards the northern end of the beach a trench dug by the Maori is clearly visible. Time has made it shallow but the mounds of soil built up on either side still make it three feet deep. With the rugged coastline protecting the seaward side of Okukari, the inhabitants must have felt secure.

When Captain Cook visited New Zealand in 1774 he referred to a number of pa built along the shores of Tory Channel as he passed through in his eight-oared pinnace on his way to Queen Charlotte Sound where his ship lay at anchor in Ship Cove.

On Cook's previous visit to New Zealand he'd spent three weeks in Ship Cove where he had caulked and careened his ship, *Endeavour*. He'd described a place where trees grew to the water's edge and birds sang their morning hymns to the sound of the fresh water as it ran down the hillside to the sea.

On 12 February 1996, Lisa, Haydn, Danielle and I went out in the *Felix* to watch the replica, *Endeavour*, sail into the northern entrance of Queen Charlotte Sound on its way to Picton. The day was overcast and the 30-knot northerly wind built up a big sea, making me glad that I wasn't a Maori paddling my canoe out to meet Captain Cook. The seas were made even more confused from the wakes of the hundreds of boats that had come out to meet her. The spars and rigging stood out in relief against the leaden sky and the wind rounded all her sails except her tops'ls which lay furled along the spars. I tried to imagine what the Maori must have thought when they saw a ship like this coming in their bay. Was it excitement, fear or wonder? All of them, I'd think.

The *Endeavour* anchored in Ship Cove and a pilot boat kept her accompanying flotilla well away. I watched the waka, *Te Awatea Hou*, paddle alongside the ship to board and challenge the crew. I shifted my position to block out the sight of Cook's monument on the shore so when I looked towards the beach all that was visible was the waka and *Endeavour* against a backdrop that must have been similar to what Cook saw. I thought of the modern conveniences we have today, with electricity, fast boats and the pollution that accompanies them, and how in gaining these we have lost a great deal of the natural beauty that was our world just over 200 years ago.

In the next weeks my mind started to feel as if it would burst, as every night I'd lie awake trying to put Okukari's history in order. I had stories that had been told down through whakapapas, the skeletons and artifacts found at Okukari, all the land formations - but these weren't enough. I needed facts. Something which I could use as a platform to build the modern history of Okukari.

The timber to build my platform arrived in the mail when I received some printed notes from Mike Taylor, Picton's local historian, taken from Wakefield's *Dispatches*. I could begin.

On 31 October 1839, Wakefield anchored the *Tory* in East Bay, rowed ashore to Grass Cove, and walked over Arapawa Island to Okukari with a chief from Waikanae, Wiremu Kingi Te Rangitaake. When they came in sight of Okukari the chief ordered Wakefield and his party to discharge their guns. From the flat there was a continued discharge of muskets until Wakefield reached the pa where they found 200 men preparing to cross the Strait to carry on the war against Ngati Ruakawa at Waikanae.[4]

As I learn more of Okukari I find myself wanting to slip back into that time frame. Days when I've walked along the beach in a thick fog I've found myself straining to catch the faint melody. The muted thump of the waves hitting the sand, then the whisper of the sea as it draws back over the sand followed by the sighing of the gravel as it chases the water down to the sea - these could be murmuring voices. In these conditions, surrounded in silence, it is easy to imagine how Okukari must have been in the 1840s.

In December 1840 the Reverend Octavius Hadfield crossed Cook Strait in his open sailing boat, even though experienced sailors at Kapiti had advised him against it. At Okukari he found a carved church 60 feet in length, and which had been built by the Ngati Awa.[5] "I spent about a week at Okukari where there are a great many natives. Here they have built a very large place of worship and are very regular and attentive at school and are well behaved." Hadfield wrote that it was not unusual to have a congregation of 800-900 people. On this trip he baptised 17 people.[6] Where did the people come from? Was the beach covered in canoes? Did people walk over the hill from the Queen Charlotte side of the island?

I feel like two people as my mind slips from the 1840s to the 1990s

---

[4] *Wakefield Dispatches* Supplementary Information 1839 p 137.

[5] Church size length - Letter written to Miss O Hadfield 30 January 1841, by Hadfield.

[6] *Rangiatea*, Eric Ramsden pp 49-50. Reed 1951.

to our own church services in the Sounds, when we are pleased if there are 20 or 30 people. Our church isn't carved, and the services are held in a home or outside in a garden and people don't paddle their canoes. They arrive by boat, motorbike or on foot.

Our 1996 Easter service was to be held at Marcia and Roy Rowe's in Aotea, East Bay. As we drove up the farm road to the boundary gate on our motorbike my eyes followed the skyline as I thought of Wakefield walking this distance to the sound of muskets being discharged. Arapawa would have been covered in native trees, making his trip very different from ours. Our road had been bulldozed by following the bridle track that was cut as bush-fellers cleared the island. Workers camped close to the sites.

Recently Lisa and James had come across a fireplace, about five feet long, two feet deep and 15 inches high. It was built of stones in one of the gullies at the back of our farm. A few days later I rode up the road on the motorbike with Lisa, Danielle, Haydn and Angela to see it for myself. It lay in a clearing about 15 feet below the road. A few stones had fallen out but once these had been put back to their original position it was easy to see its size. I picked up a stick and dug the soil inside the fireplace and discovered it was lined with flat stones. The children were intrigued when we explained how it had come to be there and that it was probably more than 100 years old. The nearest thing to any home comforts was a fast-running stream nearby.

I had perched on the grassy bank above a large rock pool that had formed on the edge of the creek and listened to the children's high-pitched voices as they decided this was the bath and that one of the smaller pools was where those early people had probably washed the dishes. Manuka and tawhina touched overhead, the black tattooed trunks of pongas leant out over the dappled water and a tree fuchsia's gnarled trunk grew from the creekbed. The light southerly breeze carried the faint rumble of the Wellington-bound ferry to our quiet place, and our laughter sounded invasive when Haydn asked if Grumps had lived up here when he was a little boy.

At our boundary gate we met up with the McPherson family on their bike and we rode in convoy over the rougher track down into East Bay. Marcia and Roy had planned a barbecue following the service. Our sausages were well thawed out by the time we'd travelled the 10 kilometres through scrub and over washouts where everyone piled off the bikes and walked, leaving the driver to negotiate the difficult places.

The service was held in a clearing, and a forest of manuka formed the backdrop. We sat on planks and chairs. Tree-stumps made up a number of seats. The sound the water made as it threaded through smooth grey boulders towards the larger creek, the shrill calls of the wekas as their natural inquisitiveness overcame their fear, the discordant shriek the peacock made as he strutted in between the seats and the quacking as ducks fought for position, all these made up the overture to our service.

The Bishop of Nelson, Derek Eaton, and his wife Alice had come in a boat with David Hastings, our vicar in Picton. Dressed in sandals, shorts and an open-necked shirt, the bishop looked totally different from his predecessors who had visited Arapawa Island, Marcia's electronic keyboard had been set up, and I played the music for the hymns with a clothes peg holding the music open at the right place. Towards the end of the service the southerly clouds that had been rolling over the hill from our side of the island brought misty rain. A sun umbrella was held over the organ as we sang the last hymn shortened - and we held our barbecue indoors.

In my research for this book I'd earlier read William Elvy's book *Kei Puta te Wairau*, (A History of Marlborough in Maori Times). On page 91 he wrote that while he was living with the Love family on Arapawa Island he saw a square-rigged boat enter Anatohia Bay, and went outside to investigate. There was nothing to be seen but Mr Hector Love remembered his father seeing a similar ship soon after they arrived in the bay and he had described the crew as "some fair and some darker than the Maori". He also stated that their clothes were "old-fashioned dress and were armed with swords and spears, and some appeared to be in armour". The sighting disappeared before Mr Love could launch his boat but when he'd described the 'ghost ship' to other Maori friends, many claimed to have seen it in the same place.[7]

When Mr Elvy was working in Lands and Survey in 1931 he spoke of the ghost stories.

I forgot the barbecue as I stared out the windows overlooking Anatohia Bay. Low cloud clung to the land, and mist rolled down the gullies to the sea. A perfectly formed rainbow lifted from the sea and draped over the three small islands behind which the ghost ship is said to sail. The changing patterns on the water from the light wind, mixed with the swirling mist and rainbow, had me straining my eyes for a

---

[7] *Kei Puta te Wairau*, W J Elvy p 92. Whitcombe and Tombs 1957.

glimpse of the old square-rigger. I understood why Elvy later admitted that what he had seen might have been low drifting cloud.[8]

Pam Davies from East Bay believes she saw the ship in the 1980s. "I was asleep when the sound of strange voices woke me up. I sat up and looked out the window and I saw an old-fashioned sailing ship in the bay." Before Pam could wake her husband, it melted from sight.

On 8 March 1842 Hadfield once more made the journey across Cook Strait to Okukari. "I started early in my boat and reached Okukari in Queen Charlotte Sound in the evening and here I was again pleased at the feeling manifested towards me by these people." [9]

I'm always exhausted the day after a trip in to Picton. It's always such a rush trying to fit in everything I want to do. But the day after his all-day trip across Cook Strait, the Reverend Octavius Hadfield spent the day preaching to a congregation of more than 700, then baptising 42 adults and 12 children. Afterwards he administered the Lord's Supper to 28 persons.[10]

The church was also used as a school, with the books and slates for lessons supplied by Hadfield. Riwai Te Ahu was 20 when he first met Hadfield and soon became his right-hand man. Riwai trained people to teach school and assisted Hadfield in setting up several schools in the area. The most successful was at Okukari where, within three years, no fewer than 2,000 could read and write.[11]

Hadfield spent 12 days at Okukari during January and February of 1843, preaching to 300 or 400 daily, and about 700 on Sundays. He must have been very satisfied with what appears to be his last visit to Okukari as on that occasion he baptised 45 male and 15 female adults, and 21 children.

Today nothing remains of this Okukari church yet once it was linked in significance with the Maori church at Waikanae, and Otaki's famous Rangiatea church which was burnt to the ground on 7 October 1995. The years, the wind and the weather have removed any visible sign of what once stood at Okukari, and I can only close my eyes and try to visualise where it might have stood within the palisade, and how our beach must have been crowded with the worshippers' canoes.

---

[8] Ibid

[9] Letter from Kapiti 5 May 1842 to the Church Missionary Society, written by Octavius Hadfield (1814-1904)

[10] Ibid

[11] *Rangiatea*, E Ramsden pp 292-293. Reed 1951.

The Reverend Charles Lucas Reay, an Anglican minister, visited Okukari after Hadfield, and from September 1843 to April 1846 he baptised 76 and performed three marriages. Records do not say where all these people came from but it must have been from a wide area.

Captain Augustus Alexander Hood arrived in Wellington as a Wakefield Company immigrant aboard the *Slain's Castle* in 1841. He worked in Wellington covering houses with zinc, and later began trading in the Marlborough Sounds, Wellington and Nelson aboard his ketch, the *Augusta*.

The next significant date I can find in Okukari's history is 1853 when Captain Hood founded a whale fishery at Okukari.[12] That same year he brought Archdeacon John Salisbury and his brother across Cook Strait to Okukari aboard the *Augusta*, on the first leg of their journey to Nelson. The flood tide also played an important part in Captain Hood's life, as Archdeacon Salisbury writes: "Off the entrance to Tory Channel, we had to lay to, till the flood tide should carry us in, and no lights were to be seen."[13]

Once again it is presumption, but it seems as if there were still a Maori settlement in Okukari in 1853 because the two brothers describe coming into a cove (Okukari) where Hood lived and being met by a native canoe. Hood spoke with the occupants and arranged for them to take the two brothers by canoe as far as Anakiwa, from where they'd be able to travel overland to Nelson.[14]

It was difficult to adjust to life at Okukari when I married Joe in 1963, but leaving my Auckland home at the age of 20 and living on an island without electricity, phones or roads seems minor compared with what English-born Carolina Bertha Sawyer must have endured. In 1855, at Nelson, she married Captain Hood, and I can't begin to imagine the feelings of this 18-year-old from Kent. Her husband's trading must have taken him away for weeks at a time, and the death of their daughter at the age of two in the early 1860s made my life in the 1960s seem so lucky and pampered.

On 20 May 1858 the first Crown Grant for land in Okukari was issued to Captain Hood, and five years later another was issued. His house was licensed in 1864 and 1865, and in 1864 Captain Hood employed J A R Greensill to manage his sheep and cattle station.

[12] *Linkwater*, A History, Geoffrey Wilson p 68. Marlborough Express Printing Works 1962.
[13] *After Many Days*, John Park Salisbury p 69. Harrison and Sons 1907.
[14] Ibid p 70.

Caroline became a widow at 29 years when Hood was found drowned at The Grove, near Picton, in 1866. Goodwin George Hood established his right to his brother's estate and title to possession of the real estate on 3 September 1867. I hope Caroline found happiness when she married a Blenheim man in 1871.

A Captain Louis Pike supplied the next firm date in our bay's history when his ship, *Canterbury*, blew ashore in a southerly gale and was wrecked on the pile of rocks in the middle of the beach in 1855. I've heard stories that the rocks are the ballast of the ship, and another is that she broke up on the rocks and they were given the name of Canterbury Rocks. Paddling through the large rock pools and catching little fish caught by the tide, or showing excited city children the brightly coloured waving tendrils of sea anemones before they close over a finger bravely stabbed beneath the rocky shelf at low tide, makes me believe that these rocks have always been here and will still be there for future generations to explore.

On 19 August 1880 the secretary for the Marine Department recommended to the Minister for Marine that two leading beacons, plus a 10 x 8ft shed for the use of the keeper, be erected near the entrance of Tory Channel in Whekenui, the bay next to Okukari, and ordered that tenders be called for them. No longer would vessels have to rely on the blow-hole rock about a kilometre up the coast from East Head, "where as the surf broke it gave a thundering fog-horn sort of sound. A warning to skippers in dark thick nights," as Captain Augustus Hood informed the Rev John Salisbury.[15]

A tender received for 75 pounds and 10 shillings was accepted. This included providing 3878 super feet of rough totara, 829 super feet of dressed totara, 4561 super feet of dressed kauri which included weatherboard and tongue and groove flooring, and 218 super feet of rough rimu. Also there were the windows through which the lights shone, three doors and two ladders with ironbark rungs.

The Notice to Mariners No 38 of November 1881 read: 'Notice is hereby given that on and after the night of 1 January 1882, leading lights will be exhibited from beacons which have been erected at the entrance to Tory Channel, Cook Strait. They will be fixed white lights and will be exhibited from two pyramidal-shaped beacons painted white. The beacons will lead through the centre of the entrance to Tory Channel. The upper light will be 36' above high water mark and 497'

---

[15] Ibid

from lower beacon. The lower light will be 22' above high water mark.'

Charles Godfrey assisted in the beacons' construction and was the first keeper, employed full-time to tend the kerosene lights. On 22 September 1881, with his mother, Emma, as witness, he married a widow, Ann Tetley.

The Runholders' and Sheepowners' Directory, within *Wises' New Zealand Directory of 1880-81*, states that Charles Godfrey of Okukari had 612 sheep which he ran on Bayonets Run, a small piece of land between Okukari and Whekenui. His parents, Daniel and Emma, were English immigrants who arrived in New Zealand about 1854. Daniel's other descendants are not known, but as there is no record in the New Zealand Lists of Freeholders, I think he may have leased some of the land from the Maori owners around 1873.

Beneath an old macrocarpa tree above the lagoon in the paddock near the boundary of the block known as Bayonets Run, words inlaid in lead on the white marble stone tell us that Daniel Godfrey died at his home in Okukari on 29 December 1885. He was 66.

Ann Godfrey died in 1893 but her grave isn't in Okukari.

From the archives in the Picton Museum I obtained a copy of a tape recording of an interview with Gilbert Perano of the whaling family with Joe Timms, who early in his life was placed in the care of the Godfreys by the Rev John Sedgewick. Charles Godfrey became blind and six-year-old Joe Timms became his eyes. They would go over to the beacons, and Joe climbed the stairs first to get to the other side of the light. Godfrey followed, lit it, and Joe would say, "Peek on your side, Dadda," and he would trim that side with his thumb. Then he'd turn around the other side and tell Godfrey, "Peek on my side, Dadda," and Charles trimmed that side of the wick.

Charles's mother died in 1899 and she is buried with her husband, Daniel, on our property.

Okukari must have had two families living in it in the 1890s because a lease in perpetuity from the crown was issued to Charles Godfrey for his block of 126 acres, Bayonets Run, on 14 June 1897. The annual rent was two pounds four shillings and sixpence. At the same time other blocks of Okukari were farmed by a Tom Mailing and Bob Temple.

One of the most exciting letters I received after my first book was published was a letter from a Mr George Barker. His grandfather, Bob

Temple, farmed Okukari in the late 1890s and his mother was born in 1898 while they were there. His great-grandfather, Captain E F Temple, was an artist and Mr Barker sent me a negative of three paintings Mr Temple did of Okukari. The house which stood until 1952 is in one of the paintings, and another could have been painted from my own windows. Now I have a copy of my own living painting, done more than 100 years ago.

At the turn of the century Okukari had new owners, George and Florence Kenny, and Charles Godfrey, at 54, married Emily White, a maiden aunt of Florence Kenny's, at Okukari. He kept the lights until one week before he died, on 30 December 1907, and is buried with his parents at Okukari.

After Charles Godfrey's death, George Kenny was appointed keeper. With his sons Oswald and Max, they hand-lit the lights until March 1930, when automatic flashing lights were installed. The same beacons, still with vents on the top from when the lights were kerosene, guide ships into the narrow channel entrance.

I am still discovering things my children did when they were young. One weekend in 1996 when Pauline was home we walked up the head of the flat to where Joe was working on the bulldozer. "Come and I'll show you our camping site," Pauline called as she jumped down a bank into a fast-flowing creek. The scrub growing over the bank had us on our hands and knees in places as we carefully pushed through tentacles of stinging nettle growing in the bushes until we broke into an open space. Pauline excitedly pointed out the area they'd built up with stones. It was marked out into rooms like a house. Most were still standing while a few drunken-looking stones, covered in lichen, leaned against each other.

"Everyone of those rocks is a forfeit," Pauline replied when I asked her how long it took to cart the rocks. "The penalty was to bring up a rock from the creek." Their 'forfeits' also edged a track down to the water.

I lay back on the light green grass that grew tall in its search for sun and watched two fantails hopping from tree to tree while Pauline wandered around the campsite, pushing over the odd stone with the toe of her boot.

Her "We did some crazy things," had me rolling over and watching her face as I waited to hear some of them.

"We used to play truth, dare or promise, and one of our dares was going down to the Godfrey graves at midnight. Alone."

And all those times I'd taken for granted that the girls were safe, I thought, as I imagined a 10 or 12-year-old taking herself down the flat, in the dark, to an old grave.

"We had to knock three times on the tombstone."

I laughed out loud as I pictured the scene and imagined the fear they must have experienced. As proof they'd been down to the grave near the beach they had to bring back a handful of sand.

I found it difficult to gather 20th century history of Okukari. Up to the turn of the century, as our nation formed, history was important, and is recorded in archives. Now it was as if I'd reached a solid wall, behind which the pioneers of the new century immersed themselves in hard work. I realised the tangible history of Okukari was gone with the church and the pa, and now sheep and cattle grazed where bush-fellers once had lived, but the history of Okukari still haunted me when I'd find a piece of blue patterned china, an old bottle with a glass stopper or old lamps, or stumble across old farm machinery that lay around.

One story I heard happened during the First World War, but even this seemed to have a wall of silence built around it. I found it incredible, but correspondence I received after my book was published gave it credence.

A worker, I was told, got up early one morning to see a float-plane in Okukari Bay. He rang the authorities and was brusquely told to go back to the bottle. An enemy float-plane in our bay!

The letter I received that tied in with this incident came from Eileen Swanson. At one time her father was the mailman for the Queen Charlotte Sounds, and her grandfather had surveyed much of the Marlborough Sounds and placed his sons on likely properties. Eileen wrote that around the time of the First World War her parents, Tom and Catherine Carkeek, lived at Wharehunga, land we now lease on the Queen Charlotte side of Arapawa Island, where, Eileen, added, "my mama was postmistress stationed with the only phone in the Sounds at that time". I wrote to Eileen to ask her permission to write her story. These are her words:

My story is told as I have so often heard it as a small child.

The German boat, Wolf, had been concealed in the coves of our bay, plainly visible - I should think - to the local settlers. Who could really hide the Wolf?

Then the story as I recall. Someone - probably crew - would request fresh supplies from the local settlers who were very nervous but never threatened. Of course they complied. Who wouldn't?

They complained to the Picton authorities and were ignored. They were believed only when a letter of appreciation for their hospitality arrived after the war.

My mother suffered a severe fright one morning after the menfolk had rowed from the homestead to another venue. She went out the back door to empty her teapot and observed two strangers with guns across their knees, observing her. Terrified, she ran to the beach waving a tea-towel to the disappearing row-boat. Fortunately they saw and understood, making great haste to return.

Of course the men disappeared. Our brave forbears went in search but found no trace. Maybe just as well they didn't.

But there was a small plane, part of the Wolf's equipment, which was often seen about the Sounds. Throughout the stay people were both scared and thrilled by such a scary happening amongst them.

I believe it to be absolutely authentic for I heard it told so often to guests and relatives. Each time I am filled with horror and wonder at the whole thing.

I still needed facts, and during a visit by the Marlborough Historical Society to Okukari I was given what I'd been searching for. One of the members, Jack Andrews, phoned me the following day with the history of the German raider, *Wolf*, a large steamer built in 1913. She was 5925 tons with a speed of 10 knots and a crew of 300, and was under the command of Karl August Nerger. She was heavily armed with seven 150-millimetre guns and four 560-millimetre torpedo tubes, and she carried 465 mines. And for me, the final cornerstone in my mind, a Friedrichafen E33 seaplane which was called *Wolfchen*.[16] This boat had come around the Cape of Good Hope into the Indian Ocean, sinking several vessels before heading for the south of New Zealand and up the coast to the Kermadecs where she'd had an overhaul before steaming back to New Zealand.[17]

The *Wolf* spent time in the Cook Strait area, and during June 1917 laid 25 mines off Farewell Spit, of which 17 were swept up by fishing trawlers.[18]

---

[16] *German Raiders of the South Seas - The Naval Threat to New Zealand 1914-1917*, Robin Bromby. Double Day Australia 1985.

[17] *Shipwrecks - New Zealand Disasters 1795-1936*, Chas W N Ingram and P Owen Wheatley p435. Dunedin Book Publishing Association 1936.

[18] *Cook's Wild Strait*, David MacIntyre and Michael Field with Christine Quinn p154. Reed 1983.

After reading my book, Neroli Rose, George and Florence Kenny's granddaughter, phoned me from Blenheim. Neroli, and Ian her brother, had lived in Okukari until 1941, moving to town for their schooling. Their father, Max Kenny, was dead and their mother, Margaret, yearned to come back to Okukari. Now I had the missing link.

Margaret Kenny had come to Okukari as a young bride in 1935. She belied her 87 years as Ian and Neroli helped her off the yacht they'd steamed in from Picton. We were told the smile on her face had grown with the day.

Once she was off the wharf, her trip down memory lane began. "There was a steep-sided creek down here," she told us as we strolled over the culvert and up the wide track Joe keeps clear with the bulldozer. A grey head nodded its approval at the work Joe had done.

"When I lived here the men used a bullock to bring firewood down from the paddocks. They'd have to unload it on one side, walk the bullock over the creek and load it up again before bringing it up to the house."

As we passed the back gate that leads into our two sons' homes, Margaret pointed out the place where the old laundry used to be. When I arrived at Okukari it was Charlie's and Ruby's woodshed, and Joe said as long as he could remember it had been the woodshed. Today it is a paddock with the water running through buried pipes.

"We dug holes in the creek that used to be there, and stood the cream cans in it to keep them cool - 14 to 20 cows were milked, all by hand. That was my first job and if I wanted to go out for the day they had to be milked first."

Before the final climb to the house we stood and rested for a few minutes and Margaret gazed across the bay. "Mailday was the highlight of the week. You know, I never saw my mother-in-law down on the beach to meet the boat without her hat and gloves. She didn't row out to it but always went down to make sure the cream made it safely out in the dinghy."

We turned our backs on the bay where gusts of wind swept across the water, purple today from the ominous clouds building up to the south, the forerunner of the predicted southerly buster, and carried on up to our home.

Stories flowed. There weren't any generators in those days and Margaret made her own candles, and baked bread every day. I thought of the days when I couldn't even get my oven warm enough to raise my yeast let alone bake the daily bread, and how I moaned if the generator broke down and we had to use candles. And I didn't have to make mine.

Church services were held in people's homes and Margaret's smile grew even wider as she told us the story about her in-laws' pet parrot. "The Bishop of Nelson was down. When he began his sermon the parrot kept interrupting, 'What rot. What rot.' " The parrot was banished for the afternoon.

If I thought it was a marathon task bringing my piano to Okukari, it would have been nothing compared with conveying the grand piano Florence and George Kenny brought into the Sounds by barge. It wasn't worth carting the old one back to Picton so it was carried to the woolshed and, Margaret recalled, chopped up. "I think ours was the first grand to come into the Sounds."

Bringing a grand piano from the beach seemed minor when Margaret told us the story of a Maori canoe which her in-laws found on a ridge on a block of the farm, well away from the water.

"It was when men were in, clearing the land," Margaret mused. "I never saw it myself but I remember the men often speaking about it." This canoe was lying in the bush, and it was easy to see where a fire had been lit in it to hollow out the centre. The bush-fellers were asked to leave the bush around it standing, and to leave it where it lay, but a large tree had fallen and smashed it.

I wondered why it had never been finished - perhaps the Maori owners had decided it was too heavy to get it out to the sea, or perhaps they left in a hurry.

Margaret gave us a copy of a photo of the house her in-laws had lived in. It was the same house as in the paintings by Captain E F Temple except that by now a wide verandah had been added.

"Did you live in this house?" I asked Margaret.

Her reply stunned me. "No. We lived in your little house. I remember it was built by Tom and Cyril Flood, and a relation of yours, Eric Heberley."

The missing link snapped shut.

Jim Heberley, Charlie's brother, took over the farm in 1941 but stayed only four years. Jim always claimed to have seen a Japanese submarine enter Tory Channel during the Second World War, as he was rowing across the bay. It was just on dark and he says he heard a loud rumbling. He saw a submarine surface, and the sight of water streaming off its deck as it steamed down the channel had him digging his oars into the water. The authorities dismissed his story even though it coincided with a number of similar reported sightings in the Sounds. Molly Webster, whose husband, Jack, owned Webster's Butchery in Picton, was staying at Blackwood Bay in Queen Charlotte Sound at the time. Today Molly can still recall her fear at the close proximity of the Japanese navy. It made her pack her bags and return to Picton.

Much of the land was covered in secondary growth when Charlie and Ruby took over Okukari in 1945. Ruby has told me the sickly sweet smell of the gorse flowers on a hot sunny day, and the popping of the seed pods as they burst open, always brings to mind her first visit to the place they were to make their home. "We walked up a track through the gorse to reach the house. Up the flat it grew with trunks like trees." It was to become the evening's entertainment. "Every night we'd go up the flat with our bucket of kerosene and a dried gorse stick to burn it."

Gorse was a source of wood for the range that my mother-in-law relied on. When I feel stressed out preparing the smokos for shearing in my electric stove and being able to freeze my baking, I often wonder how Ruby coped. For her, shearing meant cooking food daily, and I think of the sponges, cream cakes and pastries she fed the shearers as well as breakfasts, lunches and dinners. "Breakfast was always bacon and eggs. I'd have to light the coal range, get it roaring to cook their breakfast, and then scrape out most of the fire to make the toast on the embers."

I love to listen to stories of a way of life people lived not so long ago. This is history, and the thought of its being swallowed up by our computerised and space age society has compelled me to write it down. Now it is obvious to me why it wasn't recorded at the time - where would they have found the time?

Stories of Ruby's trips to town had me cringing. "Twice a year we went for our 'big shop' when we'd bulk buy." This was easy to understand when I heard of the 4am start to a day in town, milking eight cows. Clothes and shoes to wear in town were packed the night before, and kindling was heaped in the oven to ensure a quick fire to cook breakfast.

"A two-hour boat trip was too long to keep them clean," Ruby decided, and the children would get changed as they were entering

Picton harbour. The stores were bought in Blenheim. They didn't own a car so they had to be in Picton in time to catch a bus which left Picton at 7.45am.

"I'll never forget those trips. I always had to stop the bus and get out to be sick. In town we'd tear around, and I'd be sick coming back to Picton."

Our lives ran parallel with the other town trips Ruby made. Times during the whaling season when she'd go in to Picton with neighbours but there was always the same trip home in the boat and the children going to sleep. They'd howl when they were woken up to go ashore, and still be crying when they arrived up at the house. And we still have to cart everything up to the house.

There the parallel stops. Until Ruby and Charlie bought their first generator for electricity in 1952, Ruby would arrive home to a stove which had to be lit before a meal could be cooked and laid on the table.

There were no such things as drip-dry fabrics or the knit fabrics on the market today. All the girls' dresses were starched and ironed, Ruby using two flat irons heated on the top of the coal range. "Nothing made me madder," I was told, "than times I'd be finishing off a dress and the iron would leave a greasy sooty smudge on the dress."

As it is today, the phone was the most vital link. In the early days the Post and Telegraph Department built all the toll lines to serve telephone offices, and from these offices the settlers were obliged to build their own lines. A family in Wharehunga was on a private line to Okukari. Incoming calls for them had to be answered by my in-laws. They switched the call through, and outgoing calls were dealt with in the same way.

The phones improved over the years. I still remember turning the handle to generate one long ring to reach the exchange in Picton, and the different Morse code rings to reach someone on our party-line. Thunderstorms always put the phones out but not before we'd have our private display of blue flashes at the fuse-box on the wall, to the accompaniment of broken rings from the phone.

Those phones are now history and I'm thankful we can now direct dial through a radio-link to a receiver above our shed. From there, lines go out to the houses on our end of the island.

The advent of electricity to Arapawa Island in 1982 made most of these things history, and we joined the computerised and space age society. But living where we do, we can choose to pedal our bikes in the outside lane if we feel like it, and let the Rolls-Royces, Lamborghinis and Ferraris pass us by.

I'm glad history itself will not pass us by. Instead it will continue to grow with each generation and keep on being recorded. Days when the sea has matched my despondent mood and I've sat on the sand I've thought how I'll miss this place if a time comes when I have to leave. Writing this chapter has made it easier to come to terms with that possibility. Now I'll be ready, because I understand that history is a continuing record of events, and I must move over to let it grow.

CHAPTER SIXTEEN

Birth of a Boat

OUR new fishing boat which Joe had signed up for while we were down south on my author-tour in May was due to be launched in February 1997. Eight weeks before the boat's completion, Joe had to be in Invercargill to work on the final stages.

Memories of my stay in Invercargill in the weeks before *Te Wai* was launched were still vivid in my mind. A strange city where I didn't know a soul was a lonely place. I walked to parks and wandered through beautifully kept gardens. I went to movies and window-shopped. Hard pavements, traffic and people made me long for the quietness of Okukari where I could leave my shoes at home and wander along the beach, lifting the sand with my toes and feeling its warmth beneath my feet. This time, I told Joe, I'd come, but only if I could bring my machine and work on my book.

At this stage I was working on the history of Okukari so the keyboard and screen along with a carton full of reference books, notes, photocopied historical papers, notebooks, dictionary, paper on which to print out my words, a two-way plug and extension lead filled up the back seat. I'm sure I had a smile as wide as the Cheshire Cat in *Alice in Wonderland* as I thought of all the writing I'd accomplish with Joe working on the boat from 7am until after 6pm Monday to Friday, and none of the familiar emergencies to break into my time.

I still hadn't seen this boat. The last time Joe had been to Invercargill I'd asked him to take plenty of photos. He came home and excitedly showed me the boat. "This is the engine. This is it arriving at Goughs. Unloading at Goughs. Next to the boat. Lifting it up. Going in the boat." Then two more photos of it in the boat.

"But where's the boat?"

The last three photos were the ones I wanted to see. In Goughs shed it looked much bigger than its 50 feet, and the morning after we arrived in Invercargill I came down to the shed to see it for myself. I've often asked myself why a boat is referred to as a 'she' and I noticed we spoke of this boat as 'it' while it was in the process of being built. The day it is launched it's like a prisoner being released from jail. Freed of all chains and on the water, it becomes she. She leaves her inanimate form behind, and becomes a living thing.

Joe and I planned to stay in Invercargill for about two weeks this time. We'd go home for Christmas, and after New Year Joe intended going down again. For this period we decided to rent a flat. I didn't really mind what it was like as long as I had a table for my word processor and electricity to make it go. Two days after we arrived we found a fully furnished flat in an apartment building with a very good landlord and I could start work at once. As well as my two most important things, the building also had 19 other occupied flats, and, right next door, rap music that started up about 3pm most days with at least six or seven teenagers accompanying it by beating out the rhythm on the steel balcony rail outside our door.

Ear plugs jammed in my ears dulled the beat as I tried to concentrate on my writing, but as the afternoon wore on every beat jolted through me like an electric current and I wanted to hold my head. Young people came and went all afternoon. Mothers came with babies' bottles clutched in their hands. There were all shapes and sizes, with hair that was shaved, bleached, plaited or coloured. One tenant must have been determined to have curly hair. He wore curlers in it for a whole weekend.

Joe arrived at the flat to a wife teetering on the edge of insanity but when I opened the door for him and saw the incredulous look on his face I burst out laughing. I turned my back on him and jerked over to the couch in time to the thumping music.

Okukari seemed a very long way off. So did other things such as the solid elements I have on my stove top - I'd forgotten how quickly coil elements heat up. The film of oil I'd poured in the pan to cook our wiener schnitzels burst into flames. The frying-pan lid, flour, anything to smother it were in my kitchen at the other end of the South Island. Joe carried the burning pan over to the bench and tipped it upside-down in the sink where the oil soon burnt away. The music thumped on.

After our meal we drove down to Bluff to see what fishing boats were in port. The pan catching fire had been the last straw. I'd snapped. I'd remembered as a child having a ukulele. One day I'd tightened a string too much and when I'd been playing it the string broke and wrapped around a finger on my left hand. I felt that pain again as I rubbed the tip of my third finger when we walked along the wharf. The creak of the mooring-lines as the boats lifted on the tide and the smell of the sea in the wind which blew up the harbour made me feel normal again.

It was quiet when we went to bed but I think our laughter would have had our nextdoor neighbours wondering what was going on. When I turned off the light in our bedroom, the ceiling glowed with stars, Christmas trees, moons and suns. We lay on our backs and laughed until we could laugh no more and I felt tears running down my face. There is no doubt about it - my world does grow bigger.

My days took on the same pattern. Joe started work at 7am and from then until lunchtime there was little sign of life. Joe decided our fellow tenants were hedgehogs - awake only at night. I wrote. Afternoons varied, depending on the noise level. My education was completed as I watched a young man peg dry clothes on the line, *dry*, before unrolling the fire-hose and washing them. I realised why the youngsters sat on the balcony listening to their rap music. A car stopped at the adjacent intersection and the next thing one of the boys ran down the steps, over the road, across the grass strip in the middle and got down on his hands and knees and began combing the grass. It intrigued me as I unashamedly watched from behind the net curtains as he picked up something from the grass. As he came back past our window I saw he was puffing on a cigarette. "Heaps left on this one," I heard him tell his mates who still sat on the deck, elbows resting on the bottom railing, as they maintained their nicotine vigil.

Ten days away from Okukari and off the water was making both Joe and me tetchy, and we accepted with delight the invitation for us to join Goughs for their Christmas function aboard the *Southern Express* to Stewart Island. For Joe and me it was an unexpected pleasure but it must have given the men who had worked on this boat a deep satisfaction as they steamed down Bluff Harbour and out into the rip at the entrance of the harbour, knowing that at some stage they'd helped create her.

The seas turned a few faces green and a few more even greener while we fished for blue cod. I was sorry for the blue cod trying to swim through the passage where we fished - they would have had a hard job getting past all the hooks that hung over the side. The fishing over, we steamed close to Stewart Island and headed into Patterson Inlet to tie up at the wharf in Miller's Bay which had the most golden sand I've ever seen. It wasn't a sand that would trickle between my toes but a more coarse composition formed from tiny ground pebbles. One of the island's well-maintained walking tracks led through bush filled with ferns, moss and the tiny orchids that grow on the ground as well as in the trees, many of which were old rimus.

A 10-minute walk took us to the next inlet where we stood in history, surrounded by ships' propellers, an old rusted boiler, the remains of a slipway and the foundations of a house and shed. On a noticeboard we read that Norwegians had brought their whaling boats up from the Antarctic to this bay for repairs. The depot closed down in the 1930s.

Although I didn't catch one, I was relieved to find I was allowed to sample a filleted blue cod, sprinkled with lemon juice and with a piece of lemon on the fish, then wrapped in foil and cooked on the gas barbecue which was set up on the stern deck. Meat patties, sausages, bacon and steak were cooked, and salads of every description were set up on a table along with smoked salmon, locally caught, and mutton birds.

We ran with the sou'westerly wind on the return trip and as we came up the harbour I felt a flutter of anticipation - this could be us in another month. Our new boat, still in its growing stage in Goughs shed at Invercargill, was waiting to be given life.

Nine months from the time Joe and I had been in Invercargill and he'd placed the order for the boat, it was lifted by crane along the length of Goughs shed and placed on to a trailer with a notice saying '22m long'. Because of the boat's height it was a close call getting it to fit beneath all the stays between power poles that were strung across the road between Invercargill and Bluff, and some of the power lines were low too.

I sat in the car and watched the preparations for the journey. The mast, radio aerials, engine exhaust - all top fittings were laid down flat on the roof. A person from United Electricity checked that everything was lowered as far as it could be and then two wooden battens were lashed to the rails at the bow of the boat. They lay over the roof where they hung down over the back of the verandah on the stern deck. These allowed the boat to slide beneath any low wires without anything getting caught up. This was our baby in the next stage of labour - the rounded battens were there to assist the birth.

A police car, and one of Goughs vehicles carrying a warning of the wide load following, as well as the United Electricity van which kept ducking in and out of traffic as it kept ahead of the convoy to guide the truck driver under low wires - all these could have been the maternity medical team.

Joe and our two sons travelled on the boat, with a cellphone, to make sure that nothing broke free. Our family and friends followed. I remembered the time we had brought *Te Wai* down this same road, and I wouldn't have missed this impressive sight again for anything.

The usual 20-minute trip took more than an hour. The truck with the boat on the trailer was parked in a sheltered corner on the wharf where all the gear could be put back in position. Some fuel and oil was pumped aboard, enough for tomorrow when family, workers and friends could be taken out.

The next day as we drove down to Bluff in time for the 10am launching the smoke from Tiwai Point's high chimney drifted straight up. The harbour was smooth, the only movement the flood tide as it pushed into the huge basin covering the mudflats at its head.

The truck drove to the edge of the wharf where men lifted the boat off the trailer, using two cranes, and then lowered it until it nearly touched the ground.

Joe, Young Joe and James stood on the boat while everyone else gathered around to listen to Joe's speech of thanks and Tony Gough's reply. Then the Rev Neil Cowie blessed the boat. Hanging from the bow, the bottle of champagne was dressed in all its ribbons - the same ribbons I'd kept from the launchings of every boat we'd had built. Joe referred to them when he said there were ribbons tied to that bottle from four boats, and that the last three had all been designed by Colin Neill.

As I've been writing this book the past has been invading my mind more and more, and it did again as Joe's words reminded me of the time when he was thinking about replacing the *Tineke*, another Colin Neill boat, but one we'd bought. It had become too small for our needs, and Joe and I went to the sale by auction of a boat that had been confiscated by MAF for a serious fishing offence.

Joe decided the asking price was too much and as we came out of the room we met Colin. I saw the look in Joe's eyes as he spoke to Colin, and I laughed when I told him we didn't want a new boat designed for us. I knew what would happen. That look became a boat, *Te Wai*, launched on 26 March 1994.

Now our older daughter, Helen, stepped up to the new boat. She grasped the neck of the bottle and said the same words that have been spoken at launchings for hundreds of years. "I name this boat *Te Awa*. May God bless her and all who sail on her."

236

Fragments of glass flew through the air. Frothing champagne coated the bow. She was well and truly christened.

The two cranes lifted her up and swung her out over the water. Slowly she was lowered into the sea and tied up to the wharf while our family jumped aboard. It was our privilege to have the first ride.

The 680HP engine drove the 15-metre *Te Awa* through the water at a speed of 20 knots. We were thrilled. Not even the professional critics who seem to gather at any launching could find anything to criticise. I'd had to make so many decisions about the colours of her interior when Joe was too busy to help. His words of confidence, telling me he trusted my judgement, made it more difficult and I'd worried about my choice of turquoise vinyl on the wheelhouse floor, and the burgundy carpet in the accommodation area. But even the upholstery with its contemporary floral design on a navy background looked right.

The following day we took her out to Stewart Island with family, friends and some of the staff from Gough Brothers. The weather was perfect. Foveaux Strait was glassy-calm. Joe and I wanted to take his father to the Norwegian whaling base in Patterson Inlet, and all day I had a strong déjà vu feeling as we did exactly the same things Joe and I had done seven weeks previously when we'd come out with Goughs staff on the *Southern Express*. The feeling stayed with me during the day and jumbled through my mind with the memories of those early whalers from Tory Channel who with John Thomas Heberley, Charlie's uncle, as their leader had gone to Campbell Island in 1909. They didn't have warm showers or the convenience of a fridge and a five-ton ice hold we have today as they steamed much further south to the Campbell Islands aboard the *Hinemoa* and later the *Amokura*. Their comforts would have been sparse compared with ours. My eyes swept around the wheelhouse of *Te Awa* where as well as all the latest electronic equipment there was a diesel-fired stove, microwave, television, full-size sink and bench, carpet and the soft seat I was lounging back on, built around the table - I enjoyed living at this end of the 20th century.

This time I wasn't coming up the coast with the new boat. I had opted to bring our vehicle back with Lisa, Haydn and Danielle. There was a part of New Zealand I hadn't seen and we travelled through the inland road, passing some of the sheep stations I had only read about when we were buying in our merino sheep. Through Cromwell, Tekapo and Omarama, stations with the names of Bendigo, Streamlands and Grays Hills became real.

We arrived back at Okukari in the dark, aboard the passenger boat *Felix*. So much had happened and I felt drained. Haydn's voice as he told the skipper, Sam Edwards, about our new boat pushed sleep back, and had me wide awake, listening.

"Grumps's got a new boat. It's coming from Bluff. Aunty Helen smashed a bottle of wine on it - we didn't need it. It didn't make a hole in the boat but it made it go fast. It's got two bedrooms, you know."

Our grandson might be one of the computerised and space-aged generation but I was glad to hear he still lists creature comforts near the top of his list.

The trip up the coast took 40 hours, and this time the men steamed into Okukari Bay during daylight. My daughters-in-law and grandchildren were all down on the wharf with me to see *Te Awa* round the point from out in Cook Strait, the stretch of water where a great deal of her fishing would be done, and steam into the bay.

Joe had pushed the throttle down and as she surged ahead she cut a clean path in the water. Her bow wave rose up her stem slightly, then curled over to meet the sea. She suited her name. It means the channel, or stretch of water.

CHAPTER SEVENTEEN

Changing Tides

FROM the beginning this book was going to be called *Flood Tide*. I loved Shakespeare at school. As a fifth former trying to understand his plays I always looked for meanings as I grappled with words which turned ordinary things into something rare and beautiful. Lines are lodged firmly in mind, and of course they describe many of my feelings so much better than I could ever do myself.

I remembered these lines so well:

> *There is a tide in the affairs of men*
> *Which, taken at the flood, leads on to fortune;*
> *Omitted, all the voyage of their life*
> *Is bound in shallows and in miseries.*

The lines kept coming into my mind when 1996 grew to be one of the most exciting years for the Heberleys, first with *Weather Permitting*, and then when Joe was awarded the Queen's Service Medal in June. Our friends kept reminding us, "What a year it's been for you." Now I needed to know which play these words came from, and what came next.

I took the *Complete Works of Shakespeare* off the bookshelf and every night I turned over about 30 pages. The dog-eared pages were easy to read because they'd been my favourites, but the clean stiff pages took longer. I read 738 pages before I found the lines I'd been searching for, in *Julius Caesar*. It was worth the effort when I read on:

> *On such a full sea we are now afloat;*
> *And we must take the current when it serve*
> *Or lose our ventures.*

Again Shakespeare had said it all.

Every day I see the flood tide pour into Tory Channel, bringing with it logs washed down from rivers, kelp and plastic rubbish dumped by unthinking people. Along the edge of the current, where the water from the bays meets the flowing water on the channel, seabirds bob up and down, in anticipation of what the flood will bring. The rush of the tide reminds me of giant breaststrokes as they push out from the chest before sweeping round in a wide arc, filling the bays as the swimmer moves on down the channel.

I've heard people describe dying as life ebbing away. I hear the gentleness and feel the sorrow. But when I wake in the morning and feel the excitement and anticipation of the day ahead, open the curtains and see the wonderful scene from our window, the power of all this beauty makes me want to raise my arms and clench my fists and just shout out loud. Then I know my life is flooding.

So often a southerly buster comes in on the flood tide. From our windows we watch as the thin wreath of navy clouds builds to bulging black clouds that finally pour over Oyster Bay, bringing the southerly with them. We can usually predict its arrival by the start of the flood but, like the weather forecaster, we sometimes get it wrong.

On this particular day, for instance, the boys had a net set. While they waited to pull it they had put *Te Wai* on her mooring in the bay and come ashore for a cup of tea. We'd seen the southerly clouds starting to build but the wind came in sooner than we expected. Young Joe rowed frantically out to *Te Wai* to bring her into the wharf to pick up James so they could go and pick up their net before the seas built up too much. He tied the dinghy to the mooring and in his haste he cast off *Te Wai* before he'd started the engine up. A panic-stricken voice came over channel 8 on our VHF in the kitchen.

"Boat won't start!"

Joe wasn't too concerned. The same thing had happened to him that morning.

"Wriggle the wires around. It's something loose in the starter."

"Still won't start."

Then Young Joe asked his father if he wanted to hear the bad news.

"I've cast off! The dinghy is out here and the anchor's not holding."

Joe threw the microphone down and shot out of the kitchen. James was waiting on the end of the wharf, wondering what was going on, when his father arrived. They dragged an old dinghy, with half its topside missing, down the beach and later when I asked Joe how they managed to reach the boat in half a dinghy with only one oar, and the head sea, he could only grin as he said desperate men do desperate things. When they reached the *Fugitive* they clambered aboard, started her up and towed *Te Wai* back to her moorings. The net was pulled and early next morning Joe got *Te Wai* going and steamed into Picton to have the starter replaced.

Writing this book has been an extraordinary experience. It's been like watching an old film, and at times when my mind has been blocked with the weight of the responsibility of bringing our history alive it's been as if the film has jammed in the projector and jumpy images have filled the screen, or the film has broken and only a blackness remained.

I have felt such joy when I've discovered old sepia photographs. As I studied them, although faded they brought back memories that were as evocative, clear and sharp-edged as ever.

I have learnt how important it is to keep family photos and diaries, and how important are newspaper cuttings which earlier generations had gathered and kept in old boxes. Anything kept is a part of tomorrow's history. It lives on as part of the past and becomes part of a future generation.

When my father died in 1978, it was left to my only sister Betty and me to clear out Dad's home. A few days after a death is too soon to think rationally, although at the time Betty and I thought our father would be pleased with what we did. He had kept a log of his many years' yachting aboard the 28-foot yawl *Mangawai*, and Betty and I took this log book around to a very special friend of our father's. The tears in his eyes as he flicked through its pages while we were there told us it was right to give it to him.

Years later I wished I still had my father's log. I heard that Dad's friend had died, and I kept wondering what had happened to the log. This was a personal record my father had kept, a record of a way of life long gone. It was a part of my father, and I wanted it to be a part of my family's future generations. I wanted my children to read of my life as a child. But efforts to track it down proved futile.

Then a phone call came in February 1997. Friends in Auckland told me there was an article about my father, with photos of him and the *Mangawai*, in the February issue of *Marine Scene*. It referred to the log, and the last paragraph, read out to me, said: "I feel the family should have this rather personal narrative returned to them and I often wonder how it came to be sold in a garage sale. I ask that they contact me so they can have back, with my compliments, this so lovingly inscribed log."

Tears came to my eyes. Trembling fingers pushed the Auckland phone number I'd been given and I soon learnt from the writer, Paul Titchener, how the log came to be in his possession. A friend of Paul's had bought it in a garage sale, for 20 cents, and he'd handed it on to Paul as a regular contributor to many boating magazines.

I can't describe my feelings when the log book arrived in our mail. Just holding it in my hands took me back to Christmas 1955 when I'd given it to my father. The black leather cover with the gold lettering, *Log Book, Yacht Mangawai*, still looked rich, and I traced over the words with my finger. It smelt old. I shut my eyes and saw my father sitting at the table in the cabin, writing up his log in an early morning light, his glasses on the end of his nose, and I felt a rush of love as I saw him biting down on his lower lip as he concentrated. The scratching of his fountain pen blotted out the day's sounds. So deeply engrossed, Dad wouldn't hear me slide from my for'ard pipe-berth, pull on my swimsuit and dive into the calm water in a bay where there would be only one or two boats anchored.

I turned over pages and tasted the freshly caught snapper and smelt the whiff of kerosene from the lamp set in gimbals that hung in the cabin. As I closed the book I heard and understood my father's words, "Nothing good is ever lost." His log book had come home, but the memories of my childhood remain forever.

At different times when I've been the speaker at functions, the person introducing me has read from the blurb on the back cover of *Weather Permitting*, listing what I call my pedigree. I have been asked what I don't do. There are hundreds of things I still want to do, and at 55 I'll have to hurry, but two things I'll never do. One is shear sheep, and the other is become an electrician.

When all the men are away there are times when I'll have to use the shearing machine, to clean up a sheep with flystrike. Any farmer will understand when I describe the 'hum and crackle' maggots make as they bury themselves in the wool and eat into the flesh. It makes me set up a handpiece. The size of rams make them much harder than ewes or wethers. I can't sit a ram against my legs and bend over it to shear around its tail and up its back, so while Lisa and Joy hold it I'll push the handpiece over the flyblown area. It's never the most elegant ram that joins the flock again, but I'm sure it is more comfortable. That is as far as I ever want to go with shearing.

I'm not allowed to be an electrician. Once we had a two-bar heater, and only one bar had worked for years. I got fed up with pushing the spare bar out of the way every time I opened the cupboard where it lay. Joe never seemed to have the time so I decided to fix the heater myself. It seemed easy. All I had to do was take out the old bar and replace it with the new one. I plugged it in to try it and two bars soon glowed, but as it wasn't cold I turned it off at the wall and put the heater away. I didn't tell Joe. This was to be my surprise for him, but I didn't realise just how big the surprise would be.

The first cold morning he was home he took it from the cupboard, plugged it in and picked it up to shift it, at the same time brushing the chrome leg of the table with the heater. There was a blinding flash and a loud bang. The heater crashed across the dark room, and I could hear Joe staggering outside for fresh air. This was when we were on generated power, and it had blown the main switchboard. Well, how was I know I had left off the earth wire? When the heater had touched the chrome leg, Joe became earthed.

Joe recovered. I got into awful trouble. The plug was cut off the lead before the heater was dumped, and I was forbidden to touch anything electrical again.

Another part of our history left Okukari Bay on 17 April 1997. *Fugitive* was sold and when I heard her engine start up for the last time in our bay as her new owner began the trip down the east coast to Stewart Island, her new port, I felt quite nostalgic for what many people would say was only a piece of wood in the water. To us she was more than that. She had brought many boats back into the safety of the Sounds, and the times she was involved in the saving of life helped us through the searches involving death.

Newspaper cuttings, photos and diaries of her lifetime that I've kept since her launching in 1974 have been carefully stored. They are now a part of our family's history.

Te Awa has now taken over the role of *Fugitive*, and three days later on 20 April 1997 she was called out on her first search.

It began as a normal day for that time of the year. Our first frost of the winter lay on the ground. All traces of the southerly buster that had ripped in the bay the previous afternoon, bringing rain and hail, were gone. The power of the sea crashing on the beach was the only sign of the southerly and I'd opened the curtains to a beach that still lay in shadow and rimmed with white foam as the swells lifted then dropped at the top of the beach. They clutched at the grass before running back to sea where they gathered force to tear up the beach once again. From my bed it is a lonely sound but when I see it the sight of such power fills me with the joy of life. It was the last of the flood tide.

A Picton-based charter boat left Picton with a group of 10 divers aboard, bound for Walker Rock, one kilometre off Cape Jackson. At 9.15am the divers entered the water. It was 10.30am before anyone realised anything was amiss. Two of the divers had failed to surface. No assistance was called for until 12.30pm when the police in Picton were alerted. Then, at 12.40pm, the Marlborough Coastguard was called out.

I had been up the paddock and arrived home to hear the phone ringing. A commercial fisherman had heard what was happening on the VHF and asked me to let Joe know. By 2pm he, Joy and I, all of us with a pair of binoculars, were aboard *Te Awa* and heading north. Young Joe and James were away fishing down south on *Te Wai* - they couldn't help.

Outside in Cook Strait the two or three metre-swells looked even bigger through binoculars and both Joy and I jammed ourselves behind the wind foil out on the wheelhouse roof as we tried to shelter from the cold wind. I found if I held the binoculars on the edge of the wind foil with one hand, and hung on with the other, I could follow the swells as they swept over the sea. There were eight to ten boats searching, but the sea remained empty.

Later in the afternoon two fixed-wing planes were called out, and the Westpac Rescue Helicopter was allowed to search for one hour. Nothing was sighted. It seemed hopeless. The sea was so large and the day was so short. My eyes felt as if they were being dragged out of their sockets but I was scared that if I didn't keep looking I might just miss them. Just outside of us I could see the bright yellow of the *Tranz Rail Rescue* and it was from her that Dave Baker was on-scene co-ordinator for the search. Dave kept in constant touch with Joe, and with Dave Fishburn who was aboard his charter vessel, *Cygnet* - two men who between them have more than 70 years of knowledge of the tides in the area. The smaller *Interisland Rescue* combed the shoreline.

As the planes and helicopter flew overhead I found myself in anticipation of a voice coming over the VHF, saying that they'd spotted the divers. There was nothing. As the flashing light of the helicopter disappeared on its way back to Wellington and the planes left the darkening area I felt sick. Even when Joe told me to climb down from the roof when we came to Tory Channel entrance I swept the glasses over an empty sea once more, just in case.

Rowing ashore I trailed my fingers in the cold water. It felt warm. Scared of making a fool of myself I squeezed my eyes shut so no one would notice my tears. It was 6.30pm and the men had been missing for nine hours. I knew their dive suits would give them some buoyancy. I imagined them bobbing up and down in the swells, freezing, hungry, thirsty, believing, but now all 12 search boats had left the area. To make matters worse, a southerly gale was predicted to come in that night.

"All those boats," Joe said, "as well as the planes and 'chopper. I'm sure if they'd been on the surface they'd have been seen."

Now I wondered and almost hoped that they'd died beneath the sea. Surely, I thought to myself, that would be a more merciful death than drifting around on the surface of Cook Strait.

"Still," Joe's voice broke into my thoughts, "I find it hard to believe two men would get into difficulties on the seabed at the same time."

We had been told they were both experienced divers and that they each carried a diver's safety sausage, a bright orange buoy, like a fender, about two metres tall. If these were inflated they should have been spotted easily. Half of me thought they must be dead while the other half told me they were still alive somewhere in Cook Strait, in the dark.

Dinner was a quiet meal and any conversation we did have was centred on the missing men. Joe kept asking himself where we went wrong. After I'd washed the pots I rubbed my crinkled hands from the water down my jeans, and thoughts of the divers washed over me again. I felt guilty sitting in the lighted lounge, enjoying the warmth from the fire and my hunger satisfied.

Pauline's husband, Dene, was on the Interisland ferry bound for Picton. As she approached the channel entrance at 7.30pm, Dene went outside. North, between the Brothers light and Perano Head, he saw a flare followed immediately by another. A passenger next to him also saw them. Dene reported it to staff at the information bureau but he told us later they seemed sceptical so he rang Joe from his cellphone.

Immediately hope for the men was re-kindled. Everyone asked questions. "Did they carry flares?" Hopes plummeted when we were told that although some divers do, these men probably didn't. That didn't alter the fact that flares had been sighted, and by a reliable source.

"Someone must be in trouble out there," Joe told Dave Baker when he rang him in Picton. "They're not saying these guys haven't got flares. It seems reasonable to me to think they would have waited until dark to set them off, and that ferry Dene was on was the first one to pass since it became dark."

Joe, Young Joe and James decided to go out again, regardless. The southerly was holding off and they were aware time was limited before it began to blow. A fisherman in Kaikoura told them it was still calm there, so they were hopeful they'd have time to find the source of the flares. The coastguard boat, *Tranz Rail Rescue*, came out from Picton again, and so did Dave Fishburn from Dryden Bay aboard *Cygnet*. My pleas to go too went unheeded because of the strong southerly predicted.

Once again I was the one who waited, following their progress on the VHF. I heard Joe talking to Dave Baker, telling him that they were heading out towards Terawhiti until they could see the Brothers light and then they'd head north on the line where Dene had seen the flares.

Joe told me later he'd been so certain they were going to find the men. It was bright moonlight with excellent visibility, and he said that as they were heading back towards the channel entrance about midnight he heard the *Straitsman* give the compulsory 10-minute call on channel 16 of the VHF. All vessels are required to do this to advise others what time they will pass through the narrow entrance. Joe said he called them up and told them what was happening, and asked them to keep watch.

Fifteen minutes later a crewman on the *Straitsman* saw a flare. It was in the same area as the ones Dene had seen, and they estimated it to be north of Tokori. This sent the three smaller boats back to resume the search, but a dark bank looming up from the south with a freshening southerly wind sent them home at 2.30am.

I knew how Joe felt when I heard the fall of his footsteps. Even the simple act of sitting on the edge of the bed and dragging off his socks was despairing. "They must be alive. It seems awful leaving them out there but with the freshening wind we can't put more lives in jeopardy."

We woke to a brilliant day. The southerly had missed us and gone up the Wellington side of the Strait. The thought of those flares kept hope alive but from the warmth of my bed I was filled with doubt. *Tranz Rail Rescue* and *Interisland Rescue* were out on the water again and Joe rode his four-wheel motorbike to the top of Perano Head on the road that had been put in when the Döppler for Civil Aviation had been installed. From there he'd get a commanding view over Cook Strait.

His cellphone was his link with the crew of *Tranz Rail Rescue*, and a pair of 10x50 binoculars his eyes.

The *Morning Star* set off from Mana with seven men aboard for a fishing trip in the Marlborough Sounds. They called Kevin McBrydie of Marlborough Marine Radio with their TR (time report). On our VHF in the kitchen I heard Kevin asking them to keep a watch for the two missing divers.

My morning wouldn't come together. I'd start one thing and wander off to another. I sat at the kitchen table, gazing down the channel at the moving water. The sun streamed in on my back from the side window and I wondered how long it takes before a body gives in, and if it just goes to sleep or does it struggle. The voices on the VHF faded as my thoughts scrambled through my mind.

Suddenly - "Have one aboard! In wonderful shape! Just grateful to feel something firm under his feet and wants a hot cup of coffee!"

I was at the VHF waiting to hear more. "Just going over to the other." My heart plummeted. Perhaps one is dead.

"Have him aboard! He's great too!"

The *Morning Star* had steamed past them when a man on the stern had noticed one of the orange safety sausages. Thank goodness they carried flares, I thought, and when Joe reached the Döppler and heard they'd been found he shared in the excitement too.

The divers' story unfolded. When they surfaced after a dive they found themselves 40-50 metres away from their charter boat. They were being swept out to sea in the strong ebb tide which the divers described later as a rogue tide, probably brought about by the continuing southerlies. It took them outside Cook's Rock, outside the Brothers, and as far south as Tokori. Then they were carried up and down with the tide in a big arc. Just on dark they floated past a six-metre log which they clung to during the night. At one stage they were so close to Mana Island that they considered swimming to it. During the night squid boats passed by. One was only 250 metres away. Seals and dolphins kept them company. Talking about their families, about previous diving experiences, and other survivors from diving mishaps kept them awake. They always expected to be rescued. Twenty-six hours after entering the water they were plucked from it. The Coastguard boat took them back to Picton, and the men on the *Morning Star* continued on their fishing trip in the Sounds.

Everyone was to receive one last surprise. The divers had not let off any flares. Questions, all without real answers, were asked. There is no doubt in the minds of everyone who was involved in the search that something was seen. And seen by at least three different people at two different times, and all in the same vicinity as the divers were picked up, eight miles north of the Brothers. The flares kept the men searching. I jotted down some of the comments I heard from these men of the sea.

"I'm not a religious man but I believe we were being told something."

Another, "Something out there was telling us to keep on looking."

A longtime fisherman, "We were being told something."

I liked my Joe's comment best of all. "Miracles still happen."

Eight days later a debrief on the search for the divers was held in Picton. All those involved in the search and rescue operation met at Picton's fire station to see what everyone could learn from this remarkable happening. Before this rescue, the longest time Marlborough searchers had known anyone to survive in the water was 18 hours. These two men had been in the waters of Cook Strait about 26 hours.

The police search controller, liaison officer, and officers from the Wellington police launch *Lady Elizabeth* were present. The police launch was on her way to Walker Rock on the Monday morning with a dive team when the two men were found. Also present were the two divers who'd been rescued, coastguard, pilots of the planes, Dave Fishburn, my Joe and Young Joe, and Lisa and myself. The skipper and crew of the charter boat also attended, as well as members of the dive club.

Nobody was blamed. The debriefing was a sharing of information: everything the searchers had learnt, and we hoped could benefit from. One thing was apparent. The length of time that passed before the alarm was raised was crucial. It could have cost two men their lives.

The culmination of 1996 had been the announcement that Joe had been awarded the QSM. When I wrote in my first book about many of the search and rescues, I wanted everything to be accurate. I wanted people to read about them and realise what our family goes through, and what I go through as a wife and mother. I didn't exaggerate. Everything was written exactly as I'd witnessed it, or according to what I'd been told. When the news broke that Joe was to receive a medal for his work at sea, I was overwhelmed by the numbers of people who wrote to us after having read my book and then learnt that

Joe was a recipient of the QSM. They said they now understood why he'd received it, and all agreed - he deserved the honour.

His investiture took place at Government House on 15th May 1997.

I had counted down the days. Everything else that had happened in my life was in the shade in comparison with the pride I felt for Joe. I was glad he'd accepted the medal, particularly for his words when he said he'd accept it for our sons and for his father, but mostly for his Uncle Joe, drowned while trying to save a life. But it is only since I've learnt so much about the Heberleys because of researching and writing this book that I can see that the giving of themselves at sea goes back further than that, and I'm in no doubt that it is a tradition that will continue as long as a Heberley lives here, at the doorway of Cook Strait.

Getting ourselves organised to go over to Wellington for Joe's investiture was as bad as getting to Picton for a family wedding. As we were booked on the 5.30am ferry on the day of the investiture we went into Picton the day before, to unload fish and stay overnight. Our family decided to make it a special time and stay overnight at Picton's Beachcomber Inn, and I'd grinned when I'd heard the boys discussing who'd get the best room on the top floor with its panoramic views of the harbour. Joe and I enjoy being able to stay on the new boat. It has all the comforts of home with its double bed, shower and diesel stove which keeps the cabin warm. Ruby and Charlie drove over from Nelson, and stayed with Pauline and Dene.

What should have been straightforward preparations turned into a nightmare.

These Heberley men rarely wear suits so they all hired them, as did Dene. Young Joe picked up his suit, checked that the tie he'd ordered was with it, noticed that it was a dark suit and took it back to his room. Pauline was busy at work so I told her I'd pick up Dene's when I collected Joe's. I also took James's with me. None of the suits had a name on it, and back at the boat I quickly checked that Joe's was the one he'd ordered. Joe's pinstripe was easy to recognise, as was James's navy suit, but the remaining one was black and I knew Dene was wearing a dark green suit. A quick phone call to Pauline had me worried. Dene's *was* green and he should have had a shirt and tie with his. Another phone call, this time to the Beachcomber Inn, hoping I'd catch Joy and Young Joe in their room. Young Joe's colour blindness hadn't let him pick up the fact his suit wasn't black. He hadn't realised there was a shirt with it, and thought the tie was his.

None of this would have been a problem if it hadn't been nearly 5.30pm. So rarely do the boys wear a tie that they usually have to buy a new one, as the old ties have dated since they were last worn. I left their room with Dene's suit, tie and shirt, followed by Joy and Young Joe racing out to buy a tie before the shop closed.

Both Joe and I must have grown into the computerised and space-aged society without realising it, because when it came time to set the alarm clock for 4.15am we couldn't work out how to set the manual clock. We'd become so used to setting our electric clock at home. The simple act of setting the alarm seemed out of our field and I had visions of being awake all night in case it wouldn't go off. We tried setting it and then turning the hands to a couple of minutes before it should go off. The minute hand slipped past and nothing happened. Just when in desperation I told Joe that I'd go up and find Young Joe, he finally worked it out and we wondered why it had taken us so long.

My body was exhausted but my mind was wide awake. I lay beside a sleeping Joe and counted the hours of the night by the distinctive rustling sound created by the propellers of the ferries as they came in and out of the harbour. I'm always nervous sleeping on the boat when we drift out at sea, but the boys always tell me I'd hear a ship coming. Joe describes it as bubbles rushing past, sounding as if they are scratching the hull. To me it was almost like an electric jug boiling just before it switches itself off. The gentle rocking and occasional bump as *Te Awa* stretched her ropes finally sent me to sleep and my dreams had me back in Auckland on board the *Mangawai* with memories of my parents crowding my mind. They'd loved Joe, and I'm sure I saw their pride when their faces merged into my dreams.

We didn't need the alarm clock. Both Joe and I were awake at 4am. Excitement kept me from feeling tired and we sat in the quiet of the wheelhouse, enjoying a cup of tea. The only thing to make us feel sad was the fact that Helen and Peter weren't able to be with us. Farming commitments kept them in Maruia. Joe and I picked up James and Lisa. Then, when James took the suit bag out of our vehicle he tripped up on something. It was a shoe, and I saw his tie dangling from the bottom of the bag as well. Lisa had put all their clothes in this one bag without realising it had a hole. Scrambling around in the darkened carpark, looking for one of James's shoes, didn't seem an auspicious start to our day.

"It's probably in our hotel room and I've locked the door and everyone there is asleep." Lisa was so upset, but at the same time I glanced down at James's feet and thought that at least he was wearing shoes, even if work shoes, which he could wear at a pinch. It could have been worse - he could have been wearing sneakers. As they drove back to the hotel to retrace their steps, Joe and I collected our boarding passes.

Perhaps it is a sign of age but I'm noticing more and more how long-ago memories keep crowding back into my mind, such as how Heberley men seem to have bad luck with shoes. I remembered how Joe and I were walking up the stairs to where James and Lisa were having their wedding reception. I could hear Joe clumping up behind me and I laughed out loud as I recalled Joe's words when I told him to pick up his feet.

"It's pretty hard when the soles are hanging off." I turned and looked at his new shoes in disbelief when he held up a foot to show me. Both soles had come unstuck, nearly to the heel. It meant a trip up to our hotel room and a quick change of footwear. I was glad the main table had a long tablecloth as I thought of the old tan shoes peeping out beneath Joe's smart navy pinstripe suit.

This time there was a happy ending - they found the lost shoe outside their room.

Ten casually dressed people boarded the ferry in Picton. Ten smartly dressed people disembarked in Wellington. We left our bags in two lockers at the terminal, and, as Joe's parents hadn't been in Wellington for 23 years, we decided to hire a shuttle bus and have a short tour of the city before the investiture. At 9.50am, all of us rather conscious of our numbers and our vehicle, our shuttle bus was ordered to stop at the gates of Government House. Joe presented his invitation and we were waved through with a laughing proviso to keep those in the cab in order. Someone suggested that the guard probably thought the whole mob of us were intending to stay as our bus was towing its covered trailer.

I'd caught glimpses of Government House at times when I'd been watching TV cricket being played at the Basin Reserve, and the cameras had swept around the grounds. But nothing had prepared me for the grandeur as we swept through the gates up the drive into the park-like grounds and came to a stop outside the reception area. Joe was whisked away, and after presenting our invitations we were led into the ballroom. My first impression was space and timeless beauty.

It was all cream and light. My eyes followed a strip of salmon-coloured carpet from the doorway to the end of the room, where there was a dais. White ropes twisted with a gold thread, with tassels at each end, made a barrier across the front.

Two sets of panelled wooden doors were at the end of the room at either side of the dais, and between these a huge painting of Queen Elizabeth hung on the wall. Mirrors seemed to be all around the walls, and an elegant chair with a red leather seat and back with the monogram G VI R sat against the wall. I felt proud to be part of our country's heritage. Marble pillars reached to a magnificent plastered ceiling, decorated with ornate designs, from which hung two crystal chandeliers. When we stepped off the carpet to take our seats my eyes took in the highly polished dark timber floor. I wondered if all the darker spots were from years of dancing, and it was easy to imagine hundreds of beautifully gowned women on the arms of their partners as they swayed to the music of an orchestra.

Today our music was coming from a woman playing a grand piano. Voices faded as I drank in the sound and when I heard the beginnings of Chopin's Nocturne my emotions raged. This was a piece I'd always played on my sad days. I still felt the sorrow but this was a happy day and my mind was confused. The notes became jumbled as I tried to blot out those memories and bring back today. The music stopped and we were advised of the programme for the investiture.

At 10.30am His Excellency the Governor-General, accompanied by Her Excellency, members of the Vice-Regal household and Officers of the New Zealand Order of Merit and the Queen's Service Order, entered the ballroom. The first verse of God Save the Queen was played, and the Governor-General gave a short address.

Forty-one men and women were invested. As their names were read out and they moved towards the dais, a brief statement of their services was read out. My heart was full as I watched Joe move up the dais to stand in front of the Governor-General. He bowed his head and stepped forward. His medal was hooked on his left lapel. Words were exchanged, and hands shaken, before Joe stepped back, bowed his head once again and left the dais to take up his seat. The ceremony concluded with the singing of the first verse of God Defend New Zealand.

Refreshments were served in the green sitting room and the dining room. To walk down the hall was to step into history. Photos of previous Governors-General hung on the walls. Cases with glass fronts held treasures. I saw Maori carvings and many other pieces, all with display cards. I didn't have my glasses on and I didn't like to hold up the crowds so I had to feel the atmosphere - and that was easy. All around the walls of the dining room were oil paintings of old-fashioned people. They reminded me of miniatures I used to have of the Blue Boy and the Pink Lady. Everything seemed to be old and solid, and every room looked out on to sweeping green lawns. It was hard to imagine we were in the middle of the capital city of New Zealand.

With one of the letters I'd been sent after my book was published I had received some old photos from a relative who'd stayed at Oyster bay when Joe's grandparents were running their guesthouse. I was told that the man in one of the photos was Sir Michael Hardie Boys's father, as well as Sir Michael himself as a young boy. They were fishing from the *Oria* while holidaying in the Sounds. There was a second group photo, with the same people in it. The Governor-General knew about these old photos, and as we were lining up for a group photo with him, I handed him an envelope containing them, saying that perhaps he'd like to put it in his pocket to look at later - I was rather conscious of all the people waiting for their turn to be photographed. But no. Sir Michael wanted to look at the photos right away. I watched his face and could see that these old faded sepia photos brought back the same sharp-edged memories for him as old photos do for me. He said the photos were of his father, mother and brother, and he recognised many of the others. He was genuinely pleased to see Charlie and Ruby, and they easily bridged the 50-year gap. And he remembered my Joe as a little boy. I left them laughing over many happy memories. Charlie didn't stop smiling all day.

Although Helen and Peter couldn't be with us in person they arrived in a different form. Someone tapped Dene on the shoulder and asked if he was with the Heberley party, because there were some flowers in the reception for Joe. The words on the card brought a lump to my throat: 'Congratulations. Hope you have a lovely day. Love Helen, Peter, Amanda, Carl and Glen.'

We knew they were with us in spirit and sharing in Joe's special day.

Later we all went out to lunch. Ten of us sat down and it was easy to see we were celebrating. We even had the flowers. When Pauline ordered the wine she told the waitress they were celebrating their parents' wedding. Joe cringed, but I'm sure the waitress noticed Joe's medal was much shinier than my wedding ring.

Before we boarded the ferry for our trip home we changed back into our casual clothes. We all became Cinderellas as our finery was packed away into bags. Our wonderful day was over.

We arrived back in Okukari at 11pm. As we lay in bed, going over the day, I asked Joe what his feelings had been as he walked towards the dais.

"All I could think was 'Bill Gibb, Bill Gibb.' He was one of the main reasons I was there today. I know he did a lot of work to get my name put forward for this medal. I'm honoured to have known him."

I am often asked, "Will there be another book?"

Not for a while, but I've kept the door open. In 10 or 15 years I'll be getting older. Lots more things will have happened. My tide will be on the ebb. I could write another book, and call it *Ebb Tide*. Or I could be caught up in another tide, another venture, that as yet I do not know.

RECIPES

MANY PEOPLE have asked for more recipes which we use here in the Sounds. These come from people who appear in this book.

Bill Gibb loved seafood so it seems right to begin with some of his favourite recipes. Mussels were one of his specialities. "But you must use Marlborough greenlip mussels - as many as you can eat."

CRUMBED MUSSELS

1 tbsp water	1 egg
Garlic salt	Celery salt
Seasoned flour	Dried breadcrumbs

Double or treble these quantities, depending on number of mussels available. Wash and cook mussels, six at a time in the microwave, or steam in a saucepan.

Lightly beat egg and water, adding flavoured salts. Coat mussels in seasoned flour by shaking in a plastic bag. Coat mussels in the egg mix by shaking in a lidded bowl and then coat them with breadcrumbs by shaking in a plastic bag.

Fry coated mussels in about 1cm of oil until light brown (about half a minute each side).

MUSSELS IN CHEESE SAUCE

Cooked mussels	2 tbsp butter
2 to 3 tbsp flour	1½ cups milk
Large onion, sliced and cooked	1 cup grated cheese
Salt and pepper	

Prepare white sauce adding cheese along with the salt and pepper. Stir in cooked onion and whole or chopped mussels.

Serve on toast or with hot chips or rice - or anything else you fancy.

COOKING CRAYFISH - BILL'S WAY

Drown crayfish in fresh water. Place them in electric frypan with about 2cm of water. Cover with lid and steam for 12-15 minutes.

A little vinegar in the water prevents the surface of the pan from blackening.

HEATHER'S SAUCE FOR CRAYFISH (nice with oysters, scallops and salmon)

100g mayonnaise
50g tomato sauce (not homemade)
50g whipped cream

Combine mayonnaise and tomato sauce. Add cream and mix.

LISA'S WILD PORK CHOPS

James brings home the bacon and always asks Lisa to cook the chops the following way.

Spread out the chops on the bottom of an oven dish. Cover with two medium chopped onions and one 225g tin of crushed pineapple.

Pour over 3 tbsp soya sauce and sprinkle with celery salt. Cover and cook 180° C for approximately 1½ hours.

SAUCE TARTARE

With all the fresh fish we eat I like to ring the changes with different sauces. This is one of my favourites.

Use a white sauce made from milk in which one chopped onion and one chopped carrot have been boiled. Strain and season. Add one measure of gherkins, capers and parsley. Cool.

MARCIA'S FISH DRESSING

½ cup mayonnaise   ½ cup sour cream
2 tsp lemon pepper   1 finely chopped gherkin

Mix all thoroughly. Gherkin optional. Use on cooked fish.

MANGAWAI **ROOTAGOO** - my father's special for yachties.

Into one saucepan put enough potatoes, onions, carrots, and any other vegetables you wish. Enough for four people.

When cooked, strain and mash. Add one tin of corned beef and mix through. Serve with tomato sauce.

PAULINE'S REALLY EASY PASTA

1 tin tomato soup (425g)	1 tin tomato puree (410g)
1 small tin peas (310g)	1 dsp sugar
1 onion (chopped)	pasta

Brown onion in small amount of butter or oil. Combine with remainder in heavy-base pot. Simmer for approximately 40 minutes.

Cook one packet of pasta of choice (eg 500g spaghetti or macaroni elbows). Mix pasta into sauce.

Serve hot with grated cheese.

OFFSHORE ISLAND PUDDING - Margaret Hopkins, Stewart Island

¾ pint water	Two eggs
¾ cup sugar	1 tbsp (large) cornflour
Juice two lemons	Grated rind of one lemon
1 tsp butter	

Put water on to boil and add it to the other ingredients already mixed. Return mixture to saucepan and stir over heat until it thickens. Put aside with lid on to keep hot.

Crust:

1 tbsp butter	2 tbsp sugar
1 beaten egg	1 cup self-raising flour
Milk	

Beat butter with sugar, add egg. Stir in self-raising flour and enough milk to make a soft batter.

Spread the bottom and sides of ovenware dish with the mixture except for about two or three tablespoons.

Pour hot lemon mixture into dish and drop remaining cake mixture in teaspoon lots into the lemon mixture. Bake in moderate oven until 'islands' of cake mixture are nicely browned.

MAUREEN'S APRICOT SAUCE - lovely on cold wild pork

6 lb apricots	6 large onions
3 pints vinegar	1 tsp pepper
3 lb sugar	2 tsp ground cloves
2 tsp ginger	2 tsp common salt

Cut apricots in half and remove the stones. Slice fruit and onions. Boil all ingredients together for 1¼ hours. Strain through mouli or put through food processor.

Bottle and cork when cool.

RUBY HEBERLEY'S PAUA PICKLE

6 lb minced or chopped paua (cook the paua first)

½ tbsp curry powder	½ tbsp mustard powder
1 lb sugar	1 pint vinegar
1 tbsp salt	

Boil paua with vinegar for half hour, then thicken with 3 tablespoons of flour mixed with vinegar and 1 dessertspoon of turmeric.

RUBY'S HOT CRAYFISH SAVOURIES

½ oz butter or substitute	1½ tbsp flour
½ cup chicken stock	¼ cup mayonnaise
1 cooked chopped crayfish tail (8 oz)	¼ cup cream
2 tbsp chopped mushrooms	1 dsp chopped parsley
Salt, pepper, seasoned flour, oil for deep frying	

Melt butter, blend in flour. Cook one minute. Remove from heat. Blend in chicken stock. Return to heat and cook stirring until sauce boils and thickens.

Sauté mushrooms in a little butter, add to sauce with mayonnaise, cream, parsley, crayfish, salt and pepper. Refrigerate until mixture is firm.

Place heaped teaspoon lots in seasoned flour and coat well. Fry in hot deep oil until golden-brown.

Makes approximately 18 savouries.

JOY'S POTATO DISH

Potatoes (amount needed)	3 tbsp butter
Cheese	500mls milk
Dried tomato soup mix	Bacon bits or chopped bacon
1 onion - chopped	Salt and pepper
Parsley, chives, fresh tomatoes (optional)	

Mix soup and milk together. Peel and slice potatoes and layer into a large ovenproof dish.

Sprinkle 1/3 of bacon, onion, cheese and butter over (plus the optionals if desired). Pour half of the milk-soup mix over. Repeat for two more layers.

Cook for approximately 1½ hours at 180°-190° C until potato slices are soft and the milk has nearly evaporated.

HELEN'S BIG BANANA CAKE

6 oz sugar	¼ lb butter
2 eggs	3 cups flour
2 tsp baking soda	1 tsp vanilla
2 tsp baking powder	3 ripe bananas
1 cup milk	

Cream butter and sugar. Beat in eggs. Add mashed bananas, vanilla, sifted flour and baking powder. Warm milk, stir in baking soda. Add this mixture last. Cook 35 minutes at 350° F. Helen uses her expandable baking tin.